SOCIETY
AND
SETTLEMENT

SUNY Series in Israeli Studies

Russell Stone, Editor

and

A Publication from the
Center for Study and Documentation of Israeli Society

SOCIETY
AND
SETTLEMENT

Jewish Land of Israel in the Twentieth Century

Aharon Kellerman

STATE UNIVERSITY OF NEW YORK PRESS

Production by Ruth Fisher
Marketing by Theresa A. Swierzowski

Published by
State University of New York Press, Albany

For information, address State University of New York
Press, State University Plaza, Albany, NY 12246

Library of Congress Cataloging-in-Publication Data

Kellerman, Aharon.
     Society and settlement : Jewish land of Israel in the twentieth
century / Aharon Kellerman.
        p.   cm. — (SUNY series in Israeli studies)
     Includes bibliographical references and index.
     ISBN 0–7914–1295–4 (alk. paper). — ISBN 0–7914–1296–2 (pbk. :
alk. paper)
        1. Zionism—History. 2. Land settlement—Palestine.
3. Agriculture, Cooperative–Palestine. 4. Kibbutzim. 5. Land
settlement—Israel. 6. New towns—Israel. 7. Jerusalem. 8. Tel
Aviv (Israel) 9. Israel—Boundaries. I. Title. II. Series.
DS149.K489   1993
307.1'4'08992405694—dc20
                                                                                91–47853
                                                                                CIP

10 9 8 7 6 5 4 3 2 1

For my wife, Michal

"Our lives go there in transition."
("Unser Leben geht hin mit Verwandlung.")

—*Rilke, from "Seventh Elegy"*

Contents

Tables

Figures

Preface

The objective of this study is to present a bridging experiment between general essays on the geography of Israel, such as Karmon (1971), on the one hand, and general works on Israeli society in the past and present, such as Eisenstadt (1967b) and Horowitz and Lissak (1978), on the other. The bridge itself consists of relationships between the two bases. These interrelations are in themselves complex and multiple. On the geographical side, attention will be focused mainly on Israeli settlements: the system, cores, peripheries and frontiers. From the social perspective the discussion concentrates on two parameters of the country's majority Jewish society: ideologies for spatial development and organization and the role of economic activities in the evolution of the Israeli spatial system.

This book is not a general essay on the geography of the Land of Israel. Such general works usually treat the subject on a regional or systematic basis; they scan the country region by region or describe or analyze it from several perspectives, such as population, economy, political structure, and so forth. This book does not relate to all parts of the country, and those regions discussed do not necessarily receive equal attention. Nor is this work an attempt to present systematically the various aspects that together make up the geography of the Land of Israel.

The focus here on the interrelationships of society and settlement posits a basic assumption; namely, that such interconnections do exist. In other words, it is assumed that national space does not provide merely for a required national existential element; that is only for a "passive" locational context for society and its activities. The assumption rather is that national space in general, and its constituent regions in particular, present several challenges and various opportunities to the national society and its components. These challenges and opportunities, which change over time, create different societal conceptions of space. Furthermore, they contribute to the evolution of social values, economic activities, and cultural myths. This is true not only for the "raw," initially used space, it also applies to settled space in different periods—perhaps even more so. At the same time, space serves as a social arena, and the settlement activities taking place reflect societal values, myths, and economic activities. Thus, space and spatial organization are not independent entities; they are elements inseparable

from the society at large and from the activities of the collectivity in
particular (see Soja, 1980).

The importance of illuminating the interrelationships of society and space lies in the fact that they formed the basis of developments in modern social theory in the 1980s (e.g., Giddens, 1984).
This characteristic provides the background to the present attempt
to describe, analyze, and assess some of the interrelationships
characterizing the Land of Israel and Israeli society. The first
chapter will outline the various components employed for this
sociospatial analysis of the modern Jewish Land of Israel. The suc-
cessive chapters will present aspects of society and space relations
in Israel. Part 1 will discuss the connection between transitions in
Zionist ideology, on one hand, and the development of different settlement types, on the other. Part 2 will put forward several perspectives on the cores of Jewish Land of Israel—namely,
Jerusalem and Tel Aviv—in order to highlight the development of
the two cities and the relations between them. Part 3 will introduce
frontiers, peripheries, and previous cores in the new Jewish Land
of Israel. This discussion will be devoted both to general, nationwide elements and to specific processes for major regions: the
Galilee, the Valleys, Haifa, and the Negev. The concluding chapter
will present an integrated summary covering four periods and provide some clues for possible future developments. As such, the
chapter will raise some questions as well as arrive at general conclusions, stemming from the discussions in the earlier chapters.

As the title of the book implies it will focus on Jewish Land of
Israel in the twentieth century. An interrelated and intriguing topic
is Arab Palestine during the twentieth century from the perspectives of interrelationships between society and settlement. By the
same token it would have been of interest to examine the impact of
the Zionist settlement enterprise on Arab settlements (Arab
impacts on Zionist settlement efforts will be discussed in the next
chapter). The exposition of these issues would require, however, a
completely different framework, given the traditional nature of
Arab settlements and the many centuries of relationships between
society and space in situ. Needless to say, the evidence materials
would also have come from completely different sources. For these
reasons it was felt that these issues deserve a separate treatment.

The development of the idea that lies at the foundation of this
work took place while I was spending a sabbatical year at the University of Maryland, in College Park, back in 1982–1983, when I
was exposed to social theory. The initial framework for the book
was crystallized somewhat later, but my research efforts between

1984 and 1986 went into its development, particularly on the more general relationship among time, space, and society (Kellerman, 1989). I felt that before attempting to decode some of the society-space relations in Israel, I had first to understand and develop the topic within a more theoretical and general framework. One chapter in that earlier work, though, was devoted to temporality and spatiality in Israeli society. From 1987, I began to devote most of my efforts to the Israeli subject, the fruit of which is this book.

The cooperation and assistance extended by colleagues and professionals in the various stages of writing and production of this book are gratefully acknowledged here. David Amiran, Nurit Kliot, Ruth Kark, and Shlomo Hasson read chapter drafts and made constructive comments and criticisms. Baruch Kimmerling read several drafts of the full manuscript and provided profoundly useful comments and insights, as well as encouragement, throughout the revision phase. Various referees put forward important comments and suggestions that enhanced the rewriting process. Editing was dedicatedly performed by Asher Goldstein, and the artwork was skillfully prepared by Aliza Shtokelman, both at the University of Haifa. The difficult and demanding typing was professionally and devotedly carried out by Pat Leedham and Suzan Kelly, at the University of Maryland, College Park.

An earlier version of Part 1 was previously published in Hebrew in the Monogeography series of the Department of Geography, University of Haifa. One section of Chapter 5 was published in a different version in the Hebrew journal *City and Region*. Table 1.1 and a number of paragraphs in Chapter 1 were part of an article in the Hebrew journal *Horizons*.

Modest financial support at the research stage was received from the Hecht Foundation at the University of Haifa. At the production stage support was provided by the Research Authority and the Faculty of Social Sciences, both at the University of Haifa, as well as by the Dr. Irving and Cherna Moskowitz Chair in the Land of Israel Studies, at Bar-Ilan University. The generous hospitality of the Department of Geography, University of Maryland, College Park, headed by John Townshend, is gratefully acknowledged here.

This book is dedicated to my wife, Michal. Numerous ideas in this book crystallized through long and insightful conversations with her. My thanks go to her and to our daughters, Tovy, Miriam, and Noga for their patience and understanding throughout the preparation of this book.

Chapter 1

Setting the Scene

Several basic questions may be posited on the interrelationships between society and settlement in general and those pertaining to Israel in particular. Which perspectives have been developed for the study of such relationships, and which course has the recent exploration of society and space taken? In which ways do the various basic components of society and settlement in Israel lend themselves to mutual relationships? Answering these questions will provide an elaboration of frameworks and contexts for the succeeding chapters, and this is the objective of this introductory chapter. The next section will briefly review approaches to the study of settlement processes. The discussion will then turn to four basic elements in the analyses developed in the chapters to follow: space, ideology, economic structure, and Arab impacts. These elements, especially space and ideology, will be highlighted again in subsequent chapters. Finally, the rationale for the three more specific parts of the book will be introduced.

A general comment must be made at the outset in regard to the use of geographical value-loaded terminology throughout this book. This refers, first of all, to the general name of the territory studied, a problem discussed elsewhere (Kimmerling, 1985). The sovereign unit under study will be called the State of Israel or Israel. Reference to either pre-state Israel or the current equivalent area (i.e., the State of Israel and the territories under its control since 1967) will be made through the names *Land of Israel* or *Palestine.* The territories under Israeli control since 1967 will be referred to as either *the occupied territories, the administered territories,* or just *the territories*—these terms being used both in Israel and abroad. By the same token, the area previously governed by the Kingdom of Jordan will be referred to either as *the West Bank* or as *Judea and Samaria.* The use of all these terms, representing several political camps in Israel and opinions abroad, is made to avoid any political judgment concerning the future status of these areas.

Approaches to the Study of Settlement Processes in Geography

The processes of modern Jewish settlement in the Land of Israel through rural and urban settlements, constitute a basic aspect of the human geography of the country. The topic has been discussed at the national level by several approaches: policy assessment (Shachar, 1971), regional analysis (Karmon, 1971), historical evolution (Reichman, 1979), Marxist perspectives (Hasson, 1981), positivist analysis (Shachar and Lifshitz, 1980; Bar-Gal, 1982; Bell, 1962; Grossman, 1977), and cultural-behavioral evaluation (Waterman, 1979). Another viewpoint is Kliot's (1978), which analyzes trends and changes in the political symbolism of landscapes in light of socioeconomic transitions. The approach proposed here partially complements that perspective. Whereas Kliot's analysis starts in specific landscapes, their symbols and political elements, moves to society and then back to the landscape, the starting point here is the settlement process, the various ones being discussed simultaneously with societal values. This difference stems mainly from the fact that Kliot's study focused on the individual settlement (or the micro level) through a comparison of villages representing different settlement types; the discussion here, in contrast, includes the whole country as well as some of its regions (or the macro and meso levels). This approach meets Ben-Arieh's (1982, pp. 8–9) observation that current study of the historical geography of the Land of Israel focuses on the twentieth century, looks for general frameworks, and examines social-cultural aspects, with an emphasis on locational and pattern processes.

The variety of approaches to the study of Jewish settlement processes in modern Palestine attests to a more general transition; the study of settlement processes over a national territory has undergone numerous transitions in modern geography, reflecting epistemological changes in the discipline in general (Table 1.1). The deterministic approach, which dominated geographical study from the end of the nineteenth century until the 1930s and 1940s, emphasized the importance of site and location as determinants of population dispersion (e.g., Weber, 1899). The emphasis in both the deterministic approach and the regional, which followed (e.g., Dickinson, 1964), was on distribution as a given situation (through the description of patterns) rather than as a process (or the analysis of dynamics). This latter emphasis had to await the positivist approach, which emerged in the 1930s with Christaller's (1935) theory and reached dominance in human geography in the 1950s and 1960s. The approach put a special accent on the precise description of geographical distributions and dynamics, and on the use of economic laws (like economic distance, spatial supply and demand) and social laws (like invasion and succession) for the explanation of distributions. The criticism of positivism in the 1970s brought with it attempts to study distribution processes by using Marxist or behavioral notions. The Marxist approach focused on long-range societal processes at the macro level, mainly class struggles and structural changes (e.g., Harvey, 1973). The behavioral approaches, on the other hand, dealt mainly with short-run processes through the treatment of small geographical and social units, down to individual behavior (e.g., the geography of time; see Hagerstrand, 1970). Within and beyond the behavioral approaches humanistic geography evolved, putting at its basis the concept that patterns and processes are inseparable and that human experience is the preferred element of study.

The 1980s found geography in general, and that of settlement processes in particular, coping with a variety of historical-material-istic approaches. Marxism in general claimed that socioeconomic structures ("the infrastructure") are responsible for societal development. There are those who would argue that these structures, which are systems of rules and institutions, predominate over all other social elements (Althusser and Balibar, 1970), a claim constituting the basis of the classical Marxism that influenced geography in the 1970s. On the other hand, there are those who would posit additional elements that act simultaneously with the socioeconomic infrastructure; namely, "the social superstructure" (religion, culture, etc.) (Giddens, 1981).

Structuration theory, as this last approach is known, suggests that structure and infrastructure, on the one hand, and human agency, on the other, operate continuously and simultaneously in society. In other words, daily human agency occurs under the impact of socioeconomic structures and the superstructure, while this human agency cumulatively creates new structures. A duality exists here, by which structure is at the same time both a medium and an outcome of social activity. This duality was termed *the duality of structure* (Giddens, 1979, p. 5; 1981, p. 19).

The symbiosis between society and space may be called spatiality or the societal conceptions and uses of space (Soja, 1980; Kellerman, 1989). According to Soja (1985, pp. 94–95), spatiality (and temporality, for this matter) are not merely social aspects; rather, they constitute society per se. One may better say: they are

Table 1.1. Changing Approaches to the Study of Settlement Processes in Geography

PERIOD	APPROACHES	FOCI	CHARACTERISTICS	METHODOLOGIES
Until the 1930s	Determinism	Patterns	Site and location	Verbal and map analysis
From the 1930s to the 1950s	Regionalism	Patterns	City-region relations	Verbal and map analysis
The 1960s	Positivistic theories and models	Factors and patterns	Precise description. Use of neo-classical economic and sociological theories	Quantitative (statistical) analysis
The 1970s	1. Behavioral study	1. Processes and patterns	1. Short-run processes	1. Social analysis
	2. Marxist approaches	2. Processes, structures, and patterns	2. Long-run processes	2. Social analysis
	3. Humanistic approaches	3. Processes and patterns	3. Processes and patterns are interwoven	3. Cultural analysis
The 1980s	Structuration	Patterns and previous patterns, values, structures, processes and catalysts	Patterns, values, structures and processes are interrelated	Social analysis

Source: Following Kellerman, 1984b.

the concretization of society. It is impossible to separate space and its human uses, on the one hand, from societal structure and conceptions, on the other. Space is both a medium and an outcome of social activity and relations; therefore, space is in a constant structuration process with society and, as such, constitutes an inseparable part of it. From these notions, it is possible to define the societal conception and use of space. The *conception* of space is the process through which the spatial becomes social. Uses of space contribute to the development of conceptions of space. Simultaneously, the *uses* of space turn the social into the spatial. In other words, societal conceptions of space result in varying uses of space.

Giddens's structuration theory is of special importance to geography, because it attempts to tie together patterns and processes (an element emphasized in humanistic geography) and since it acknowledges the importance of space and spatial organization as integral patterns and processes in the changing formation of society (an element emphasized by Marxist geography). Then too, the broad comprehension of social change as an outcome of both socioeconomic structures and human agency appeals to geographers, who have been typified by a holistic tradition. It is interesting to quote, in this regard, Gregory's (1978, pp. 88–89) definition of structuration: "Man is obliged to appropriate his material universe in order to survive, and [because] he is himself changed through changing the world around him in a continual and reciprocal process." The chapters that follow will attempt to develop this definition from the perspective of Jewish settlement processes in the Land of Israel during the twentieth century.

The development of social theory renewed attention to historical geography, as geographical research anchored in social theory implies the investigation of a *historical process* and the study of the social status of time. The need for an integrative study of society and space over time was also raised within the subdiscipline of historical geography itself. Thus, for example, Meinig (1978) proposed to study U.S. core-periphery relations over time as well as the impact of culture and ideology on the national landscape. Mention was made earlier of Ben-Arieh's (1982) assessment that such a study was necessary for the twentieth-century Land of Israel. Special importance has also been attached to the historical perspective by geography students of structuration theory (Dodgshon, 1987, p. 1), one of whom has even claimed that "all geography *is* historical geography in the most profound sense" (Gregory, 1982, p. 17). Obviously this historical geography is diachronic in nature, with its focus on process, rather than synchronic, reconstructing space and its organization during a given "static" period. Sociospatial analysis also includes a historical geography that attempts to "recruit" the past for the study of the present under the assumption that it is impossible to understand the present without "decoding" long-range processes.

A Framework for the Study of Settlement Processes in the Land of Israel

A framework for the study of Jewish settlement processes in twentieth-century Palestine is composed of two major aspects: (1) the introduction of a general research framework; (2) more elaborated discussions on the four principal elements (namely, space, ideology, economic structure and Arab impacts) in the analyses.

A Research Framework

There exists, at best, but a handful of cases in which a *national movement* directed a migration to a territory overseas, being both old (in the collectivity's memory) and new (for the actual settlement effort). It is, therefore, difficult to compare the *totality* of the Zionist enterprise to other new societies, though several of its dimensions may be couched within more general concepts, such as cores (see Part 2) and frontiers (Part 3).

The analysis of society and settlement in Israel obviously consists of these two basic dimensions, the spatial and the social. The spatial dimension refers both to national space (discussed mainly in the next part) and to regional (the subject of Parts 2 and 3). The social dimension, too, relates basically to the macro or national collectivity as well as to several large internal political or social segments. In the social sphere, the discussion will concentrate in the main on ideological elements and economic structures. The temporal dimension will be treated only passively, by outlining changes and transitions over time. The active role of time as a cultural and social dimension has been highlighted elsewhere (Kellerman, 1989).

The discussions will be informed by a simultaneously social and spatial perspective. Naturally, there will be some bias toward the spatial owing to the very nature of the topic, which has a profound geographical connotation; but this bias is also influenced by the disciplinary identity of the writer. The next part, devoted to ideology and settlement types, carries a stronger social accent, whereas Parts 2 and 3, dealing with cores, peripheries, and frontiers, bear a more spatial character. The discussion in general will move between the ideological-cultural and the spatial, or between the social and the spatial, with the economic dimension serving as a kind of bridge. Both society and ideology need an economic structure for their welfare and survival, whereas the development of space brings about economic challenges. The initial formation of society and space along specific economic characteristics may influence the continued evolution of that space and society, and vice versa.

Superstructure in Palestine would relate to nation, religion, language, and basic cultural values. It further includes the natural physical structure of the Land of Israel, especially its basic divisions into plains, valleys, and mountainous areas, and into settled and desert regions (Figure 1.1). It would be impossible to study the relationships between Israeli society and its settlements without looking at the cultural superstructure concomitantly with the physical-geographical system.

Structures in Israeli society contain two central aspects: socioeconomic and ideological-political. The socioeconomic structure, in its part, has two facets: one is the political-economic system, which in the Israeli economy and in the economic behavior of its citizens has both socialist and capitalist accents; the other is the preferred or senior sector among the three classical sectors (agriculture, industry, and services). Inseparable from the socioeconomic structures are the ideological-political structures or the different and changing priorities in Zionist objectives and the changing relations among them. Together, the two aspects of the structures in Israeli society determine the preferred settlement forms and patterns from an institutional perspective (e.g., rural, development town). They also exert widely varying impacts on the residential and economic location decisions of individuals.

Paralleling these two aspects there exists the cumulative activity of human agency, in our case the choice of residential and employment locations. This decision does not necessarily correspond to the structures and preferences advocated by institutional or political ideology.

The unfolding of sociospatial change over time consists, therefore, of two central parts. One part is mostly social: the system of structures relating to the predominant economic ideology, sector and Zionist objectives, which in different periods have con-

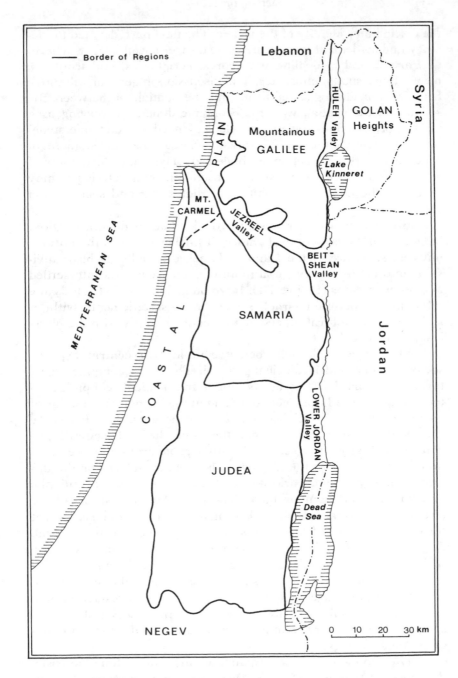

Figure 1.1.   Major Natural Regions in the Land of Israel

strained human agency in space. At the same time, human agency in space has contributed to structural changes in society in the form of the choice of residential and activity locations. The second major part of the sociospatial change process finds Israeli space to be simultaneously a medium and an outcome of the social activities of both the collectivity and its individual members. The Land of Israel as a national territory and the several regions of the country serve as a means of realizing ideological and private wishes. At the same time the spatial organization of the country is an outcome of these social activities as undertaken in a continuous process. More attention will be given in the following chapters to this part of the sociospatial process, because it is the one that constitutes the core of society and space relations. We turn now to four elements that have played a major role in the interface between society and settlement in the Jewish Land of Israel. The role of space, ideology, economic structure, and Arab impacts in the shaping of spatial organization in Israel will be surveyed to provide some general background. In doing so, special attention will be given to the highly influential political dimension. The discussions on space and ideology are couched in appropriate theoretical concepts and classifications, whereas the purpose of the discussion on economic structure is to highlight a "hidden," but crucial, sector in the Israeli economy, the service sector; theory on the role of this sector is scant (Kellerman, 1985b; 1986a).

Space

The role of space in the Israeli national context may be illuminated through the eight meanings ascribed to national space by Williams and Smith (1983). The eight were classified into two groups: one group relates to given objective aspects (physical habitat, popular culture, size, and location); the second to more abstract and subjective aspects (boundaries, autarchy, motherland, and nation building).

National space as habitat is the natural environment—the topographical structure, the climate, the land. All these facets are meaningful, not just as physical elements but also for the context of national culture. Thus, for example, the "proper" habitat for the nation of Israel in biblical times, were the mountains. It is not surprising that Scripture addresses this physical element. Thus, "But you, O mountains of Israel, shall put forth your branches and bear your fruit for my people, Israel" (Ezekiel 36:8). The spiritual peak was Jerusalem, which is described in mountainous imagery throughout the Bible: "The mount of the Lord," "Mount Zion," "Mount of the temple of the Lord," and so on.

In the modern Jewish resettlement of the land, however, the national habitats were different, as judged by the settlement accents. As of the beginning of the twentieth century, priority was accorded to the valleys (Jezreel and Jordan), which became the theme of many popular songs; for example, "the sea of wheat is moving, the song of flock rings—this is my country and its fields, this is the valley of Jezreel" (Nathan Alterman, "The Song of the Valley"). The connection between the people and its land still carried an agricultural connotation, as it had in ancient times. A second modern preferred habitat was the South and the Negev, which have developed since the dawn of statehood. "The command of existence for the State of Israel, both an economic command and a security one, is to go South" (Ben-Gurion, 1979, p. xiv). This dictum came from Israel's first prime minister, who also practiced what he preached. In reality, the national habitat in modern times has emerged neither in the valleys nor in the Negev, but along the coastal plain. Because this region was not preferred for settlement by the Zionist establishment after the 1930s, it is difficult to find popular or programmatic expressions in its favor. Moreover, the popular-mythical attitude is lacking despite the region's being the core of a typical modern Israeli agricultural symbol—the citrus fruit.

National space also serves as an arena for the development of popular culture on a regional basis, in the context of soil conditions, climate, agricultural crops, and seasons of the year. The long separation of the Jewish people from its land makes it difficult to identify Jewish regional traditions in Israel. Had such traditions existed, they would have had a mountainous character, given that Jewish settlement in most historical periods concentrated in the mountains. Modern Jewish settlement tended, in contrast, to concentrate in the plains, which in the very distant past were less-Jewish areas. Nevertheless, there have been attempts to renew the cultural attachment between the people and the land when it comes to Jewish holidays (e.g., Omer—an ancient grain measure—ceremonies during Passover, and First Fruit festivities on Shavuot, the Feast of Weeks). This trend has developed principally in the mostly secular kibbutz movement, which has attempted to create a new Jewish mode of life in Israel in part by developing festival traditions, at the center of which was the contact between humankind and land, rather than the religious Human-God relations. The First Fruits, for example, were brought to kibbutz members or to the Jewish National Fund, an organization that aimed at the "redemption of the land" (purchase and development of land). The diffusion of such traditions to the nation as a whole or their development into significant regional traditions, however, has been very limited. This lack of acceptance may be attributed to the newness of these ideas and to the urban preference of most Jewish settlers in Palestine. The partial or full conflict with religious tradition constitutes an additional factor in the restricted development and diffusion of these festivities.

The "size" dimension of national space has to do with both the size of the national territory and the size of the population living on it. These two aspects have been of particular importance for the Zionist attachment to the Land of Israel in the past and present, and they will be elaborated on in the next chapter. It will suffice to state here that the size of the national territory, and not necessarily its precise boundaries, has been a major problem both in the past (e.g., the slogan and anthem of the major rightist movement were "two banks has the Jordan") and in the present (the status of the West Bank and Gaza). The question of the size of the Jewish population in the national territory has also been a central though a consensual issue to the evolution of an Israeli nation in Palestine, given that only about 30 percent of the Jewish people currently reside in Israel.

The location of the Land of Israel is of profound significance in what this site can and cannot offer. The geopolitical location of Palestine in a junction of three continents and in the center of the Middle Eastern fertile crescent was of much commercial-cultural importance in many historical periods. In the modern era, until the mid-twentieth century, this location was of value, especially for the city of Haifa. It largely diminished in value with the partial or full sealing of road and air connections with Arab countries after Israel attained statehood in 1948. Even under these circumstances, though, the location of Israel between the Mediterranean and the Red Sea permitted relatively varied international contacts. On the other hand, this location has blessed it with but little of the richest natural resource in the Middle East: oil.

First among the four abstract-subjective characteristics of national space are its boundaries. In terms of the meaning of national space, boundaries are determined by three components: geopolitics, bureaucracy, and ethnicity. The geopolitical characteristic has importance for the security and vitality of the national political unit, the state. This characteristic has turned out to be a central issue for Jewish national space in Palestine, especially following the establishment of the state and even more so after the 1967 war. Currently, the State of Israel has only one fully recognized international border, that with Egypt, and even this one was finalized only in the late 1970s. The bureaucratic and ethnic characteristics are interconnected in the Israeli context, as they refer to the boundaries of state jurisdiction. This subject has been raised since the late 1970s, when the idea of autonomy for the West Bank and Gaza was proposed. One ingredient in such a solution is, obviously, the extent of contact between the two ethnic groups, Arabs and Jews.

The bureaucratic characteristic has an additional dimension, namely, the internal administrative division of the country. The State of Israel does not enjoy a federal structure, and several implications of the centralization of power will be discussed throughout this book. The country is administratively divided into six districts, which in turn are subdivided into fifteen subdistricts (including the Golan Heights, but excluding the West Bank and Gaza). This division was originally introduced by the British Mandatory authorities. The six districts are Jerusalem, Tel Aviv, Haifa, the North, the Center, and the South (Figure 1.2; for the list of subdistricts, see Table 6.5).

A second abstract characteristic is autarchy. National space is the primary unit for the provision of human needs—the most basic ones for human survival—originating in the agricultural world. Zionist socialist movements indeed emphasized agriculture, albeit more as "a return to the land" but also as a basis of material provision for the Jewish community (several slogans in pre-state days called for preference to be given to a "Hebrew product" or to "the land's product"). The agricultural sector received priority in Israeli economic development for a long time, and it attained a remarkable success. The preferred status of agriculture is still noticeable in regulations concerning "the freezing and defrosting of agricultural land." These regulations promulgate strict controls to prevent the transformation of rural land uses into urban uses. The importance of land as a resource was also expressed in the efforts to assure national ownership of land—an issue that was not merely political but cultural, as well. The purchase of land from Arabs was considered an act of "redemption of land." Selling nationally owned land was prohibited. Its leasing to individuals, businesses, and organizations, on the other hand, was a transformation of the biblical idea of the Jubilee Year. The original commandment not only called for the return of land to its original tribal ownership, it also pointed to its Divine ownership. The Bible commanded, "The

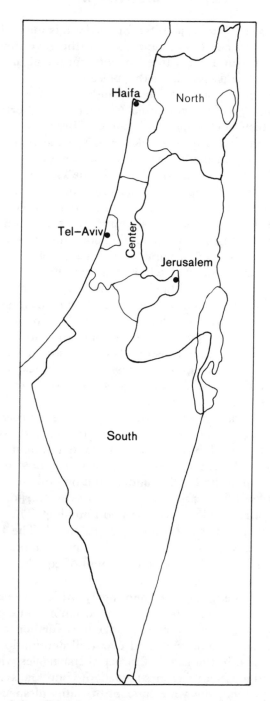

Figure 1.2. Division of the State of Israel into Districts

land must not be sold in perpetuity; for the land is mine" (Leviticus 25:25). National ownership of land vis-à-vis the government or the Jewish National Fund constituted a national-social anchoring as opposed to the biblical sacred, for this basic resource.

National space may serve as a motherland for one national unit (or nation) or for several units. As such, a motherland points to belonging: historical rights and home. This is so with regard either to national space as a whole or to specific regions or sites within it, all of which could provide memories and symbols. The importance of the idea of "motherland" in the Israeli context stems from the long physical separation between the Jewish people and their land. Also, the Arab-Jewish conflict necessitated justifying the modern existence of a Jewish entity in the Land of Israel through the use of historical rights. The contemporary meaning of the historical Jewish motherland in the Land of the Israel has turned into a major internal issue over the status of Judea and Samaria. On the one hand, these areas constituted the core of the ancient Israelite kingdoms; on the other hand, these same areas currently constitute the core for the Palestinian population. The desire to bridge the ancient Jewish past and the Israeli present in the context of national space also finds expression in the accent on renewed biblical and Talmudic Jewish place names (Cohen and Kliot, 1981) and in the conducting of extensive archaeological excavations, especially in Jerusalem.

The last characteristic of national space is its role in nation building, and this is of crucial significance for an understanding of the attachment of the Jewish community to its national territory in the modern era. The Land of Israel, as territory, has served as an element in and an arena for the modern nation building of the Jewish people. At least for Labor Zionism, however, territory and people were not sufficient elements for nation building. The creation of a new mode of life in the territory was required. The building of national space may provide for fraternity and national consciousness. It may further enable the achievement of equality among several social groups. In Palestine and later on in Israel, these aspects were emphasized mainly by the Labor party, which preferred a centralized government and which maintained labor and equality values. Nation building in and through space may further be manifested through settlers coping with and eventual domination of harsh natural conditions. In the Land of Israel, the struggles with the valley-swamps and the Negev deserts turned into national symbols.

Generally, then, the very concept of national space is multifaceted, as is its social significance. The chapters to follow will examine some of these aspects for the various ways in which they have been utilized in several settlement types, and in cores, frontiers, and boundaries.

Ideology

The role of ideology in the development of the sociospatial system in Israel will be discussed in three phases. First, definitions of ideology will be introduced and interpreted. Second, the role of ideology in geographical analysis will be explored. Third, some thoughts on a geography of ideas and ideology will be presented.

Ideology was defined by Therborn (1980, p. 2) as the "medium through which [this] consciousness and meaningfulness operate." Seliger (1976) defined an "inclusive" ideology as "sets of ideas by which men posit, explain and justify ends and means of organized social action, and specifically political action, irrespective of whether such action aims to preserve, amend, uproot or rebuild a given order" (p. 14). The "restrictive" use of ideology was reserved for extremist ideologies or for ideologies present in some groups and absent from others. This formulation may leave the impression that political action comes first and ideology serves as a kind of a posteriori justification for faits accomplis. Seliger, however, advanced four propositions on the interrelationship of ideology and social-political action (1976, pp. 15–16). First, "ideology is linked to politics no less than all politics are linked to ideology. Ideology requires politics as its mode of implementation while political decisions are, at one stage or another, related to moral principles." Second, "ideology can as little be divorced from factual knowledge as from tolerably rational justification and moral and other prescriptions." Third, different ideologies do not necessarily oppose one another. Fourth, "since ideology is action-oriented thought—i.e., thought conceived to guide political action and invoked to justify it—the way ideology functions in the political process, or is intended to function, must have a bearing on its nature." Therefore, ideology has two-way relations with political action, with other ideologies, and with factual knowledge.

Our argument, outlined earlier, is that the organization of national and regional space in Israel has been ideologically charged. The ideology in the Israeli case has had complex objectives and changes over time. It has always had the plural form; in other words, there have always existed several competing or parallel ideologies. Political action therefore mediates between ideology and the organization of space. As such, political action has a more complex role in national and regional space than merely providing for "authority relations," which are "the structures of command which maintain order in both work and non-work activities" (Wolch and Dear, 1989, p. 10).

Society and space relations at the meso and macro levels may call for two-way flows of ideas and spatialities, from ideology as structure to political action and from there to spatial organization and back. These flows may be controlled and restrained. First, there is space as superstructure; that is, the almost absolute constraints that space may impose on social action in terms of size, shape, topography, fertility, and so forth. Second, and even more important, there is human agency, which may act in ways not "approved" by ideology and political action or structures. Third, there are economic conditions, which supply another set of structures. Fourth, there is the possibility that several ideologies will prevail in parallel or in conflict with one another. Political action may permit spatial activity (in the form of settlement, agricultural, industrial, and other construction activities) for single ideologies only, or it may implement several ideologies in parallel or in compromised or intermingled ways through the political process.

Modern Israeli society, since its inception at the end of the nineteenth century, has displayed several characteristics that have permitted such relationships among ideologies, political action, and spatial organization. The political organization of Israeli society both in pre-state times and afterward was based on competing political ideologies. The "play" among those ideologies was through open, democratic elections even before statehood. Following the establishment of the State of Israel, all governments were coalition governments. The democratic nature of Israeli society permitted actions of human agency side by side with and in contrast to the political ideologies, despite the role of institutions as ideological controls in the form of laws, education, and the media (Anderson, 1973).

The construction of Jewish space in Palestine was executed under the umbrella of Zionist ideology and within a short time span. The development of villages, development towns, frontiers, and peripheries were pursued until recently almost exclusively with profound ideological loadings, both sectoral and state oriented. Part of the evolution of the cores in Tel Aviv and Jerusalem in fact originated directly or indirectly from this ideology. On the other hand, most of the population throughout the 110 years of modern Jewish settlement has preferred big city over rural or town residence, which latter were preferred by the ideological and political establishment. A possible interpretation of this trend may lie in the dissonance between ideology and spatial organization; however, the long duration of this seeming dualism points to the existence of a structuration process. On the one hand, a leading ideology and the economic and political resources at its service influenced the employment and residence locational decisions of some of the population. On the other hand, the evolution of large and modern cities contributed to the recent decline in status and importance of rural and town ideologies and to the rise of urban ideological elements relating both to residential values and patterns and to social-cultural values in various spheres of life.

Geographers and social theorists alike have not paid much attention to the link between political ideologies and spatial organization. Taylor (1985, p. 158), for instance, noted that "political geography has totally neglected the study of political ideologies." This absence of study almost seems inexplicable, given the notion that "space has been shaped and molded from historical and natural elements, but this has been a political process. Space is political and ideological. It is a product literally filled with ideologies" (Lefebvre, 1976, p. 31). It seems that geographers (and social theorists, for that matter) assumed that one leading, spatially simple ideology prevails at any given time and is gradually taken over by another (religion, nation-state, capitalism, in this order) (see, e.g., Taylor, 1985, pp. 164–166; Soja, 1989; Giddens, 1985, pp. 16–17, 219–221). Often a reader is left with the impression that ideology has been treated in its restrictive sense; namely, as "their" ideology.

Two exceptions may be noted in this regard. The first occurs when some reference is made to the micro level, or the local, "ideological landscape" (see a study on Israel by Kliot, 1978). Giddens (1985, p. 17) briefly mentioned that the "physical lay-out of many traditional cities has ideological effects...[in the form of] state and religious edifices, giving a visual representation of power." The second exception is an approach put forth by Guelke (1974), entitled "an idealist alternative in human geography." Guelke did not refer to ideology per se, but to the analysis of space vis-à-vis the rational intention of the actors; Gregory (1978, p. 133) termed this an *idealist geography*. Both Harvey (1969, p. 56) and Gregory (1978, pp. 132–133) noted the problems of validation encountered in such a *verstehen* approach. In addition to this difficulty, an idealist geography seems to be based on a number of hidden assumptions that are not too realistic: (1) What is observed in space fully or partially reflects that which was intended. (2) What eventually occurred in space is fully or partially influenced by that which was intended.

(3) There is no room for conflicting thoughts and intentions (or ideologies), which would create more complex spatial outcomes. (4)
There is no room for a case in which one person or group would
do the thinking while another would be in charge of implementation (presumably in deviation from the declared intention). (5)
There is no place for the possibility that thinking on spatial action
will occur in one location and implementation in another.

The neglect of the ideological aspect in the literature on spatial organization and social relations may be attributed to Western
spatial experience in general and the urban Western experience in
particular. As previously mentioned, this experience displayed in
each period one prevailing ideology centered on a specific dimension, whether socioeconomic (class society), religious (traditional
society), political (nation-state), or economic (capitalism). Thus, all
cities and most regions within a certain society at a given time
could present similar trends. The Israeli experience in the twentieth century has been more complex, however. It involved a multi-
faceted ideology (Zionism), subdivided into several ideological-
political groups, all of which have enjoyed access to space in terms
of space formation. Hence, at given times, the spatial organization
of the Land of Israel reflected several ideologies simultaneously.

Space may be seen as both absorbing and creating ideas and
ideology. A geography of ideas and ideology would thus entail three
inseparable dimensions: first, ideas about space and geography,
namely, where and how spatial organization should take place; second, a geography of ideas, namely where ideological centers are
located in general and those emphasizing geographical development
in particular; third, the evolution of a spatial organization as a result
of the first two dimensions, namely, where and how it did evolve.
That these three dimensions may be suggested implies that the location of thinking about geography, the conceived target areas, and
the eventual location of geographical change do not necessarily
have to be identical sites. Furthermore, our analysis of the process
leading from ideology through political action to spatial organization implies that the "what" and "how" at the a priori stage do not
necessarily have to be identical to the practical outcome. Thus, if
spatiality means the conceptions *and* uses of space, then these two
components do not have to occur at the same location. The tensions
between spatial vision and reality, as well as those between places of
geographical thought and implementation are reflected in Israel in
the changing roles and status of cores and frontiers.

One should not mistakenly equate these societal transmission
and structuration processes with urban and regional planning,

since the latter constitutes the professional element of political action. Planning may be restricted by legal regulations and it may sometimes be bypassed by human agency. One should also not conceive of ideological centers only as capital cities, as the geographical location of ideological centers may potentially be varied. Obviously, spatial change whether as a direct or an indirect result of ideology and human agency, may bring about a change in the location of future ideological centers.

Economic Structure

The economic element has been considered central to the structuration process that operates between social structures and human agency in Western society (see, e.g., Giddens, 1981; 1984). Economic structure has been tied to social theory, and its examination pursued in relation to the evolution of modern capitalism.

In Israeli society, a stronger relationship exists between economic structure and ideology than it does in Western society because of the process of nation building. Generally, such a process requires the sacrifice of the individual's interests in favor of the collectivity's, and the determination of economic activities is at the mercy of the latter (Kimmerling, 1983a, p. 155). Until recently, this process was expressed in Israel through socialist accents in the social ideology, so that institutions and rules were established for cooperative agriculture, union-owned industries and services, and government ownership of manufacturing and commerce. Thus, at one time about two-thirds of the Israeli economy was publicly owned, and governmental involvement in the licensing, control, and operation of economic activity was quite strong. This process peaked in the 1950s, a slow relaxation of public involvement then set in, and signs of more radical change emerged in the late 1980s. From the perspective of individuals, the economic system has altered from one that has rewarded through participation in the economic process and through the creation of economic power to one that rewards by money compensation, profits, and economic success (Kimmerling, 1983a, p. 160).

The vast amount of capital imported by the public sector for direct investment in manufacturing since 1948 has not necessarily resulted in the development of flourishing national peripheries with advanced and core-integrated plants. It might well be that the application of an alternative development plan calling for the investment of imported funds in infrastructure, especially in transportation and telecommunications (the Thron plan), would have facilitated more extensive flows of people and resources to the peripheries (Zohar, 1974). On the other hand, the massive urban concentration of the population throughout the evolution of the modern Jewish entity, coupled with the development of a vigorous private sector in large cities, contributed to the gradual transition from a socialist to a capitalist accent in the Israeli economy.

Another structural economic aspect is the relative status of the major economic sectors. Until the late 1950s, agriculture was the ideologically preferred sector, and the one that was thus supposed to receive priority in human and economic resource allocation. Since the 1960s, this status was reserved for manufacturing. As things turned out, however, the unpreferred, even condemned, service sector has always been the senior sector in terms of both investments and employment concentration (Kellerman, 1986a). As such, this sector reflected the heavy idelogical-political accent in Israeli public life; on the other hand, it also contributed to the emergence and dominance of the urban cores. It deserves, therefore, more detailed attention here.

As far back as 1931, 45.4 percent of the Jewish labor force was employed in services (the equivalent general percentage for Palestine was 27.9 percent) (Gur, 1967, p. 87). In 1987, the percentage of service employment in Israel had reached 65.5 percent, comprising 29.0 percent employed in public and community services; 6.4 percent in personal and other services; 13.9 percent in commerce and lodging; 6.6 percent in transportation, storage, and communications; and 9.6 percent in finance and business services (Central Bureau of Statistics, 1988). The overall percentage of service employment has been constantly on the rise (Kellerman, 1986a). A slight transition could also be noticed in the composition of service subsectors since the mid-1980s: employment in public services has decreased slightly, whereas more people are employed in commerce and lodging. An increase in service employment is typical of developed countries; until a few years ago, however, in these countries employment in services was lower than employment in manufacturing (Kellerman, 1985b). In Palestine and later in Israel, the percentage of employment in manufacturing has never been higher than employment in services (Kellerman, 1986a). During the critical years of Jewish nation building efforts, 1917–1939, 42.5 percent of Jewish Agency investments in Palestine were in services, whereas only 38.4 percent went to agriculture and rural settlements (Olizur, 1939, p. 273). The Jewish tendency to service employment, before and following statehood, has been in sharp contrast to the ideological wish of Labor Zionism to turn the Diaspora Jewish employment pyramid upside down, so as to create a wide basis of employment in agriculture and manufacturing. This contrast is of special importance, given the ideological value attached to agriculture and manufacturing, and the condemnation of the urban tertiary sector. It may be explained from several perspectives: historical, economic, social, and political.

From a historical perspective, the 1920s witnessed the evolution of a double establishment, a civil-British one coupled with several Jewish-Zionist establishments. As such, this decade was a formative one for the evolution of the service sector in Palestine and, later, in Israel. The British prepared the infrastructure for modern municipal government, a planning administration, a judiciary system, a constabulary, and religious services. Simultaneously, the organized Jewish community in Palestine (the so-called Yishuv) established its own segmented and multifaceted administration. In addition to local "community committees," there developed a central Zionist establishment through the Jewish Agency that dealt with land purchase, settlement, foreign relations, immigration and security. The evolving Jewish labor union (Histadruth), however, constructed its own service system in areas as varied as housing, education, health, publishing, employment placing, banking, commerce, and insurance. Several political parties also became involved in the provision of services for their members in housing, employment, banking, and so on. A lion's share of these establishments continued to exist after 1948, when the State of Israel was established, despite the nationalization of education and employment-placing services. The union economy today still amounts to about one-third of Israel's manufacturing, almost all of its public transportation, and about one-third of the insurance business; it also includes the largest bank, and the most extensive department store, supermarket, and hypermarket chains. The attempts to build labor-owned and party-controlled economies brought about an increased concentration of employment in services. When competition was absent, the result was at times redundant services and inefficiency.

From an economic viewpoint an important factor in the development of services was imported capital, which amounted in 1983 to 9 percent of GNP, a very high ratio compared to other countries. In pre-state times, most imported capital was private, and only 15 percent-30 percent was public (Gur, 1967, p. 111). The ratio of private to public-national capital imports had constantly declined, from 8.5 in 1898 to 1.5 in 1945 (with the exception of the mid-1930s during the Jewish emigration from Germany, when the ratio reached 10.5!) (Weintraub, Lissak, and Azmon, 1969, p. 27). Following statehood, however, this ratio was reversed; about three quarters of current capital imports are public-national. Before 1948, most public capital went to services, whereas most of the imported private capital was invested in manufacturing and housing construction, but not in commerce (Kellerman, 1986a). After 1948, some of the imported funds went directly to the service sector without government control (these were mainly monies imported by the Jewish Agency and the Histadruth). At the same time, government-imported capital permitted the evolution of central and local bureaucracies without regard to the domestic tax base.

The social perspective presents aspects of supply and demand in the development of the service sector (Gur, 1967, p. 39). On the supply side was the immigration to Israel; this, in turn, led to a rising demand for services, especially education and health services. The social character of the immigration to a large degree suited employment in services, and the willingness to avoid unemployment contributed to the evolution of services. These factors decreased in importance from the 1960s, with the decrease in immigration. Nevertheless, given additional factors, the service sector has not declined. From a demand perspective, Israel is still a state with a large segment of minors in its population, about one-third, a high percentage relative to developed countries. When coupled with a desire to provide complex educational and health services, this fact increases the service sector.

Politics have also played an important role in the development of the Israeli service sector, despite its inferior ideological status. Mention was made of the extensive development of services by the political sector. The emerging Jewish establishment did not inherit the British *service* tradition in the civil service. Rather the emphasis was *domination* through service provision, a tradition imported through immigration from Eastern Europe and later on from Mediterranean countries. Moreover, *activism*, being a central element in Jewish political culture (Akzin and Dror, 1966; Segre, 1985, pp. 138–139), contributed to the flourishing of bureaucracies. While the production sectors in the economy have adopted productivity as a major value, given domestic and international competition, this outlook started to make headway in the public service sector only in recent years.

The Israeli service sector basically represents an immigrant society based on ideological motivation more than on economic stimulation. Again, a slow process of change has characterized the decades since the 1960s, and there are increased signs of a more radical change beginning in the late 1980s. Government has been under extreme pressure to cut expenses. The change of power from Labor to right-wing Likud in 1977 reduced governmental economic support for union and party services; therefore, further change, even of a structural nature, may evolve in upcoming years.

The historical evolution of the service sector and its current transition are related to the modern spatial organization of Israel. As we shall see in Part 2, a separation developed in the 1920s between what became the largest city in the country (Tel Aviv) and the capital (Jerusalem). This separation contributed to the development of services. Related to it, and to the creation of a double core, was the evolution of Tel Aviv into a primate city; some 40 percent of the Israeli population live in its metropolitan area. The existence of a primate city tends to increase the service sector, as has been the case in France and Britain (Singlemann, 1978, pp. 90–91; Daniels, 1982, p. 37; Kellerman, 1985b). In relatively small Israel, this development is expressed in the concentration of finance and business services in Tel Aviv, which is also the headquarters of labor union services.

The evolution of a privately owned service sector side by side with all the publicly owned systems accompanied the growth of large cities and the modernization of agriculture and industry. A demand subsequently rose for modern producer services in several areas, such as advertising, marketing, computers, and consulting. As of 1974, the percentage of employment in business services was higher than that in agriculture, and employment in commerce and lodging had started to rise as well. As already noted, the public sector has declined somewhat since the mid-1980s. In 1980, 20.8 percent of computer workers were employed in the business sector, 7.3 percent in government, and just 14 percent in the public sector. These changes might point to a deeper, structural change of the Israeli economy and society. The 1950s were devoted to the absorption of extensive waves of immigration; in the 1960s, the agricultural sector underwent modernization; and in the 1970s, a similar process occurred in industry, especially through the development of high-tech industries. The 1980s marked the beginning of a change in the service sector. The transition from a largely public, politically and ideologically loaded service system to a modern, privately owned and competition-based system might be very difficult, however, because of the political power that has accumulated in the service sector and because this sector *is* the Israeli political system. The pressures for regional rather than relative nationally based elections and coalition governments as well as pressures for the direct election of the prime minister are related to an oncoming transition in the structure of a service system that allocates power to political sectors.

Arab Impacts

The three elements described so far relate to the Zionist entity per se and its attitude to the land. The impact of indigenous Arabs on the Zionist settlement process has been both external and internal to the Zionist enterprise. The external impact was manifested in two main ways. First, though living in the country, Arabs were external in the sense that the Zionists attempted to establish a Jewish homeland with increasing emphasis on the separation of the indigenous Palestinian Arab population. Second, Zionists had to respond, beginning in 1948, to threats, wars, and eventually peace originating in the neighboring Arab countries. The internal impact came in the very presence of Arabs in Palestine, Arabs who would have had to live next to Jews, whether under any division of Palestine into two states or, obviously so, within the same political entity. In other words, when the first Jewish immigration wave began some 110 years ago, the newcomers found an already settled Arab population that could be neither ignored nor eliminated, as occurred in other new societies.

The distinction between internal and external impacts with regard to Palestinian Arabs also reflected a double interest on their part in relation to the Zionist enterprise. The internal-domestic interest consisted of the national aspirations of the Palestinians, which emerged at the end of World War I. These aspirations were fed to some degree by the perceived threat of a gradual Zionist takeover of lands; for that reason, too, the Zionist enterprise engendered feelings of antagonism among Palestinians toward the Jews. On the other hand, as will be demonstrated later in this section, Palestinian uprisings have themselves contributed to the enhancement of Zionist settlement activity. Though each national movement was kindled and nourished by many other factors, it is interesting to note that the actions or reactions of one group influenced the other group, often in opposite ways than expected.

The international Arab dimension has been of major importance for the Palestinian cause, because it reflects a Pan-Arab objection to the Zionist enterprise on cultural-religious grounds, not just national-political motives. This disapproval is based on the holiness of Jerusalem to Islam and the inferior status reserved for Jews.

The double-edged sword of the Arab dimension has presented a variable importance to Jewish settlement activity over time. It has had an impact on all three major sociospatial dimensions, as will be seen in the three following parts of the book. Still, the over-all Arab dimension was there and not there at one and the same time. On the one hand, it did and does hold various implications for Zionist settlement; on the other hand, the predominant willingness to build a *Jewish* society and sovereign entity has made Zionist leaders frequently ignore the Arabs' very existence (inside the Land of Israel) and concentrate attention and activity only on the Jewish sector.

Four aspects of the Zionist settlement enterprise may be attributed partially or wholly to Arab impacts: (1) the distinction among phases in the settlement process; (2) the contribution and status of kibbutzim as a settlement form; (3) the increased geographical separation between Jews and Arabs in Palestine until 1967; (4) the persistent Zionist policy until 1948 of buying land from Arabs. These aspects will be briefly treated in the remaining paragraphs of this chapter and referred to again from different perspectives in later chapters.

Although one might assume that the growth of a settlement project would naturally involve various phases, it is a matter of fact that the expansion and development of Zionist settlement occurred in reaction to various periods of Arab hostility and violence. The major outbreaks of riots and wars between Jews and Arabs and their impacts on settlement are outlined in Table 1.2. Three riot periods prior to the establishment of the state moved Zionist activity from an emphasis on single settlements (1920–21) to the creation of settlement regions (1929) and finally to the shaping of a national settlement map (1936–39). The 1920–21 Arab attacks on settlements in the North, in the Upper Galilee, notably on Tel-Hai, resulted in the inclusion of the Huleh Valley within British Mandatory Palestine and demonstrated the crucial importance of single settlements. Furthermore, the 1920–21 riots turned Tel Aviv into the major Jewish center; and it received, following the riots, a status of township. The 1929 riots, which for the first time were nationwide, led to a decision to develop two concentrations of settlements: along the coastal plain and in the Jezreel Valley (Avneri, 1980). Between 1929 and 1936, 80 new settlements were added to the 100 already in existence, and 60 of the new ones were located in the two preferred regions (Avidar, 1980). It was because of this decision, too, that the destroyed mountainous Jewish community of Hebron was not reconstructed (Sela, 1989). As a

result of these decisions, geographical separation was increased
between the mainly mountainous Arab community and the Jewish
concentration in level regions. Following the 1929 riots, the need
also emerged to stress security considerations in the siting of new
settlements (Kimmerling, 1983b). Another interesting development
was Ben-Gurion's (1963, originally written in 1929) early call for a
national settlement map, which was adopted only in 1936 (in this
connection see Figure 2.1).

Table 1.2. Impact of Palestinian Riots and Arab-Israeli Wars on
Zionist Settlement Activity

YEAR	EVENT	IMPACT ON SETTLEMENT
1920–21	Riots	1. The concept of single settlement as boundary creators (Kimmerling, 1983b). 2. The importance of single-settlement defense for settlements at large (Kimmerling, 1983b). 3. Tel Aviv becoming a town and a major Jewish center (Ram, 1982).
1929	Riots	1. Emergence of settlement regions (the coastal plain and the Jezreel Valley) (Avneri, 1980; Avidar, 1980; Kimmerling, 1983b). 2. Increased regional-rural separation between Jews and Arabs (Sela, 1989). 3. Early conception of a national settlement map ("Ben-Gurion Plan," 1963). 4. Settlement siting according to security considerations (Kimmerling, 1983b; Avidar, 1980).
1936–39	Riots	1. The creation of a national settlement map (Avneri, 1980). 2. The isolation of Jerusalem (Paz, 1989).
1948	War	1. The defense of boundaries via settlements. 2. Separation between Jews and Arabs in the urban sector.
1967	War	1. Jews and Arabs in a unified city of Jerusalem.
1973	War	1. Cancellation of the separation between Jews and Arabs in the rural-mountainous sector.
1987–	Riots	1. Increasing separation between Jews and Arabs in Mixed regions.

The concentration of Jewish settlement activity on the plains and valleys together with the Arab economic boycott of the Jewish sector increased separation between Jews and Arabs even further. An interesting issue concerned the isolation of mountainous Jerusalem. Ben-Gurion, in his 1929 "plan for security and fortification" proposed to strengthen and expand Jewish Jerusalem, but not as part of the national settlement map, with its focus on the plains. Attempts to purchase land along the "Jerusalem Corridor" leading to the coastal plain did not result in extensive settlement (Paz, 1989; Avneri, 1980).

The need to cope with the Arab internal challenge, which was being posed at an ever-expanding geographical scale, added to the importance of kibbutzim as a preferred settlement form. Given its strong ideological spirit and tight collective structure, the kibbutz could best fit the settlement task. Therefore, 68 percent of the kibbutzim were established at times of security problems, compared to 38 percent of the moshavim, and but 8 percent of the moshavot (Weintraub et al., 1969, pp. 29–30).

The establishment of the State of Israel in 1948 and its first war against the Arab countries yielded two settlement results. First, border settlements were now built to *defend existing* borders rather than to determine new boundaries. Border settlements have been established close to all borders throughout the history of Israel (see, Efrat, 1981; Newman, 1989). The second result was the separation of Arabs and Jews in the three large cities, much like the earlier separation in the rural sector. Arab Jerusalem was now ruled by Jordan, and almost all the Arab residents of Jaffa (adjoining Jewish Tel Aviv) and Haifa had fled during the war. Between 1948 and 1967, then, the impact of Arabs on settlement trends was mainly external, the hostility of Arab countries yielding hundreds of border settlements.

The 1967 war renewed close settlement contacts (as well as other renewed or reinforced contacts) between Jews and Arabs; it also expanded Israeli settlement efforts in two phases. The first phase came about in the urban sector in reunified Jerusalem, it led to a larger and stronger city, the capital now being well connected with the coastal plain. The second phase, which occurred in the wake of the *shock* of the 1973 war, manifested itself within the country rather than along the borders—the settlement in the mountainous and Arab Galilee and also in Samaria and Judea. With the exception of the efforts in the Jerusalem Corridor in the early 1950s, the post-1973 activity amounted to the first systematic Zionist attempt to settle the mountainous and Arab parts of the country. The result has reversed the very first stage of Zionist settlement activity by causing proximity between the Arab and Jewish rural sectors.

The Palestinian riots known as *Intifada* that started in 1987 *did not* bring about any *new* Jewish settlement effort (at least it had not as of early 1991) that could have signaled either a weakening of the Zionist-Israeli settlement effort or spirit or the possibility of establishing some kind of political solution. Two developments should not be ignored in this regard. First, the Intifada intensified the paving of roads that connected Jewish settlements in the occupied territories directly with Israeli centers. This action was due to attacks on Jewish traffic on roads passing through Arab settlements and may have enhanced the creation of two completely separated settlement sectors despite their interwoven locations in the disputed regions. Second, as the settlement enterprise is still young, the Soviet immigration wave beginning in 1990 may cause a major increase in the Jewish population in the territories, this population consisting of both veteran and newly arrived Israelis (though the officialy announced policy up to the 1991 Gulf War was not to deliberately settle Soviet immigrants there).

The dependence of the Zionist settlement enterprise on land purchases from Arabs caused, among other things, the concentration of the settlement effort in the plains and valleys of Palestine, areas that were only sparsely settled and less favored by the Arabs. As will be seen in the next chapter, the Zionist movement had attempted since its early work in Palestine not to hurt individual Arabs and their property. This approach, it was believed, might convince the Arabs that Zionist projects would benefit them, too (Avneri, 1980, pp. 208–209). Although this policy was not changed as a result of the various riot periods in the pre-state era, the State of Israel has been involved in sometimes massive Arab land confiscations for the establishment of new Jewish settlements. The mountainous West Bank project, however, was based on land purchases and government-owned land that was almost always unsuitable for agricultural purposes. One effect has been the non-agricultural basis of this settlement project. The new trend, for its part, has brought about a transition in rural settlement patterns in Israel proper, as well.

Conclusion

This chapter has introduced some basic elements and frameworks for the upcoming, detailed analyses. Essentially three major

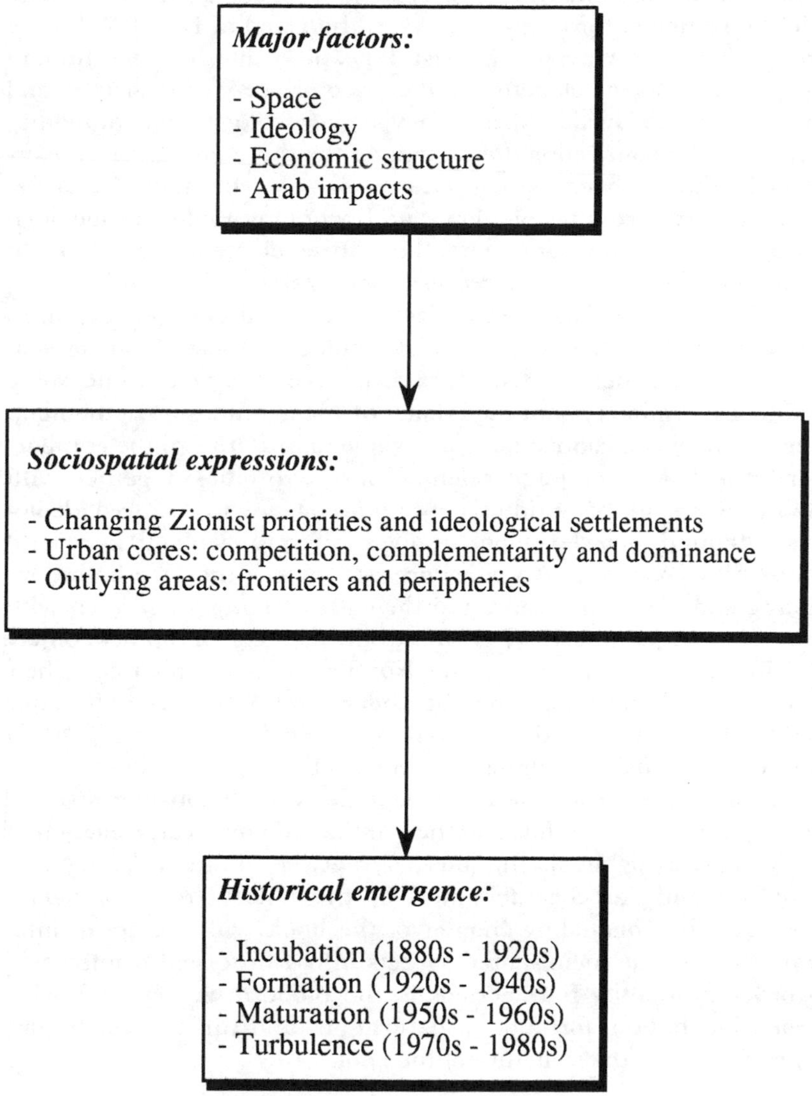

Major factors:

- Space
- Ideology
- Economic structure
- Arab impacts

Sociospatial expressions:

- Changing Zionist priorities and ideological settlements
- Urban cores: competition, complementarity and dominance
- Outlying areas: frontiers and peripheries

Historical emergence:

- Incubation (1880s - 1920s)
- Formation (1920s - 1940s)
- Maturation (1950s - 1960s)
- Turbulence (1970s - 1980s)

Figure 1.3. Society and Settlement in the Modern Jewish Land of Israel

dialectics are assumed to have been in operation throughout the modern settlement process by Jews in the Land of Israel. All three are strongly interwoven. The first dialectic is that between human agency and social structures; the second, between society and space; and the third, is between vision (ideology) and outcomes (reality). The connecting thread among the three processes in operation in the evolving Israeli society may be summarized as the attempt to suppress people, land, and economy under an ideological umbrella. At the same time, these three elements have "fought back," in different ways, to redress social values.

The next part will directly continue the discussions begun in this chapter by introducing Zionist ideologies, their changing spatial objectives, their settlement records over the years, and some initial observations about the impact of social values on settlement. The emphasis on Zionist ideology will lead in Part 2 to the comparison of Tel Aviv and Jerusalem. These two cities, together with Haifa, represent the antithesis of human agency to declared ideologies, although their development owes much to ideology, in several ways. Moreover, the two cities present images that are both conflicting and complementary, and their growth implies conflict with frontiers and peripheries. Part 3 introduces the geographical object of Zionist ideology, namely the frontiers and peripheries. Their evolution and transitions may be understood only after two major forces are elucidated: the ideology *for* their development (Part 1) and the *competing* geographical magnets—the big cities (Part 2).

All chapters relate to all three dialectics; obviously, however, Part 1 gives more emphasis to the relationship between society and space; Part 2 highlights the interplay between human agency and structure; and Part 3 centers more on the dialectic of vision *versus* realities. The concluding chapter of the book will attempt to integrate the various socioispatial aspects into a historical framework, in order to identify four periods in the modern history of Jewish Israel: incubation, formation, maturation, and turbulence. Figure 1.3 summarizes the structure of the book.

Part 1

Transitions in the Priorities of Zionist Objectives
and in Their Geographical Implementation

Chapter 2
Pre-State Ideological Settlement Activity

Introduction

"To become a free nation in our land" is probably the key phrase in the Zionist and later Israeli national anthem. This phrase discloses three central objectives of Zionism and the State of Israel: first, the creation and nurture of freedom; second, the concentration or ingathering of the Jewish people; third, the implementation of these two goals in the country of the Jewish people, the Land of Israel. This order of the three objectives is not an order of priority; it merely reflects the syntax of the phrase. The purpose of Part 1 of the book is to introduce the thesis that there has been a changing order of priority among the three central objectives of Zionism. These three objectives—population, mode of life, and territory— which are basic to nation building in general, have a geographical context. Their implementation in Israel has been conditioned, in part, by the physical construction of the country and its several regions; that is, through the creation of settlement patterns. These patterns and the shifting regional emphases of settlement activity may be termed *settlement ideals*. The settlement pattern changed its accent from cooperative villages to development towns and eventually to community settlements, while the regional emphasis moved from the northern valleys to the Negev desert and, more recently to the mountains of the Galilee, Judea, and Samaria. As will be seen through a detailed matrix, an interrelationship exists between transitions in the priorities of Zionist objectives, on the one hand, and settlement ideals or patterns on the other (Kellerman, 1984b).

An examination of the relational system among several national objectives has rarely been pursued, whether in political geography in general or in analyses of the Zionist enterprise in particular. Zionist activity was characterized by profound ideological loading for the building of a new society (Eisenstadt, 1967a). We shall refer here to three works in this regard: Gottmann (1973) for the more general level, and E. Cohen (1969) and Reichman (1975) for Zionist projects. Gottmann noted that "the relationship between sovereignty and territory is built upon a connecting link: *the people* in the territory or, if it is devoid of permanent settlement,

33

at least *the activities* of people within the territory" (p. 4). He defined *territory* like this:

> Territory, although a very substantial, material, measurable, and concrete entity, is the product and indeed the expression of the psychological features of human groups. It is indeed a *psychosomatic* phenomenon of the community, and as such is replete with inner conflicts and apparent contradictions. Territorial sovereignty is an indispensable attribute of independent nations: the territory is the very basis on which national existence rests, the "sacred soil" in whose defense true citizens will be prepared to give their lives. The concept is one of self-preservation, but also one of preserving the community's way of life, the right to self-government, freedom, and whatever opportunity a free people is entitled to. (p. 15)

Gottmann thus argued that it is impossible to make a distinction among territory, the people living on it, and their mode of life when sovereignty is analyzed from the territorial perspective. He did not refer, however, to a possible priority among the three elements as an objective of a national movement.

As for Zionism, Cohen (1969) noted the lack of clarity in the formulation of several objectives of Zionist ideology, a condition that has increased over time and with the move from a rural to an urban settlement accent. The several Zionist objectives have been interrelated, though the realization of one may have hurt the implementation of another. As Cohen sees it, "The general slogans were not interpreted properly, in a concrete and specific language"; yet in the view of the ideology realizers themselves, "it has always been possible to carry out all tasks, and at the same levels, and that one thing does not disturb another one" (p. 143). Reichman (1975) cited this example of such a view: a geographically concentrated settlement pattern is preferred for absorbing people from different exiles; on the other hand, a dispersed settlement pattern is more helpful for land acquisition and maintenance. He further noted that

> there were three central objectives for the settlement project in the country that determined the ideological framework for actual work in the country: "redemption of the land" (which, after the establishment of the state, was termed "the conquering of the unsettled"); the ingathering of the exiles or immigration; and the security of the state, which, given the circumstances, has become more and more important.

The scheme of objective priorities proposed in the following treats land acquisition and state security as belonging to the same category of obtaining territory and guarding it. A third central objective will also be added; namely, the creation of specific modes of lifes in the Jewish society settled on its land.

The focus of the discussions to follow will be on the Zionist movement; more specifically, on *transitions in the priorities* of Zionistic objectives and on transitions in their implementation. No detailed observations will be made of ideological and practical relations of the Zionist movement with other populations and political approaches, whether within the Jewish population (e.g., the ultra-orthodox) or outside it (the Arabs). Another subject that is external to this examination concerns the several boundaries options for the State of Israel, both before statehood (the partition plans) and after the 1967 war (the whole Land of Israel; partial or full withdrawal from the occupied territories). These subjects go beyond the specific interest of this study. What, then, were—and are—the the Zionist goals and what changes did they undergo?

Zionist Objectives: Territory, Population, Mode of Life

Any matrix of the connections between Zionist objectives and settlement ideals must first pay some attention to each of the objectives separately. This will be done within the context of four parameters: concepts, means, political approaches, and conflicts with other objectives (see Table 2.1).

Territory

The creation of a national territory for a long time constituted the foremost Zionist objective, even if for a while there were more important objectives, which were implemented in some of the settlement ideals. The centrality of the territorial objective in the Zionist enterprise emerged in part because of an objection to ideological approaches that argued for an extended and organized Jewish life outside Palestine (as was proposed by the autonomists, the territorialists, and those Zionists who agreed to the so-called Uganda solution).

A national territory might carry several meanings at varied levels. At the most basic level, territory is an elementary existential need, a "passive" base for the existence of all human beings and

Table 2.1. Zionist Objectives: Territory, Population, and Modes of Life

OBJECTIVES	CONCEPTS	MEANS	POLITICAL APPROACHES	CONFLICTS WITH OTHER OBJECTIVES
Territory	Existential need Resource Political identity Cultural or religious importance	Purchase Presence (settlement) Sovereignty	*Right:* Maximum territory, sovereignty as means (until 1977), purchase and presence (settlement) as means (from 1977) *Left:* Territory balanced by population and mode of life. Purchase, presence (settlement) and sovereignty as means.	(See the following)
Population	Maximum Jewish population of total population and of world Jewry	Refugee immigration Free immigration (Higher birth rate) Settlement	—	*Until statehood: With Territory:* Small population→ small territory (Difficulties in maintaining a large territory). *After 1948:* Population dispersal contradicts immigration absorption.

Table 2.1. (Continued)

OBJECTIVES	CONCEPTS	MEANS	POLITICAL APPROACHES	CONFLICTS WITH OTHER OBJECTIVES
Mode of life	Productivity Agriculture Cooperativeness Concentrated power	Cooperative organizations Cooperative settlement Cooperative production Legislation	Ideals of the Left	*With population:* Lack of sufficient readiness for cooperativeness and agrarianism. *With territory:* This lack results in scarce peripheral settlement.
	Individual decision making Free economy Commuting Status symbols	The large city Community settlements	Ideals of the Right (acceptance by the Left?)	*With territory:* Need proximity to large cities
	Civil liberty Equal rights Wide attachment to contemporary Western culture	Media Legislation Cultural activity	Evolving ideals of the Left	*With territory:* Ideals of the large city. *With mode of life:* Previous ideals of concentrated power and cooperativeness.

their several activities. Territory or land also serves, however, as an "active" resource for agricultural activity and a strategic resource for military purposes.

At a higher level of territorial significance, one finds the attachment of a people to territories as political and cultural entities, this relationship leads to the several meanings of space discussed in the previous chapter. At times, the cultural attitude of a nation to a given territory is the result of armed conquests; at other times, the relationship is the reverse, a cultural closeness brings about the political attachment of a population to its territory. In the case of the Jewish people, the attachment to the Land of Israel was preserved and nurtured for centuries on a religious-cultural basis, without almost any direct national-political presence in the country. Generally, some interrelationship exists between space, on the one hand, and human culture and the state, on the other. Space precedes culture and contributes to the shaping of the latter; on its part, culture creates, shapes, and expresses national spaces (Reichman and Hasson, 1984; Sack, 1981).

The basic cultural attachment of the Jewish people to the Land of Israel over several millennia was nurtured through the perception of the territory as a sacred national land. This sacredness has manifested several meanings and changing boundaries over the generations (Shilhav, 1986). The secularization processes that accompanied most of the Zionist movement called for viewing the Land of Israel as the national territory of the Jewish people, who had a long historical attachment to this territory. In the words of the Declaration of Independence (1948), it was a land "in which their spiritual, religious, and political nature was shaped, in which they lived life of a sovereign state, in which they created national and universal cultural assets and gave as an inheritance to the whole world the eternal Bible."

The basic need for a territory and the cultural-religious attachment to the Land of Israel yielded two major approaches in Zionism. The first one characterized Revisionist Zionism, and its heirs, the current right wing. This approach sees territory as an *absolute* value, and the need for its attainment and possession as values superior to any other objective. Until 1977, the Right saw sovereignty as a major tool for the achievement of territory and for its safeguarding. In the words of Jabotinski, the founding father of Revisionist Zionism (in 1940): "With us, this triple idea of national territory, self-government, and independence is focused on the term, 'Jewish State.' Obviously, since we do not have a state, it is our ideal, and for this we are ready to sacrifice everything"

(Jabotinski, 1981, p. 23). Since 1977, the Right has made massive use of land purchase, presence, and settlement as a basic means of achieving and maintaining territory in the occupied territories.

The Left, or the Labor movement, perceives territory as a major value, but its geographical extent and the pace of its acquisition have had to be conditioned by the status and the progress made for the achievement of the two other central objectives, population and mode of life. Moreover, the means advanced for attaining territory have been more varied in socialist Zionism, which almost from its inception has emphasized the need for settlement as a central value. As a result, transitions have evolved in the priorities of the geographical implementation of Zionist objectives by Labor. For the "classic" Right, in contrast, the order of Zionist objectives has been unchanging. As Jabotinski put it:

> Even the Jewish state is not a *final objective*; the Jewish state is just a first step in the realization of proud Zionism. Afterwards will come the second step: the return of the people to Zion, the exodus from exile, the solution of the Jewish problem. And the truly final aim of proud Zionism will appear only at the third stage—the essence for which great nations actually exist: the creation of a national culture that will shed its beauty on the whole world. (1935; in Nedava, 1982, p. 122)

In other words, the order of objectives for the Right was territory, population and mode of life. Labor movements usually preferred to start with the mode of life objective.

There are three ways to acquire and maintain territory: purchase, presence, and sovereignty (Kimmerling, 1982; 1983b). In practice, however, only land purchase is a "pure land activity" in that it aims only at land acquisition. The two other ways, presence on the land and sovereignty, are more complex activities or means, which have extensive significance with regard to population and mode of life as well. This does not necessarily imply that land purchase has always been a successful way to acquire territory for the Zionist enterprise, as several land parcels and settlements remained outside the boundaries of the State of Israel after 1948 (Gush Etzion south of Jerusalem and Neve Ya'akov, slightly to the north, are West Bank examples). Since the last quarter of the nineteenth century, land purchase in Palestine has been performed by individuals as well as by Zionist and national institutions. Similar to the trend that was noted concerning capital imports, most purchases in the pre-state era were effected by individuals. Therefore in 1915, the ratio of private to nationally owned land was 25:6, whereas in 1945 it decreased to just 1:1 (Weintraub et al., 1969, p. 29). Following the establishment of the State of Israel, the nationalization of all public land put 90 percent of the land under government or Jewish National Fund ownership. The term used for land purchase, mainly by the Left, was *land redemption* or *country redemption*. Kimmerling (1982; 1983b) interpreted this expression as displaying an ambivalent connotation. The purchase of land from Arabs was a financial-economic deal, whereas its transfer into Jewish hands was a "redemption." By Zionist socialist ideology, full "land redemption" was possible only through national land ownership.

Presence on land is achievable via settlements, though there have also existed some other, less permanent and thus weaker, means, such as afforestation, tours, and archaeological excavations. The need to show a visible presence on land as a means for its maintenance originated in the Ottoman rule of Palestine until World War I. The Ottomans instituted the notion of land possession as a proof of ownership, a concept that was enhanced by the pioneering Zionist movement; prior to statehood, the Left adhered to the idea of "the creation of facts on the land," or the determination of the political status of land through settlement. This notion was later transformed into the ideals of "frontier settlement" and the "conquest of the unsettled." Furthermore, settlements fulfilled other objectives; namely, population and a new mode of life. Frontier settlements, in particular, were believed to possess a security value in their serving as military posts; this view gained currency following the Tel Hai affair of 1921, in which a small number of settlers defended a lonely settlement; the result was that the northern border of Palestine was ammended, and the Huleh Valley as well as the Jordan River were later included in Palestine. The operative warning and fear were phrased thus:

> Since this is to be known—under both peace and emergency conditions: borders that will not be settled, next to which a Jewish plough will not deepen a furrow, next to which there will not be settler homes and fields, and children will not be educated and reared nearby, will not remain unsettled, but will serve as a breach, calling for the Arabs to fill it and move the border beyond it. (Zur, 1980, p. 41)

Right wing movements accepted presence as a means of achieving territory only much later, in the post-1973 settlement of Judea, Samaria, and Gaza. The Hebrew term used for this process was the biblical term for the settlement of the Land of Israel by the twelve Israelite tribes following the Exodus from Egypt; *hitnahalut*. The use of presence as a tool for land maintenance meant therefore, that legal ownership (purchase) and political recognition (sovereignty) were not considered sufficient for land attainment; there was a need for a permanent, continuous deed on the territory through settlement. Constant presence by settlements was believed to bring about sovereignty.

Sovereignty may seem to imply the achievement of all three objectives through state control over land, people, and modes of life. As such, it is, on the one hand, a stronger, much more drastic means than land purchase or presence. On the other hand, sovereignty might signify a minimal domination over land, while its ownership and the activities taking place on it remain unchanged. The Right conceived of sovereignty as the major means for controlling territory; when it achieved political power in 1977, it adopted presence-settlement as the central tool for maintaining Judea, Samaria, and Gaza. The establishment of the State of Israel in 1948 had gradually contributed to a weakening of the ideological tension among the Left as far as settlement activities were concerned. Hence, a certain exchange of territory maintenance means occurred between Left and Right in the 1980s. The Left accepted sovereignty as sufficient for holding onto territory, especially the Negev desert and the Galilee mountains (at least in terms of readiness to settle these areas with any density). The Right, on the other hand, adopted settlement as a tool for territorial acquisition of occupied stateless lands.

Population

The need to assure the existence of as large as possible a Jewish population in the Land of Israel has been a consensual Zionist objective (though one may sometimes wonder if the extent of the efforts made in this regard during the 1970s and 1980s was in line with such a widely agreed objective). The significance of the size of the Jewish population in Palestine may be measured by two relative measures: first, compared to the Jewish population worldwide; second, relative to the total population in the country. The first measure relates only to populations; the second also has some territorial significance, because a high Jewish percentage in the population would enhance the territorial status of this population. Thus, population, though constituting a separate Zionist objective, operates as an integrated objective with territory. As we shall see later, the desire to expand or maintain the national territory has not always gone hand in hand with the need to increase the Jewish population.

The Zionist way of coping with the two population measures has been to encourage Jewish migration to Palestine. This tendency has received a profound value loading by terming it *aliya* (going upward) and by calling Jewish emigration from the country *yerida* (going downward). The absorption of immigrants has also been ideologically termed, as *the ingathering of the exiles* and *the blending of the exiles*. These expressions refer both to the immigrants' previous condition (exile) and to their current state (ingathering or blending). Immigrants were and are either refugees or free-will migrants. Both types have been nurtured by Zionism and the State of Israel. The first type of immigration has been arranged through negotiations and financial support; the second, encouraged through education and propaganda campaigns in the Diaspora and financial support in Israel. The Israeli legal system has classified immigrants as a separate group to assist them in areas as varied as army service, taxation, employment, and residence. The Law of Return, which provides for instant Israeli citizenship to nearly all Jewish immigrants, is a unique citizenship law and reflects the priority of the Zionist objective to increase the Jewish population in Israel.

An alternative means of increasing the Jewish population could have been a higher Jewish birth rate. This issue, though, has been treated ambivalently in Israeli society. A higher Jewish birth rate in Israel would have related only indirectly to the ratio between the world and the Israeli Jewish populations. Zionism has attempted to uproot Jews from exile and bring them to their homeland, not merely increase the Jewish population in Israel. Moreover, a cultural barrier has existed in the attitude to this issue. A large family has been perceived as a too "traditional" and "primitive" characteristic. Except for a famous call by Ben-Gurion in the 1950s to increase family size, no serious efforts have been made in this direction; in fact, informally efforts were made in the opposite direction among immigrants from Oriental countries. In more recent years, especially from the mid-1970s, some change in this area could be distinguished, so that a slight increase was registered in overall Jewish family size. The increase in the Jewish birth rate was termed *internal aliya,* especially coming at a time of low external immigration. At the same time, enhanced assimilation processes throughout the Jewish Diaspora have caused a decrease in the Jewish population abroad; thus, any increase in the Jewish population in Israel has altered the proportions of the Jewish population in and outside Israel. The 1975 tax reform was supposed to provide for a relatively generous compensation for large families; however, the payment was reduced in value during the years of high inflation in the late 1970s and early 1980s. Although several organizations are attempting to promote the issue, the Israeli parliament passed a law in this regard only in the mid-1980s, and by 1991 it had become only partially operational.

The major geographical means for the absorption of a new population is the construction of settlements. As for this solution, the complementarity and contradiction between the Zionist objectives of territory and population may be noted. The two objectives were supposed to complement each other. On the one hand, there is a need for territory to settle a population; on the other hand, a population is required to create a presence on a territory. In practice, relations between these two objectives have turned out to be more complicated. Hence, until the attainment of statehood, a two-way conflict frequently evolved between the two. The small number of Jews in Palestine did not justify demands for an extensive territory; at the same time, this small population did not permit enough presence on the land (Kimmerling, 1983b, pp. 91–92; 104–105). A similar relationship was found for sovereignty. Its achievement would have increased immigration, but a large population influx could have caused a delay in the need for receiving statehood (Kimmerling, 1983b, p. 52). Moreover, before statehood and even more so after 1948, some conflict has characterized the very implementation of the two objectives (Reichman, 1975). The holding of territory in the periphery by a population living in any settlement form was a state objective termed *population dispersal*; "the ingathering and the blending of the exiles" are best achieved, though, by absorbing immigration in large and older population centers. From this perspective, the contemporary settlement of Judea, Samaria, and the Galilee have somehow been different. The attempts to maintain these territories through settlement activity have been accompanied by either sovereignty (in the Galilee) or by military occupation; the settled areas are in part located adjacent to large metropolitan areas. Ironically, most of the population moving into these areas has not been an immigrant one.

Mode of Life

The formulation of a Zionist objective concerning mode of life has proved an even more complex undertaking compared to territory and population objectives. A consensus has existed that territory is needed; the differences in approach to this objective relate mainly to justification, extent, means, and priority. As for population, the consensus extends to both the objective and the means. Mode of life, by contrast, has involved historical disagreement on both concept and means. *Insofar as geographical implementation is concerned*, the major division on mode of life has had to do with the profile and structure of the economy and with the individual as producer and consumer. (This does not imply that other central conflicts over modes of life in the Israeli society, such as the issue of religion, have been of less importance.)

Since the beginning of the Second Aliya in the early twentieth century, the several Labor movements have aimed at the creation of an economic and social mode of life in which material production and labor would play superior roles. Agriculture was conceived of as a leading production sector.

> The absolute priority given to the village in the construction of the Land of Israel by Zionist leaders was not the result of an in-depth research into the ultimate economic structure of the national economy. Images of economic sectors, in which the strength of a nation is concealed and out of which grows the ultimate human profile or which serve as a growth source for a national culture, had a crucial impact. Nobody disagreed with the opinion that the village is the construction base for the Jewish settlement. The romantics of soil cultivation played a major role in the Zionist myth. (Giladi, 1985, p. 7)

Second to agriculture was publicly owned industry, owned by the labor union or, later, by the state. Thus, an additional central issue accompanied productiveness—either full collective ownership (as in the kibbutz) or partial (as in the moshav and urban settlements) of both production and consumption. A third issue emanating from Labor ideology was the need to locate power in several centralized establishments, both cooperative-volunteer ones (the labor union and its institutions) and legal bodies (the government and its agencies). The Labor-movement socioeconomic ideology was not accepted by the several branches of the Right; the Left, though, was able through political power, education, and propaganda to put it forward as the leading Israeli ideology, the one identified with Israeli society. Israeli society was thus typified by a strong leading ideology until the 1970s, when it started to weaken.

The means for realizing this ideology were varied, and they extended over all spheres of Israeli life, from organizational institutions (the Histadruth) to production (Hevrat Haovdim—the Workers Company and its branches) and consumption bodies (the health fund, wholesale and retail trade chains) (Kellerman, 1986a). They included the establishment and development of cooperative rural settlements and development towns. Volunteer activity was also nurtured prior to statehood. Following the establishment of the state, legislation permitted the transfer of key resources to government auspices (the nationalization of water, land, and development capital).

These means facilitated to a large degree the simultaneous implementation of territorial and social objectives, because they financed land purchase and development and the construction of small cooperative and collective settlements on the periphery and along the borders. These projects involved extensive investments compared to the development of the big cities and the large population they attracted (Reichman, 1975). A conflict emerged, however, between the mode of life objectives and the consensual population objective, and it went rather deeper than differences with the financial aspects of the enterprise. The immigrants that the Zionist movement brought to Palestine were segmented by political party membership and, after 1948, were divided among political settlement movements. In both periods, most of the population agreed, freely or otherwise, with the national emphasis on rurality and cooperativeness that was put forward by the ruling establishment. Over the long run, however, these values were not implemented in the choice of residence location; in fact, the rural population percentage among Jews in Palestine never went beyond 29 percent (in 1941). Most of the Jewish population preferred large or medium-sized cities or their suburbs. Moreover, employment in industry never surpassed that in services (Kellerman, 1986a). A correspondence between population and mode of life objectives could have been created if the Zionist revolution forecast by the Left would actually have occurred, in a way that cooperativeness, productiveness, and collectiveness would have truely predominated. This lack of implementation of leftist mode of life objectives, despite the political power of the Left, left an impact on the territorial dimension, in form of a low presence on the periphery of both rural and urban settlements.

An urban mode of life, based on personal decision making and free and individual production and consumption, has existed in Palestine for a long time. In leftist ideological thought, this mode was considered the values of the Right and could not be considered as Zionist objectives. The coming to power of the right wing Likud party in 1977 and its efforts to settle the West Bank finally brought city values into the center of Zionist activity, in form of the community settlements. In this settlement type, several urban values are expressed: personal decision making, free economy, status symbols, and commuting (Newman, 1984a; 1984b).

Following the 1967 war, tendencies emerged both toward increased economic welfare and an opening to contemporary Western society. These trends served as bases for transitions in mode of life ideals as conceived by the Left. The change in political power in 1977, coupled with the rightist territorial emphasis, strengthened these trends, partially in contradiction to the territorial accent. Thus a "social Zionism" has evolved in the Left, placing at its center such as social values as civil freedom, equal rights, and a broad attachment to contemporary Western culture. We shall return to this development in the conclusion section for this part; at this stage, it is important to note that these values were those of the big city, which the Left condemned for so many years in the past.

Changing Zionist Objectives and Changing Settlement Ideals

The three central Zionist objectives of territory, population, and mode of life have received changing priorities when implemented in the three settlement ideals (cooperative villages, development towns, and community settlements/Judea and Samaria). These changes occurred even during the domination periods of each of these settlement ideals, as will now be seen.

Transitions in the priority order of Zionist objectives and in settlement ideals show an interrelationship. Hence, the transition to each new settlement ideal may also be viewed as an emphasis on a different Zionist objective (Table 2.2). The rural ideal commenced with an emphasis on mode of life; development towns started with a population priority; and the settlement of the West Bank began with a territorial accent. Generally, mode of life has lost its importance. In the rural ideal, it remained the top priority until 1936, when it was overtaken by territory. In the development town ideal, mode of life originally ranked third; whereas in Judea and Samaria, it was second, but only for a short period. Territory and population have displayed a variable importance in all three ideals.

These trends will now be examined from two perspectives: ideas and realities. Expressions, plans, and even laws have suggest-

Table 2.2. Zionist Objectives (Territory, Population, and Modes of Life) and Geographical Implementation Means (Villages, Development Towns, and the West Bank)

PRIORITY ORDER	COOPERATIVE VILLAGES		DEVELOPMENT TOWNS		JUDEA AND SAMARIA		(COMMUNITY SETTLEMENTS)
	UNTIL THE 1930s	FROM THE 1930s	IN THE 1950s	FROM THE 1960s	1967–1977	1977–1983	1984–
I	Mode of Life	Territory	Population	Territory	Territory	Territory	Population
II	Territory	Mode of Life	Territory	Population	Population	Mode of Life	Territory
III	Population	Population	Mode of Life	Mode of Life	Mode of Life	Population	Mode of Life

ed certain ideas or objectives, which have not always been fulfilled in reality. The ideological priorities of Zionist objectives, therefore, have not always been identical with the practical world. This gap sometimes received an ideological rationale. For example, the pragmatism that was attributed to the leading Labor party at the time (Mapai) and to the Histadruth "did not come instead of the ideology, as is sometimes thought, it was rather its ally" (Naor, 1983, p. IV).

The Cooperative Settlement: 1908–1936

The modern Jewish settlement in Palestine began during the last quarter of the nineteenth century, with the establishment of European-styled colonies (moshavot) by the immigrants of the First Aliya, a settlement wave that preceded the founding of the organized Zionist movement. It is possible to argue that these colonies attempted, in intention and deed, the Zionist objectives of acquiring territory in the Land of Israel, influencing many Jews to immigrate to Palestine, and creating an agricultural-rural mode of life. It is difficult to state, however, that all their activities were carried out under the auspices of a central political-organizational framework (except for Baron Rothschild's sponsorship, which was of a different type). The Second Aliya, on the other hand, started its settlement activities upon the establishment of the Zionist movement, though not all of its settlement activities were performed within the framework of the movement or according to its orders. In addition,

> the difference between the workers of the first *aliya* and the labor movement as it later evolved lies in the fact that the workers of the First Aliya did not feel like a separate social unit and did not hold any general idea on the method of settlement construction. If they quarrelled with the farmers and clashed with them, it was not because they were against the settlement system presented by the farmers,...they did not see themselves as carriers of the Hebrew work idea or as bearers of the idea of building a Hebrew labor class as the people of the Second Aliya saw it. (Kulat, 1964, p. 53)

Thus, the order of priority of Zionist objectives held by the founders of the cooperative villages set up during the Second Aliya, and later on during the Third Aliya, was mode of life, territory, population.

An Agricultural Cooperative Mode of Life

The major purpose behind the establishment of all types of cooperative villages in Palestine was the creation of a cooperative productive-agricultural mode of life. The building of such villages by Labor Zionist parties did not reflect the execution of a planned policy to create cooperative villages with a special character. Rather, the catalyst was the feeling that it would be difficult to assure the exclusive use of Jewish labor ("the conquest of work," "Hebrew work") in the colonies established during the First Aliya. Originally, then, Second Aliya laborers aimed at the creation of an agricultural Jewish proletariat in Palestine (Livne, 1969; Katzenelson, 1969).

Ongoing conflicts between farmers and labor, however, produced only frustration. The farmers perceived the laborers as an inferior, expensive, and unskilled work force; for their part, the laborers themselves felt they were being exploited. Socially, the laborers conceived of themselves as possessing a higher cultural level, to which was added the ethnic difference between Russian-born laborers and Romanian-born farmers. Moreover, and perhaps most important from a political perspective, the workers viewed their labor as a national and social value, not merely a means for survival; farmers, by contrast, expected their workers just to do their jobs.

One may identify the farmers' attitude in a letter sent by the noted agricultural scholar, Aharon Aharonson, to his sisters: "The viewpoint of our madmen [the laborers] is completely different. They have dreams, they are moonsick and dangerous. They believe that they serve a *goal*, an idea. In this area it is possible to be highly mistaken, and we have to be forgiving" (October 14, 1909; in Livne, 1969, p. 162). In a report to the Zionist leader and planner Arthur Ruppin (1911), Aharonson observed: "Under a mask of nationalism they performed a very unnational job. Under a mask of high words they waste terribly, and all this is done, I have to admit, with clean hands and without any personal motives, but this is no justification." Aharonson went on to describe an oat harvest in rocky land:

> and our workers, enthusiastic with good will, start picking, while screaming national songs with Cossack melodies.... When two energetic and intelligent men are permitted to humiliate themselves and handle the job of one primitive Arab woman—this is an antinational deed...to perform work for 25 piasters that can be done for 5; it

means throwing to the wind the poor pennies of the nation. (Livne, 1969, p. 163)

An initial call for independent laborer farming came from Vitkin (1908): "At the time when the agricultural worker, [in contrast,] makes a living by working on a private estate or hoping to achieve this,...all this should not deter 'the Young Laborer' from insisting on a different way, the only way that can get him to achieve his goal, the way of conquest of agricultural work through national colonization, which he will take in his own hands" (Vitkin, 1961, pp. 44–45). The reasoning was in the social realm, not the territorial, and certainly not the population. Vitkin advocated the "individual farm" (later resulting in the moshav, a type of cooperative village), rather than the "cooperative colony" (later, the kibbutz, a collective-type village). The first collective groups established in Palestine amounted, therefore, to an initiative from below and operated from social motives (Shilo, 1989). This motive was clearly expressed in the words of the labor leader Berl Katzenelson. "If we shall ask what came first for us in the settlement—the settlement idea, the settlement theory or the settlement *form*—the reply will be, as strange as it may seem to you, that the settlement form came prior to the settlement idea" (Katzenelson, 1969, p. 10). And in the words of another leader, Yoseph Tabenkin: "The kibbutz came prior to its idea. It had no preplan" (Lanir, 1979, p. 92; see also Rabinowitz, 1976).

The idea of agricultural cooperative settlements met with objections. Aharonowitz, for example, in his 1908 article, "The Conquest of Labor or the Conquest of Land" (Aharonowitz, 1941) presented powerful arguments against Vitkin's idea: "The conquest of land—though it is something needed as a goal in itself, and without which all Zionism has no value—does not solve at all the question of labor conquest, but deepens it further" (p. 12). Aharonowitz felt that trying to cope with the mode of life–labor problem through the establishment of independent villages would contribute to the territorial objective. This contribution would be made, though, only in conflict with the mode of life objective. For him, too, the "right" order of priorities for Zionist objectives put mode of life first, mainly because of the creation of a proletariate in the colonies; second was territory, mainly in the Galilee, given its particular geographical character and working conditions; and third came population, by assuring a Jewish majority in all areas of employment.

The establishment of cooperative villages by immigrants in the first quarter of the century was accompanied by a view of agricultural labor as being a superior mode of life, whether from an existential, a social, or even a religious perspective. A. D. Gordon, a spiritual leader of the early labor movement, wrote that "human improvement and the renovation of social life will not come about without a new relation to Nature, to cosmic life. From here has to start all social, national human work.... The idea of labor is the idea of the integration of human life into world life, and human creation within universal creation" (Livne, 1972, p. 209). Rabbi A. Y. H. Kook, the first chief rabbi of Palestine, made the same point, though couched in religious terms:

> The construction of the country has its central basis in agriculture, which for all other nations is just an essential economic factor. But for the nation whose being is all sacred, and whose country and language are all sacred...even its agriculture is soaked in sacredness. This sacredness in the agricultural element is given emphasis by that the festival of harvest commencement—the Omer—rises to the level of a supreme sacred service: the sacrifice sanctified with it is a collective sacrifice superseding the Sabbath. (1937, pp. 193–194)

The writer and Nobel laureate S. Y. Agnon expressed the same viewpoint: "love for the land-all other good merits are included in this merit...and you already know that there is no greater merit than this one, since the whole Jewish community exists on land cultivation, and if not for the era's temptations, all would have recognized and known that the salvation of the people of Israel is only from God above and the soil below" (1971, p. 489).

Kulat (1964, pp. 58–59; 168; 262–263) related the agricultural accent of the Second Aliya pioneers to physiocrate ideas, which had been transmitted to them by the founders of the First Aliya, who had received them from Russian national thought. These ideas obtained their final economic-ideological formulation at the hands of the economist Frantz Oppenheimer. Agriculture represented the return to the soil, low dependence on manipulation, and the provision of conditions for social closeness, modest life, and a revival of Jewish holidays. Indeed, "the status of agriculture within the national idea as a whole in the early 1880s was so strong that it enjoyed priority even over the Land of Israel" (Kulat, 1964, p. 58).

The kibbutz as a social community presented a special challenge for labor society. It required a volunteered consent for collective ownership and sharing in all spheres of life, including production, consumption, and decision making. In its early stages, the kibbutz further required extreme austerity and modesty. By the

Third Aliya, in the early 1920s, however, a socially less challenging settlement type was being sought, and it was found in the creation of the moshav. In this settlement form, there were no collective dining halls or collective children homes. Production took place in fields allocated to each family. Cooperativeness prevailed in marketing, most retail shopping activity, input purchases, and colleagueal assistance. In the 1930s a third type of cooperative settlement evolved, the *moshav shitufi* (collective moshav), which attempted to blend the merits of the two earlier settlement forms: production was collective as in the kibbutz, but consumption took place within a family household context, as in the moshav (see also Weintraub et al., 1969).

Territorial Presence

As previously suggested, the territorial and population objectives were not foreign to cooperative settlement thought before 1936, though they were of secondary importance to mode of life. Reichman (1975) has observed that it had become clear by the early days of the British Mandate that farmers needed much land and that a few farmers might maintain large parcels of land, especially when compared to urban entities. From a practicable perspective, this point was crystallized after the Tel Hai affair in 1921 (Kimmerling, 1983b, p. 85). Ussishkin warned that it was impossible to desert settlements, and Tabenkin argued that failure in the North would bring about a withdrawal from the Negev. Thus, two settlement doctrines were formed. One was that the geographical boundaries of the Jewish collectivity in Palestine would be determined by Jewish settlements; the other constituted a kind of "domino doctrine," that deserting a single settlement could lead to the complete collapse of the *Yishuv.*

At the beginning of the Zionist settlement of Palestine, programmatic elements had been proposed for Jewish territorial deployment. This was done mainly through the Palestine Bureau, set up by Arthur Ruppin, who enumerated four principles for this territorial spread:

1. Creation of two settlement blocs, one in the North and one in the South, connected by a corridor.

2. Construction of rural settlements adjacent to towns with existing Jewish communities, rather than scattered all over the country to enable the towns to enjoy an economic hinterland.

3. Not settling on land cultivated by Arabs.

4. Cultivation of large parcels of land not far from ports and railways. (Hasson and Gosenfeld, 1980)

In practice, settlement activity was determined largely by the availability of land for purchase, but a trend was apparent not to spread out all over the country. This meant, in effect that not much territory could be acquired within a short time span. Ruppin's rules served, to a large degree, as operative criteria until 1936. During the Second Aliya, an ideological principle was also established, particularly by A. D. Gordon, that the right to the Land of Israel would be determined, not by the historical past, but through contemporary land cultivation (Zameret, 1985, p. 90).

The New Cooperative Villages and Population Absorption

The idea of the agricultural cooperative rural life being superior to either urban bourgeois life in the Diaspora or farmer bourgeois life in Palestine lead naturally to the Labor view of cooperative villages as the central settlement type for population absorption. "The Young Laborer" party "conceived of an immigration that would aim at the immediate construction of the Land of Israel. They supported immigration by pioneers and not a massive popular immigration. This conception of mass immigration was explained by the fact that the Zionist movement had not yet ignited a Zionist zeal in the whole nation" (Kulat, 1964, p. 301). In taking this approach, the "Young Laborer" faction disagreed with the opinions starting to be heard in the Zionist organization, which came to be clearly expressed by Max Nordau, demanding massive emigration to Palestine "to turn it quickly into a country with a Jewish majority" (p. 302). An example of this latter view was provided by Tabenkin, who cited the "Labor Battalions" (a pioneering unit): "The major advantage of the labor battalion was not that it was a communal organization, but that it succeeds economically and facilitates immigration absorption" (Near, 1979, p. 55). This argument thrust the population objective ahead of other aims in the establishment of the first large kibbutz (Ein Harod). Ambivalent attitudes developed toward towns and colonies, the two alternative settlement types for the absorption of mass immigration. First, investments in villages were more extensive and time consuming compared to urban development, which did not require massive land development (Reichman, 1975). Second, the city was unacceptable ideologically (E. Cohen, 1970a). Nevertheless, the central institutions of the Histadruth, founded in the 1920s, such as the purchasing organizations, party centers, and newspaper head-quarters, all concentrated in Tel Aviv (Kellerman, 1986a) and to a lesser extent also in Jerusalem, Haifa, and the colonies. Finally, most of the immigrants preferred the cities.

Bourgeois Zionism and the Right developed the cities in the meantime, but "without significant involvement on the part of the settlement institutions" (Reichman, 1977, p. 3). Except for a short period in the 1920s, the Jewish National Fund did not have a department for urban land purchase, though at times it did buy large parcels of land (such as the Haifa Bay area). Nevertheless, Labor Zionism attempted to cope with the urban issue by propos-ing the creation of working-class sections or suburbs. These were called *field neighborhoods* (Luft, 1923; Hayuth, 1974) or *workers neighborhoods* (Greiczer, 1982; Reichman, 1977). Two major such suburbs were eventually constructed (Boruchov in suburban Tel Aviv and Qiryat Hayim in suburban Haifa). There, such labor val-ues as cooperation and modesty (and even agricultural elements) were supposed to be expressed. In reality, however, "the move-ment was forced to largely compromise the new social and eco-nomic principles formulated in the 1920s by Katzenelson and D. Remez" (Reichman, 1977, p. 6).

Immigration absorption by villages was small. For example, the number of immigrants to Palestine during the Second Aliya (1908–1914) was about 20,000. Only 2,000 of them, or about 10 percent, were counted as pioneers in 1922. The original number of pioneering immigrants was probably much higher, since the out-migration rate over the years was estimated to be as high as 90 per-cent (Giladi, 1985, pp. 4–5)! By 1935, at the conclusion of the first phase of cooperative rural settlement in Palestine, the settlement record was as follows: 39 Jewish colonies (of which 19 were estab-lished before 1908), 48 moshavim, 43 kibbutzim and one collective moshav; a total of 131 settlements, of which 92, or 70 percent, were in the Labor-cooperative sector (Portugali, 1976). On the other hand, the rural population percentage among Jews in Pales-tine increased less impressively than the settlement record, from 10 percent in 1900 and 14 percent in 1914 to 24 percent in 1936 (Gov-ernment of Palestine, 1938, p. 7; Bein, 1953, p. 429).

The Cooperative Settlement: 1936–1948

The Transition to Territory as the Preferred Objective

The mid-1930s were characterized by a transition in the priority order of Zionist objectives within the context of their geographical implementation by cooperative villages. Territory replaced mode of life as the most preferred objective. Population still ranked third, at least from the perspective of Zionist performance within the rural sector. This transition was not a sharp one, though the year 1936 witnessed several changes. First, though, two pre-1936 settlement processes, one of them rural and dating back to 1929 and the other urban and going back to 1933, will be examined.

Until 1929, settlement advanced slowly (Kimmerling, 1983b, p. 86), for several reasons. For one thing, funds for land development and equipment purchase for settlers were lacking. In 1927, more than half of the Jewish-owned land was not yet distributed to settlers, and only 80 percent of distributed lands were under cultivation. Second, ideological conflicts still persisted over the desirable settlement form. At the end of the Fourth Aliya, in 1929, most agriculture was still concentrated in the private sector, though conditions were ripe for a future settlement wave (Giladi, 1973, pp. 69–70, 215–227). Meanwhile, Arab riots that year were the first conducted on a countrywide scale, and they proved the importance of building settlements for security purposes. Thus, the Jewish Agency named Y. Ruttner as security consultant for settlement siting on the basis of *local* security considerations (Kimmerling, 1983b, p. 86). Third, assistance and development activities provided by the British authorities to the Jewish rural sector was coming to an end (Bigger, 1983).

In 1933, two additional, seemingly contradictory processes started to take place. On the one hand, there began the Fifth Aliya, by Central European Jews fleeing the Nazi regime. This immigration wave went mainly to the cities, the newcomers being mostly alien to rural and even more so to the cooperative modes of life, developed in Palestine (Cohen, 1970a, pp. 11–12). Though some of the immigrants went or were sent to rural settlements, the very arrival of a massive number of immigrants in the cities weakened somewhat the accent on mode of life that had been promulgated by the Second and Third Aliyas. The second event in 1933 was that Labor gained political power in the Zionist Executive Council, which permitted the diversion of more attention and resources to "practical Zionism" (Reichman, 1979, p. 45); in effect, enhancement of the particular mode of life developed earlier in rural settlement. There evolved, therefore, both internal and external conditions for the implementation of the Labor Zionist mode of life objective, albeit next in priority to the territorial objective. This occurred, of course, at a time when the new incoming population was turning to another track (the urban one) and its absorption was taking place mostly outside of organized "Zionist work."

From 1936, the territorialization process of Zionist implementation started to gain pace. Four factors were responsible (Reichman, 1979, p. 31; Kimmerling, 1983b, pp. 49; 86). First, the Arab uprising of 1936–1939 created difficult security conditions and reinforced the need to deploy additional settlements to protect existing settlements, roads, and other areas. Second, the Arab uprising was accompanied by a general strike, the aim of which was the destruction of Jewish communal existence. Jewish agricultural and urban development, however, had made the Jewish collectivity largely self-sufficient, so that 64 percent of the products and services it needed were self-provided. Third, British Mandate authorities began to limit immigration and back down from the declared National Home promise. Thus, more Jewish effort had to be invested to assure the continued development of this home. Fourth, several partition plans for Palestine drew boundaries on the basis of settlement locations.

These factors raised the territorial objective to a higher ranking than that of mode of life and led to the formulation of the "territorial concept" as a major Zionist objective (Kimmerling, 1983b, pp. 55–56). Settlements were to assist in the drawing and defense of future boundaries. Hence, the concept of "settlement N"—the letter being traced along the Jordan Valley, the Jezreel Valley, and the coastal plain—was introduced, and settlements filled in its joints, arms, and extensions (mainly along the northern coastal plain) (Oren, 1978; Paran, 1970) (see Figure 2.1). In Ben-Gurion's words, there was no need necessarily for "land for ordinary settlement—but [in] positions, key positions, for *expansion* of borders, for strengthening of *security*, for protection of traffic routes"; in other words, "not a declaration or a formula but fact creation—this has to be the goal of our policy" (Oren, 1978, p. 58, 204). The implementation of the territorial policy through settlement activity took the form of "stockade and watertower" campaigns, which established minimal settlement compounds overnight. In a rare expression of this sort, however, Ben-Gurion also called the city a partner or target in the territorial effort. In other words, the population objective was subordinated to the territorial one. Ben-Gurion demanded that all urban migration be directed to Haifa to "avoid British treason." "One has to amplify our power, number, weight, holding here," the future prime minister exhorted, "—and it is forbidden to miss even one minute" (Oren, 1978, p. 58, 64). As we shall see in Part 3, Haifa also presented a special working-class mode of life.

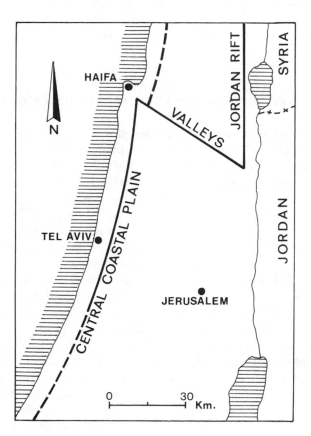

Figure 2.1.   Settlement *N* in Pre-State Israel

The Right perceived the use of settlements for "fact creation" as the wrong means of territory acquisition. Jabotinsky charged: "They [Labor] do not have a program, they have never created a program, by which they will know how to settle the Land of Israel or how to operate Zionism practically." He called the Revisionist program the first attempt to create such a program: "It is the first

attempt to translate the word 'Zionism' into a language of speci-
fied paragraphs" (Jabotinski, 1937, pp. 20–21). What was the
Revisionist program? Entitled "colonizing government," it had a
fourfold base: demand for land reform in Palestine; the nationalization of all unsettled lands and all "lands which are not satisfac-
torily cultivated—including Transjordan"; the establishment of a
"national company" for settlement that would direct the immigration and distribute lands (not free of charge, though); and payment
by the settlers themselves to cover settlement expenses). In addition, Jabotinski wanted a propaganda campaign that would force
Britain to assist the settlement enterprise (Ackerman, 1982, pp.
136–137).

Cooperative Mode of Life as a Secondary Priority

Although now second to the territorial objective, mode of life
was still of major concern to the Labor movement. Several points
should be made in this regard. First, the Arab uprising was viewed
as an opportunity for increased separation between the Arab and
Jewish societies, and for the further encouragement of productiva-
tion processes in the latter (Horowitz and Lissak, 1978). Second,
cooperative settlements, particularly the kibbutzim, were held to be
best suited to the implementation of the territorial objective, given
their strong ideological, social, and economic internal bonds (Kimmerling, 1983b, p. 86). Third, volunteerism was now encouraged in
both the urban and rural sectors, though here, too, preference was
given to the latter. "The settlers [in rural collectives] were those
who took upon themselves the defense tasks, and through their
return to their land and the construction of their settlements the
tactics and strategy of settlement grew in the 'years of turbulence.'
The growing soil of the settlement strategy was the settlement
proper, and its origin was volunteering for settlements" (Oren,
1978, p. 198). Fourth, the mode of life objective, created during the
Second and Third Aliyas, had begun to suffuse the entire Jewish
community in Palestine. The result had been concisely described
by Elon (1971, p. 145):

> No subsequent wave of immigration has had as deep an influence on
> future social structures as the Second and Third *aliyahs*. They set a
> pattern of politics and society, of habits, passions, and prejudices,
> that add up to what one loosely call national character. Henceforth,
> at least in the eyes of the founding fathers, all latecomers had to fit

themselves to it. [Examples:] 1. the party system—its unique centrality in political life; 2. the strong belief in equality; 3. the continuing
informality and simplicity in manners, dress, and language; 4. the
agrarian ritual; 5. the belief in voluntary action; the notion of an official (Zionist) "state ideology."

Some changes can be identified in Labor thinking in regard to
the creation of a socialist structure for the Jewish community in
Palestine. In the early 1920s, the expectation was "to establish a
working nation in the country on the basis of widespread cooperative-collective settlements in all economic spheres, with the power
of national capital" (Margalit, 1980, p. 82). Toward the end of the
decade, the objective became the creation of a "pluralist economy
while planning the activities of private capital or at least having
national supervision and control of private capital" (p. 89). This
approach found expression in David Ben-Gurion's leadership of
the Histadruth and in the creation of such a "controlled pluralism"
following the establishment of the state. The Right, on the other
hand, called for the establishment of a free economy (Jabotinski,
1981, p. 27).

The Cooperative Village as a Population Objective

As in the earlier period, the population objective, for most
part, was not implemented through cooperative rural settlements.
Tabenkin pointed to the goal in 1944: "The only thing that we are
attempting is that in a short period of time, there will be concentrated in the Land of Israel not merely a Jewish majority, but the
majority of the Jewish people." This people he characterizes as follows: "We are a people without a fatherland, without an element of
existence in the world; our way of salvation is first of all through
the creation of a people immersed in their soil" (1983, p. 41). As
things turned out, however, the share of the rural sector seemed to
stand still, at around one quarter: 24 percent in 1936, 29 percent in
1941, 26 percent in 1945 (Bein, 1953, p. 429). The 1941 figure
became the apex for the Jewish rural population of modern Land
of Israel.

The end of this period, namely on the eve of statehood, found
the cooperative rural settlements having achieved much success.
About 70 percent of public-national investments went to agriculture, mostly cooperative (Eisenstadt, 1967b), whose land potential
was larger than that of the private sector. In 1936, 861,000 dunams

were privately held, whereas the Jewish National Fund possessed only 370,000 dunams. By 1947, however, the JNF owned 933,000 dunams, whereas the private sector had slipped to some 801,000 (Oren, 1978, p. 210). The number of cooperative settlements of all types reached 211 in 1947, all of which had been established in less than forty years. These constituted over 80 percent of the Jewish rural settlements in Palestine. The main growth occurred in the number of kibbutzim set up between 1936 and 1947. At the beginning of this period, the number of kibbutzim and moshavim was almost equal (43 and 48, respectively); at its end, the number of kibbutzim had tripled to 127, whereas the number of moshavim had increased by about 62 percent to 78. In 1947, therefore, kibbutzim formed about one-half of all Jewish villages, moshavim about one-third (Table 2.3).

The relative contribution of rural settlements in the areas of land and population from 1900–1948 is displayed in Figure 2.2 through a percentage comparison of the Jewish rural population and cultivated land owned by Jews. Back in 1903, before the inception of cooperative settlements, the settlement enterprise was more successful in land maintenance than in population attraction. Whereas the percentage of the rural population recorded a gradual increase until 1936, the amount of cultivated land grew sharply until 1914. A steep decline followed, owing to World War I and also the lack of capital and new settlements characterizing the 1920s. Even during these years, however, massive land purchases continued. A recovery in land cultivation took place in 1927, but the large rise in settlement construction started only in 1936. In the mid-1940s, a distinct separation began to characterize rural population and agricultural land trends. The rural population became relatively smaller. This development was related to increased urbanization as well as to the high participation of the rural population in the military efforts of World War II and the Jewish struggle for independence in Palestine. At the same time, more land was cultivated, thanks to additional capital investments and technological improvements.

The implementation of Zionist objectives by way of rural settlement until 1948 may be summarized by quoting Tabenkin (1983, p. 22):

> The economic development in the world and its impact on the condition of Jews brought us to our way of implementation, through the kibbutz and moshav settlement movement. This way says—despair of exile, concentration of the nation in its country, and settlement of

Table 2.3. Jewish Villages in the Land of Israel, 1908–1987 (Selected Years)

YEAR	TOTAL	MOSHAVOT AND VILLAGES			KIBBUTZIM			MOSHAVIM			COLLECTIVE MOSHAVIM		
		NUMBER	% OF TOTAL	% GROWTH	NUMBER	% OF TOTAL	% GROWTH	NUMBER	% OF TOTAL	% GROWTH	NUMBER	% OF TOTAL	% GROWTH
1908	22	21	95.5	—	1	4.5	—	—	—	—	—	—	—
1929	71	31	43.7	47.6	26	36.7	2500	14	19.7	—	—	—	—
1935	131	39	29.8	25.8	43	32.8	25.4	48	36.6	242.9	1	0.8	—
1947	260	49	18.8	25.6	127	48.8	195.3	78	30.0	62.5	6	2.3	500.0
1956	620	38	6.1	-22.4	227	36.6	78.7	331	53.4	324.4	24	3.9	300.0
1967	660	60	9.1	57.9	233	35.3	2.6	345	52.3	4.2	22	3.3	-9.1
1985	867	62	7.2	3.3	268	30.9	15.0	411	47.4	19.1	47	5.4	113.6
1987	936	61	6.5	-1.6	268	28.6	—	409	43.7	-0.5	47	5.0	—

Sources: 1908–1947: Portugali, 1976; 1956–1987: Central Bureau of Statistics, *Statistical Yearbook for Israel.*
Notes: The total includes community settlements as of 1985 (see Table 3.6).

Jews on their land. And this way brings about a deep transition in the life of every Jew and in the life of the whole nation. It is more than a political struggle and more than territorial change.

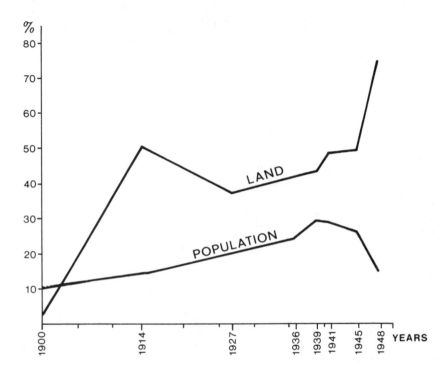

Figure 2.2.   Jewish Rural Population in the Land of Israel (Percent of Total Jewish Population) versus Cultivated Jewish Land (Percent of Total Jewish-Owned Land), 1900–1948

Sources and notes:

   Population: 1900–1914 data (Government of Palestine, 1938, p. 47); 1927–1943 data (Bein, 1953, p. 429); 1948 data (Central Bureau of Statistics, 1965–1988). *Jewish-owned land* (Kimmerling, 1974, p. 108). *Jewish cultivated land*: 1900 (1897 in the Meirovitz census), 1914, and 1927 data (*Figures and Facts on Settlement and Economy in Palestine*, p. 38); these data relate to physical area, whereas data from 1936 on relate to cultivated land and may include some multicrop irrigated land more than once; deviations, though are very small; 1936–1945 data (The National Committee, 1947, pp. 265, 535); 1948 data (Central Bureau of Statistics, 1965–1988).

Chapter 3

Ideological Settlement Activity Since 1948

Between Village and Development Town: 1948–1957

Dilemmas in Zionist Implementation with the Achievement of Statehood

The establishment of the State of Israel in 1948 created a completely new condition for the implementation of Zionist objectives. As for territory, the desire for sovereignty was satisfied over a major chunk of British Palestine. This sovereignty could, theoretically, have solved the need to acquire territory. Would Zionism see this means of territorial control as sufficient? As it turned out, not only was the answer a negative one, but the acquisition processes through lawmaking and the presence processes through settlement activity were intensified following the achievement of statehood. When it comes to population, the Holocaust refugees and Jews leaving the Arab countries flooded the new state; this human stream doubled the population in the first three years after the formation of the state. Would the State of Israel just absorb these immigrants, or would it attempt to spread them over the whole national territory? If the answer to the latter was positive, would the distribution attempt once again take place within the rural context? As in pre-state times, this latter point would become the weak link in the implementation chain of Zionist objectives, and most immigrants would reach neither the villages nor the development towns that were established in their proximity.

What of the attempt to base the Jewish community on a specific socialist structure, which action would be enhanced with the new power available through the use of the parliamentary system under the Labor hegemony in the political system and administration. Would it result in radical changes in the basis of the newly founded state, making it more egalitarian, cooperatively based, and agrarian?

As has been suggested, it seems as though the cooperative village enterprise was initially supposed to serve as the geographical framework for the implementation of Zionist objectives following the achievement of statehood. For various reasons to be outlined, however, a new framework, or settlement type, was created—the development town. During the period 1948–1956, both villages and development towns were undergoing reinforcement processes. Obviously, their starting points were not equal. Cooperative villages had already existed on the Israeli landscape for forty years; the development towns were newborn. At this stage, it would be worthwhile to check for transitions in the ranking of Zionist objectives before the implementation of Zionist objectives through villages and towns is examined. Israel's Declaration of Independence is an important document for the study of this specific point in time, as it effectively summarized the Zionist enterprise since its inception and also proposed an ideological program for continued activity within the context of state life.

In relation to the pre-state period of construction of the Jewish community, this document states:

> And during the past generations, they massively returned to their land, and pioneers, illegal immigrants, and defenders made the unsettled land flourish, revitalized their Hebrew language, built villages and towns, and founded a growing community, dominating its economy and culture, desiring peace and defending it, bringing the blessing of progress to all residents of the country, and seeking independence as a state.

The order of the objectives, as expressed here, was this: population, territory, mode of life (the Hebrew language), villages, towns, economy (socialist?), defense, helping the Arabs, sovereignty. As for the future, the Declaration of Independence asserted:

> The State of Israel will be open for Jewish immigration and for the "ingathering of the exiles"; it will persist in the development of the country for the welfare of all of its residents; it will be founded on the bases of freedom, justice and peace in light of the vision of the prophets of Israel; it will maintain complete social and political rights for all its citizens without regard to religion, race or gender; it will ensure liberties of religion, conscience, language, education and culture.

The order of objectives here was, again, population, territory, mode of life (though here this objective does not refer to language or to the economy, urban and rural life-styles, and so forth, but to citizens' rights and the foundations of government).

The heavy emphasis on population, in both the description of the past and the paving of the future road, reflected the central issue with which the new state would have to cope, beyond the basic problem of survival in its war of independence. This was the absorption of the Holocaust refugees, recently prevented from reaching Palestine by the British Mandate, and the absorption of the mass immigration of Jews from Arab countries. In Ben-Gurion's words in 1949:

> The main thing is the absorption of immigration; in this are included all the historical needs of the state.... We could have perhaps conquered the West Bank, the Golan or the whole of Galilee, but these conquests would not have strengthened our security in the same way that it may be strengthened by the absorption of immigrants. The doubling and tripling of the number of immigrants gives us more and more power.... This is the most important thing, standing above any other issue...on immigration depends, too, the fate of the state. (Segev, 1984, pp. 106–107)

The question of territory was going to be important in the 1950s, but second to immigration. The feeling prevailed that sovereignty was not a sufficient enough means for holding national territory. Again it was Ben-Gurion who underscored this point in 1949: "We won indeed in conquests, but without settlement these conquests do not have a decisive value, neither in the Negev nor in the Galilee nor in Jerusalem. Settlement—this is the real conquest" (Segev, 1984, p. 107).

An examination of the priority of objectives as listed in the policy outlines of the first government (*Government Yearbook*, 1950) shows the preference given to immigration and absorption issues. The immigrants were supposed to be directed "to the village and to agrarian settlements of all types" (p. XV). Population distribution was mentioned later on as part of a four-year development plan. The policy outlines of this first government devoted a separate chapter to civil rights, which appeared before all the programmatic chapters. In 1956, the policy outlines of the government presented immigration as its first objective and economic independence and territorial settlement as its second and third. Immigration would continue to appear first in the list of policy outlines issued by all Israeli governments until 1970.

The Attempt to Institutionalize the Preference for the Cooperative Village

The attempt to institutionalize the agrarian-cooperative mode of life, which effort had started before statehood, was now intensified, among other things to facilitate a large immigration absorption in villages. At the time, the readiness of veteran Israelis to move from cities to villages was low. Moreover,

> eight out of every ten Israelis were concerned by the flow of immigrants to the large cities. They perceived it as a threat to the economic and social structure of the national community. Nearly 100 percent of the Israelis said that the immigrants should be 'directed' to agricultural settlements. About half of the respondents thought that immigrants should be compelled to work in agriculture.... The immigrants' refusal to do what Israeli veterans did not want to do was interpreted as a harsh stand against the ideology, which was still accepted by many, and as foreign to the country's needs. One of the newspapers accused that the small number of immigrants absorbed in agriculture 'causes the lack of products in the country.' An information publication warned that the immigrants settling in cities bring about the creation of slums, 'quarters of poverty, dirt, idleness, sin and crime, a new Carthage.' (Segev, 1984, p. 151)

The attempts by the state to settle both veteran Israelis and immigrants in rural areas encompassed all relevant resources for rural development; namely, human resources, land and capital, water, and organization.

Human Resources. In 1949, the "security service law" was passed; it stated, among other things: "The first twelve months of a man's military service and a woman's twelve months of service would be mainly devoted, following basic military training, to agricultural preparation." Ben-Gurion, who at the time was in charge of the Defense Ministry, in addition being prime minister, explained the law to Israel's parliamentary body, the Knesset: "The security service law that is in front of you is directed to impart to our army two qualities which are necessary for our security: military capability and pioneering capability" (Gvatti, 1981, p. 39). This particular clause of the law has never been put into practice. The law was temporarily amended in February 1950 for a year and a half, and this amendment has been extended several

times. Only in 1986 did the Knesset initiate discussions for its cancellation. This intention to integrate compulsory military service
with service in cooperative settlements, especially for young urban
citizens, however created, one military unit, Nahal (an acronym
for pioneer fighting youth), which attempted this integration first
for kibbutzim only, then for moshavim as well, and lately even for
development towns.

A volunteer movement, active in the early 1950s, for the
mass direction of urban population to the kibbutzim, called *from the
town to the village,* failed. In 1952, only 1701 adults moved from
towns to kibbutzim (Ben-Horin, 1983). These two human resource
channels were accompanied by educational indoctrination. As
Ben-Gurion phrased it: "A human being does not become a pioneer by a command from above. All the education in the country,
in school and outside it, in the literature and in the press, has to be
directed so that we shall rear a pioneering generation" (Gvatti,
1981, p. 39).

Land and Capital.
Immediately following its establish-
ment, the state sold two million dunams of land to the JNF in a
kind of a "land redemption" transaction. In return, the JNF paid
for immigration absorption. The Israeli Agricultural Bank was
established in 1951, but the Israel Land Administration was set up
only in 1960.

Water.
The water operations company, Mekorot, was
founded in the pre-state 1940s. The governmental water planning
company, Tahal, was established in 1952. In 1959, the "water law"
was passed, nationalizing all the water resources of the country
and creating an agency in charge of its allocation.

Organization.
The Joint Center for Agricultural and
Settlement Planning was set up in 1952 to coordinate between the
Ministry of Agriculture and the Jewish Agency. The latter contin-
ued to build settlements through the political parties, as was done
during the British Mandate.

The variety of state means and tools helped agriculture to
turn into a flourishing, modern sector. It also facilitated Jewish
ownership of most of the agricultural lands and water resources of
the country.

Between 1947 and 1956, the number of rural settlements increased from 260 to 620, or by almost two and a half times (Table 2.3). On the other hand, the number of colonies decreased through urbanization processes. The number of kibbutzim almost doubled, but their share in rural settlement decreased from about one half to slightly over one-third (36.6 percent). In contrast, the number of moshavim increased more than four times, from 78 to 331, and the moshav became the dominant form of rural settlement (53.4 percent). Thus, most of the construction effort in the rural sector went to the moshavim, which being cooperative rather than collective, were inferior to the kibbutz from an ideological perspective. This practical weakening of the ideology of cooperation was necessary to make it easier for the new immigrants to adjust to their new life. Because most of these newcomers received no ideological preparation, however, the socioeconomic gap increased between the old and new kibbutzim, on the one hand, and the new moshavim, on the other. To a lesser degree this was true also for the relationship between old and new moshavim. Veteran moshavim incorporated the new cooperatives into their national political movements and into their retail and marketing organizations (Weintraub et al., 1969). It was not, though, to be the last ideological change in the rural sector. The kibbutzim were forced to use hired workers, both to assist in immigration absorption and because of their expanding operations. Most of the workers employed in kibbutzim came either from the new moshavim or from the development towns.

The rural sector, once again, did not prove to be a massive population absorber. During the first three years of the State of Israel, the country's population doubled from 716,000 (in 1948) to 1.4 million (in 1951). During the same period, the rural population also almost doubled, from about 160,000 to some 310,000. This meant that the villages absorbed only about one quarter of the newcomers (the data include natural growth). The rural population peak, as mentioned, was reached in 1941, when its share of the national Jewish population amounted to 29 percent. During the first years of statehood, the percentage ranged between 15.4 percent in 1948 and 23.6 percent in 1954. By 1956, villages had started to lose population in absolute terms, as well. In 1957, about 397,000 people lived in Jewish villages; in 1958, this figure decreased to 324,000. (The decline had also to do with a reclassification of several colonies as urban settlements; however, the drop in rural population has continued since then, see Table 3.1.)

Table 3.1. Jewish Rural Population in Israel, 1948–1987

YEAR	POPULATION IN THOUSANDS	PERCENT OF TOTAL JEWISH POP.	YEAR	POPULATION IN THOUSANDS	PERCENT OF TOTAL JEWISH POP.
1948	110.6	15.4	1970	271.9	10.7
1949	161.0	15.9	1971	275.2	10.5
1950	224.3	18.6	1972	264.2	9.6
1951	310.7	22.1	1973	264.7	9.3
1952	330.7	22.8	1974	268.9	9.3
1953	345.9	23.3	1975	273.6	9.2
1954	360.6	23.6	1976	277.4	9.2
1955	371.2	23.3	1977	283.3	9.2
1956	379.8	22.8	1978	287.8	9.2
1957	396.8	18.3	1979	291.0	9.5
1958	324.6	17.9	1980	314.8	9.6
1959	321.1	17.3	1981	320.7	9.7
1960	322.4	16.9	1982	329.6	9.8
1961	297.9	15.4	1983	329.5	9.8
1962	303.3	14.7	1984	350.9	10.1
1963	288.4	13.4	1985	356.2	10.1
1964	294.7	13.2	1986	364.9	10.2
1965	267.4	11.6	1987	370.1	10.2
1966	271.3	11.6			
1967	272.9	11.4			
1968	275.2	11.4			
1969	269.8	10.8			

Source: Central Bureau of Statistics, *Statistical Yearbook for Israel.*

The intention to increase on a massive scale the share of the Israeli rural population, though aided by extensive governmental support, has not succeeded. This failure stemmed from an unwillingness on the part of most immigrants to live in rural settlements, an attitude shared by veteran Israelis. The lack of success was also related to the high costs associated with rural development. Jabotinski's forecast is of interest in this regard. In his testimony before the Peele Commission in 1937, he argued:

We deny that in modern settlement and in the new rules for population distribution, agriculture still has the crucial role attributed to it in the past. The fact should be noted that in every country development goes hand in hand with a diminishing value for agriculture in the country's economy. Therefore, we think that as far as the Jews

are concerned—and I think that the Arabs will also develop in this
direction—the future of Palestine will be an urban one, and the value
of the industries that are not connected with agriculture will increase
more and more. (p. 24)

The lack of a proper residential infrastructure for the huge
influx of immigrants caused the Jewish Agency to house many of
them in former Arab towns, immigrant camps, and transitory communities (*ma'abarot*), especially along the central coastal plain.
This geographical concentration served as a deterrence to the
agrarian policy as well as to efforts to construct development towns
(Table 3.2). About a quarter of the immigrants in 1952 lived in
ma'abarot around Tel Aviv. The policy of directing population to
peripheral regions was called *population dispersal*; it assumed that
domination of the national territory could be achieved by rural as
well as urban settlements. This territorial approach appeared in
the policy outlines of all Israeli governments, and Israeli cooperative villages served as the leading edge in "settling the boundaries"
and "conquering the unsettled." The preferred regions were the
northern Negev (including the Lakhish region), the Jerusalem corridor, and to a lesser degree the Galilee. Cooperative settlements
thus continued the implementation of the territorial objective as
this was viewed after 1936; namely, that territorial possession has
to be achieved through presence. Once again, this approach was
accompanied by the notion that security along the borders could be
assured through civilian settlements.

As for mode of life, the 1950s witnessed the evolution of a
strong rural sector that was completely cooperative in structure,
with the exclusion of the few urbanizing colonies. The large-scale
settlement construction strengthened both regional and national
agrarian-rural organizations that dealt with production, marketing,
and consumption. This centralizing structure exerted a negative
effect on the welfare of the newly established development towns,
as we shall see later on. In its attempts to enhance a cooperative
and productive mode of life, the Labor movement benefitted much
from the establishment of the state; however, this was true mainly
for the rural sector.

In the cities, cooperativeness and Labor ownership was limited to those services and industries owned by the Histadruth. Even
there, however, cooperativeness was mostly of a different nature,
since the plants belonged to all union members, not just to the
workers of specific factories. Ben-Gurion related to this unique mix
in 1950: "The State of Israel is not a capitalist country; less than

Table 3.2. Distribution of Transit Camps *(Ma'abarot)* in Israel,
by Region and Population (December 1952)

REGION	NO. OF CAMPS	POPULATION	PERCENT
Eastern Upper Galilee	3	4,374	2.1
Eastern Lower Galilee	7	7,401	3.6
Valleys	15	13,517	6.6
Western Upper Galilee	2	4,381	2.1
Haifa Area	15	29,119	14.1
Ceasarea	9	11,144	5.4
Central Sharon	10	16,028	7.8
Southern Sharon	9	22,843	11.1
Tel Aviv Area	19	40,518	24.0
Lydda Area	19	24,057	11.7
Jerusalem Area	4	15,465	7.5
Southern Coastal Plain	5	5,950	2.9
The Negev	4	2,218	1.1
Total	121	206,015	100.0

*Source: The Inter-Ministerial Committee for the Study of Conditions of the
Ma'abarot, 1954, p. 8.*

half its workers work in the capitalist economy. This state is not a
socialist one, because in this country there exist—and the government will encourage and enhance—private entrepreneurship and a
private economy that is based on private capital and on hired
labor" (Segev, 1984, p. 282).

Along the same vein, Ben-Gurion's comment on the austerity
plan that went into effect in 1951 was that it was not meant to be
"a means to control for equality. This government does not yet
dare to take upon itself this task. Not because this task is not great
and important; it is very great. But its time has not yet arrived.
Anybody who will take upon himself this task now is either a liar
or a saboteur" (Segev, 1984, p. 299). In fact, the policy outlines of
the very first government allowed for private capital alongside with
(and even before) cooperation as a means for the construction of
the country (*Government Yearbook*, 1950). On the other hand, the
centralization that typified the organization of the rural-agricultural sector was transferred to other sectors, as well; for example, in
terms of the restricted status of local governments and the mecha-
nisms for capital allocation.

It is possible, therefore, to summarize the first decade of statehood from the perspective of the rural sector like this: Statehood

did not significantly change the status of cooperative settlements in the implementation of Zionist objectives relative to the period 1936–1947. Villages did not turn into the major absorbing settlement form for immigrants, which was, after all, the major challenge of the 1950s. On the other hand, the rural sector attained an almost utmost ability to hold territory. The rural sector also continued to develop the mode of life that was formatted in the 1920s. We will return briefly to developments in the rural sector in more recent years in the concluding chapter.

The establishment of development towns was supposed to provide an implementation tool for Zionist objectives in their new post-1948 order of population, territory, and mode of life. In practice, the development towns, too, eventually reached the "rural priority order" that had originated in the 1930s: territory, population, and mode of life. This occurred, however, only at a later stage, through the town-basing efforts of the 1960s.

The Development Towns: 1948–1961

Evolution of the Idea of Development Towns

The very idea of establishing field towns as a Zionist-institutional initiative was not new. Back in 1917, Tischler (1947) had proposed a nationwide system of such towns. It is perhaps symbolic that at the time when cooperative villages started their big leap forward, in 1936, an orderly discussion of the development town idea was modestly commenced. This was initiated by the "settlement reform circle," which started its deliberations in 1937–1938. The urban idea, in the form of several levels of field towns, was foreign to institutional Labor Zionism (E. Cohen, 1970a), but it later served as a basis for the establishment of a professional planning body for the State of Israel (Brutzkus, 1970; Reichman and Yehudai, 1984). The planning and construction of the development towns, following the Declaration of Independence, were an outcome of a change in the priorities of Zionism: population now became the preferred objective. As Cohen (1970a, p. 33) has noted, the settlement authorities did not decide to direct their efforts to urban development out of free choice. This decision was forced on them by the circumstances of immigration and settlement that evolved during the first years of statehood. On the one hand, there was the unprecedented influx of poor immigrants; on the other hand, land and water resources became scarce. It was becoming clear that agriculture could absorb only a small percentage of the immigrants, and that most immigrants would need governmental and other institutional support to be absorbed in towns and cities. The development towns would have permitted the distribution of the immigrants all over the country, rather than their possible concentration along the coastal plain. Thus, the establishment of the development towns during the 1950s was a *must*, not necessarily a matter of *will*. The towns served as a necessary means of implementing Zionist objectives, for population absorption first and for population dispersal second. Indeed, Cohen (1970a, p. 35) argued that the slogan *population dispersal*, never had the importance and ideological urgency of, for example, *the blending of the exiles*.

There were, therefore, several objectives for the establishment of the development towns:

1. Immigration absorption (population);

2. The settlement of sparsely populated regions to decrease regional imbalances (territory);

3. The settlement of frontier regions for security and assurance of sovereignty (territory);

4. Changing the primate city structure of the urban system by restricting the coastal plain (territory);

5. Creating integrated and ranked regional systems through the establishment of urban service centers. (Shachar, 1971, p. 364)

The geographical characteristics of the newly established towns were four in number:

1. The towns were located in underdeveloped or sparsely populated regions.

2. They were planned.

3. The population consisted of immigrants.

4. The towns were small in size. (Cohen, 1970b)

There were exceptions to each of these characteristics; the specific locations of the towns were determined by (1) central place theory (Brutzkus, 1970); (2) the distribution of natural resources; and (3) the location of existing towns (both Jewish and former Arab ones). The towns also had two administrative characteristics. First, a central governmental administration did not exist for development towns (Aronoff, 1973). Second, the development towns were managed throughout the 1950s from the outside by clerks appointed by the central government; thus they constituted a type of "planted" communities. As such, these communities and their population were, or were perceived to operate as, passive objects manipulated by central agencies, without having any defined role in their own planning and development (Cohen, 1970b).

It is obvious that development towns, unlike the cooperative villages, were not a settlement ideal per se in the 1950s; rather they were viewed as a necessity that turned into policy. Proof of this perhaps lies in the fact that development towns were not directly mentioned in the policy outlines of Israeli governments until 1975! Until then, there appeared expressions such as "development regions" and "immigrant settlements," which could be interpreted as referring either to villages or development towns or both together. During the 1960s, the development towns would turn into an "ideal from above," fostered and directed by government. It was not until the 1970s, however, that a local leadership emerged in almost all the development towns. Before the discussion moves to the 1960s, several aspects of the population, territory, and mode of life objectives as they related to development towns in the 1950s should first be examined.

The Development Towns as a Means of Absorbing Large Immigration Waves

Several weeks before independence was declared, Labor [Mapai] prepared the immigration and absorption policy for the first two years of statehood. The committee established for this purpose constructed a budget for the absorption of 150,000 people, but there were some members who talked about a quarter of a million. Nobody thought that the number [of immigrants] would reach 400,000. The policy outlines of the government stated that it would formulate a development plan for the next four years to bring about a doubling of the population. This, therefore, was the national target: about 600,000 immigrants in four years. This target was achieved, but the number of immigrants who came in the first year, 1949, was ten times the number of those who came during the fourth one. (Segev, 1984, p. 106)

These data show the intensity of the "population pressure" and its concentration within a very short time span. The villages, as we have seen, absorbed less than a quarter of the immigrants during the first three years of statehood. The development towns housed some 115,000 people (assuming that around 10,000 people lived in some older parts of several towns before 1948). Deducting natural growth, one can see that development towns absorbed *instantly* about 15 percent of the huge immigration wave. In other words, the rural and the new urban sectors together absorbed around one third of the immigrants.

During the 1950s, thirty-four development towns were established or declared, of which fifteen were brand new. The percentage of Jewish Israelis residing in them grew constantly. Thus, in 1948 only 1.5 percent lived in a development town; in 1950, this percentage rose to 7.1 percent; by 1956, it had reached 13.1 percent; and in 1961, some 16.5 percent of all Israeli Jews resided in development towns (Table 3.3). The development towns gradually spread over the national territory and they absorbed immigration throughout the whole decade. One disadvantage, however, was that their relatively small population size and their demographic structure, consisting almost solely of immigrants, slowed down the process of social integration (Cohen, 1969).

Table 3.3.　Development Towns in Israel, 1948–1961

YEAR	NO. OF TOWNS	POPULATION	PERCENT OF TOTAL JEWISH POP.
1948	4	11,251	1.5
1949	6	21,775	2.1
1950	16	85,433	7.1
1951	22	126,081	9.0
1952	23	136,732	9.4
1953	24	144,461	9.7
1954	24	162,125	10.6
1955	26	180,630	11.4
1956	30	218,159	13.1
1957	32	254,095	14.4
1958	32	272,984	15.1
1959	32	289,539	15.6
1960	32	303,060	15.9
1961	33	319,374	16.5

Sources: Development town population (Amiran and Shachar, 1969); total Jewish population (Central Bureau of Statistics, 1965–1988). For notes on the number of towns, see Figure 3.3.

Development Towns and Territorial Spread

The development towns were supposed to become a major building block in the population dispersion program, which became national policy after the establishment of the state. "The term *population dispersal* received the significance of a symbol, expressing the Zionist policy of wishing to achieve a Jewish foothold all over the State of Israel" (Reichman and Yehudai, 1984, p. 115). Within this context, one may interpret the development towns as a settlement form equivalent to rural settlements (Reichman, 1975). Sovereignty over state territory and even state ownership of most lands, though, were not considered sufficient to implement the territorial objective; the desired goal was to attain a settlement presence everywhere. Because the social and economic circumstances of rural settlements could not provide such a presence, development towns became the instrument to do so. The spread of development towns was as a result confined mainly to peripheral areas of the state, ranging from Qiryat Shemona in the North down to Eilat in the far South. Development towns were perceived in early national plans as facilitating population distribution (Sharon, 1951). They were also integrated into the security concept, which called for settling citizens along the borders. They permitted the use of cheap urban land (Altman and Rosenbaum, 1973), and they further assisted in efforts at agricultural land preservation along the coastal plain. Three blocs of development towns may be identified: northern, central, and southern (Figure 3.1). The central bloc, along the coastal plain, was practically cancelled during the 1960s with the removal of a number of urban sites from the several definitions of development town (see comments to Figure 3.3). Hence, only two blocs of development towns have remained, one at each end of the country.

Development Towns versus Rural Mode of Life

The objection to the urban idea by the political-Labor establishment, based on the preference for rural and agricultural modes of life, manifested itself in a resistance to dealing with urban development. Throughout the years between the two World Wars and almost until the declaration of independence, Labor Zionist leaders made no statement regarding urban policy or the need for such policy in the future (see Cohen, 1970a). In their opinion, the future

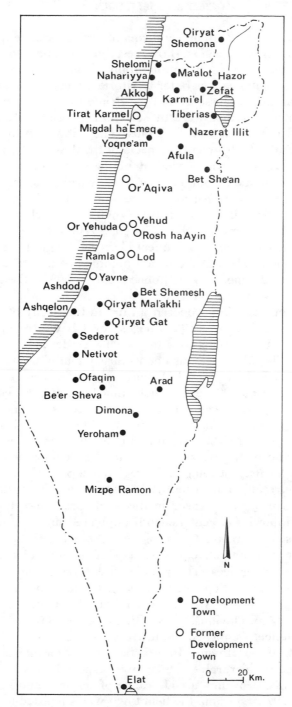

Figure 3.1. The Development Towns

was linked to new revolutionary forms of agricultural settlements, not to cities. This objection, however, had to undergo change, given the needs relating to immigration absorption, on the one hand, and the continued desire for territorial spread, on the other.

The planning professionals in the Prime Minister's Office and in the Ministry of Labor were those who proposed the establishment of field towns back in the 1930s. They now had to contend with the "rural establishment," especially the Jewish Agency Settlement Department, which viewed immigration absorption and population distribution from an exclusively rural perspective. This conflict per se has received much attention in the literature (see, for example, Brutzkus, 1970; Reichman and Yehudai, 1984; Sharon, 1951; Kellerman, 1972; Cohen, 1970a). Here, however, our concern is with attempts to inject ideas relating to the cooperative-rural mode of life into the urban planning of the development towns. These attempts may be noticed at two levels, the regional system and the single-town level.

Early national plan proposed an urban hierarchy of five levels. Level A consisted of single villages; level B was composed of intervillage centers serving four to six villages; level C were field towns of 6,000–12,000 persons each (earlier planning even called for fewer than 5,000); at level D there were subdistrict or district towns of 15,000–60,000 people each; and level E marked urban localities, with large regional or national cities of more than 100,000 people each. This structure was strictly applied to the development of the Lakhish region lying between the coastal plain and the northern Negev, as well as to the development of the northern Negev itself, leading to the regional capital of Beersheba.

Two, normally nonexistent rural aspects relating to town-village relations may be observed in this structure. First, the establishment of intervillage centers, both populated and unpopulated, were supposed to make it possible for the villages to preserve autonomy in the cooperative provision of technical, social, cultural, and educational services. The populated centers acted mainly as service providers and guidance centers for the new moshavim, and the unpopulated centers were industrial centers jointly owned by several kibbutzim. Obviously, level B, the intervillage centers, by its very existence, weakened the towns of levels C and D; that is, the regional service towns. In practice, the intervillage centers have developed a hierarchy of their own, especially in the kibbutz subsector, while providing a wide range of services and industries (Kellerman, 1972). Second, the field town was supposed to operate in such a way that there would be no place for private commerce, and the provision and marketing systems were supposed to be organized cooperatively, exactly as in the agricultural moshavim surrounding it. From a municipal viewpoint, the status of the town was similar to that of an agricultural settlement—represented by a local committee. In the new urban centers, which were established in the south of the country, this was even given validation in the "regulations code"; that is, their municipal status was one of a local committee, included in the jurisdiction of a regional council. (Reichman and Yehudai, 1984, p. 114)

The status of the development towns was also hurt by several additional factors, such as the difference in age between villages, which had been in existence for several decades, and the newly established towns; the short distances from the rural peripheries to the large cities; and the antiurban ideology of the rural sector. These aspects yielded two processes. For one thing, the towns were subordinated to the villages, not the other way around, so that town residents found themselves employed mostly in agriculture, in kibbutz industries and in the intervillage centers. For another, the old villages as well as the new ones were able to interact directly with the large cities through their centralized shopping organizations (Y. Cohen, 1967).

At the level of the single town, there were experiments with several rural ideas. One concept introduced was that of garden towns and auxiliary farming to assure the self-provision of agricultural products for the urbanites and maintain the rural character of the development towns (Altman and Rosenbaum, 1973). Not only did these ideas not prove useful, they even turned into spatial obstacles for the creation of a coherent urban space. Furthermore, the land parcels for development towns were restricted and surrounded by agricultural fields to avoid future expansion (Reichman and Yehudai, 1984, p. 114).

These rural elements, which were inserted into urban and regional planning, would cause problems in the future. They responded, however, to ideological-political objections to the urban idea, and thus permitted the use of towns for the implementation of Zionist territorial and population objectives. The Labor-rural establishment could thus view the development towns as an attempt to integrate population (immigrants), territory (population dispersal), and mode of life (preservation of the status of villages; rural elements introduced into urban entities).

The Development Towns: 1961–1987

The Increased Importance of the Development Towns

The year 1961 was a symbolic one for the evolution of development towns as a tool for the geographical implementation of Zionist objectives, side by side with cooperative villages. This year, the percentage of the Jewish population residing in development towns surpassed that in rural communities, 16.5 percent (15.9 percent in 1960) as against 15.4 percent (16.9 percent in 1960) (Tables 3.1 and 3.3). It is difficult, however, to equate the immense political status of the cooperative villages in 1961 with that of the development towns, many of which were still struggling for bare survival. One also cannot compare either the cooperative rural sector, which in the early 1960s was reaching agricultural saturation, or specifically the industrializing kibbutzim with the development towns, which still had to attain a sound economic base. The absolute and relative sizes of the development towns, however, had become significant, especially in light of the growing reluctance of the general population to continue "Zionist work" through rural cooperative settlement. Thus, the development towns started to be considered a legitimate tool for the implementation of Zionist objectives, as a kind of an "ideal from above," side by side with cooperative villages. These trends were expressed on several occasions by the young leadership of Labor (Mapai) of the mid-1960s. Moshe Dayan declared in 1963: "Deganya, Ein Harod, or Nahalal are not a symbol anymore for the essential centers, nor for our problems of national existence. Nowadays these are typified by places such as Beersheba, Ashdod, or Dimona" (Schweitzer, 1984, p. 22). Shimon Peres argued in 1964: "The development towns should be elevated...to a degree of value and property for the movement" (ibid., p. 23). These statements were made at a time when the social-political elite of the past had grown tired. Politically, it might well be that the dominant party, Mapai, did not get the message. Practically, however, much was done, especially by Pinhas Sapir, then minister for commerce and industry and later finance minister, to develop and foster industrial entrepreneurship in general and in the development towns in particular.

Since the early 1960s, the development towns have been typified by three major transitions. First, the priority order for the implementation of Zionist objectives through them has changed. No longer was it to be population first; now the descending priority order was territory, population, mode of life; in other words, the same order that has prevailed in the rural sector since the 1930s. Second, the attempts to limit the status, function, and structure of the development towns by the rural sector diminished. Development towns could now receive their own urban status, either with the assistance or despite the objection of the villages. These two trends typified the 1960s. A third trend, which became more prominent in the 1970s, was the emergence of a strong local leadership in most development towns. Some of these leaders have also found their way into national-political life, in the Histadruth, in the central government, and the Knesset.

"Population Dispersal" in Preference to "Immigration Integration"

Some elaboration of the first two trends are necessary for a better understanding of the changes that the country was undergoing. The 1960s in general were characterized by a decrease in the size of immigration relative to the 1950s. Though 43.3 percent of the immigrants who arrived from 1961–1967 reached development towns (Altman and Rosenbaum, 1973), the share of these towns in the general population did not increase by much. This was due mainly to the small size of immigration in general, but also the negative migration balances experienced by many development towns as a result of out-migration to the large cities. For most of the decade, the percentage of the Jewish population residing in development towns rose, though only gradually from 16.5 percent (1961) to a peak of 19.7 percent (1967). Thereafter, it dropped slightly, until stabilizing at 17.5 percent by the mid-1970s. In the early 1980s, the percentage fluctuated around 18 percent, and then it increased annually by an additional 0.5 percent, fluctuating at 18.5 percent in the late 1980s (Table 3.4). The decline since 1967 may be attributed to the immigration trends mentioned previously and to the exclusion of towns located on the coastal plain from the list of development towns (i.e., Tirat Hacarmel, Lod, Or Yehuda, Rosh Ha'ayin, Yehud, Ramla). The modest increase in the share of the development town population since the mid-1970s reflects the even more modest success of the several plans for population dispersal (Kellerman, 1985a). On the other hand, it also attests to a certain population steadiness in most development towns.

From the 1960s on, the policy concerning development towns

Table 3.4. Development Towns in Israel, 1962–1987

YEAR	NUMBER OF TOWNS	POPULATION IN THOUSANDS	PERCENT OF TOTAL JEWISH POP.
1962	33	360.4	17.4
1963	33	398.0	18.5
1964	34	429.8	19.2
1965	34	448.9	19.5
1966	34	459.9	19.6
1967	34	470.0	19.7
1968	30	415.6	17.1
1969	30	432.0	17.2
1970	30	447.2	17.3
1971	30	464.6	17.5
1972	29	469.0	17.1
1973	29	505.9	17.8
1974	29	516.3	17.9
1975	29	597.6	17.9
1976	29	615.0	17.9
1977	29	625.7	17.9
1978	29	641.1	18.0
1979	29	670.1	18.3
1980	29	692.9	18.4
1981	29	703.8	18.5
1982	29	626.9	18.6
1983	29	610.0	17.8
1984	29	637.8	18.4
1985	29	646.0	18.4
1986	29	664.3	18.7
1987	29	668.2	18.5

Sources: Until 1967 (Amiran and Shachar, 1969); 1968–1987 (Central Bureau of Statistics, 1965–1988). For notes on the number of towns, see Figure 3.3.

called for strengthening existing towns and not establishing new ones, given the shortage in new-immigrant population (Shachar, 1971). Therefore, only two new towns were added in the mid-1960s (Arad in the South and Karmiel in the North). With the exclusion of Or Akiva from the list of development towns in the early 1970s, there have remained twenty-nine officially designated development towns.

The 1960s and 1970s saw the offer of generous government subsidies and grants to those who were ready to move from the large cities to development towns. A similar policy was applied to industrial enterprises. In 1975 a national plan for population redistribution (the "Five Million" plan) received legal status. Development towns on the northern and southern peripheries constituted the major settlement means for the modest dispersal targets of this program.

Another trend for the implementation of Zionist objectives, and one of major geographical importance, related to the size of the towns themselves. By the end of the 1950s it became clear that the need existed for an economic base for the towns that would be independent of the surrounding rural sector and would allow for their growth. The restraints instituted earlier on the character and structure of the development towns made this task quite difficult (Reichman and Yehudai, 1984, p. 115) and were eventually relaxed. The failure of ideas regarding garden towns and auxiliary farming permitted an increase in urban density, so that these towns received an urban look and pattern. The growth in population and the removal of municipal ties to the rural regional councils made it possible to develop commerce and services for the needs of the towns themselves and, to a growing degree, also neighboring villages. The major turning point came, however, when industrialization efforts, which started in the 1950s, came into full force under Sapir's leadership in the 1960s. Most of the industry directed to development towns, however, was labor intensive and undiversified, consisting mainly of textiles and foods (Gradus and Einy, 1980). The result has been cyclical economic crises, which have slowed down growth in both the social welfare and the population of development towns.

A New Territorial Challenge: The West Bank and Gaza

The Territorial Accent

Following its victory in the 1967 war, the State of Israel was faced with a dilemma that contained some of the elements of the settlement-security dialectic that had accompanied the Zionist movement from 1936 to 1948. Should Israel expand its Zionist activity into the territories occupied during the war, or should the state restrict itself to its pre-1967 borders? The dilemma now was different from that in the 1930s and 1940s, in that the new territories were under Israeli military control rather than under foreign authority (the British Mandate). This military control by its very nature, however, represented a temporary possession of the territories until peace agreements would eventually be reached. On the other hand, the possible use of nonmilitary means for the maintenance of the territories, such as presence (settlement) or sovereignty, could have had a Zionist significance in terms of an expansion of Jewish holdings in the Land of Israel. A large-scale transfer of Israeli-Zionist population and mode of life to the occupied territories could have enhanced such an expansion.

Since 1967, this dilemma has been solved for some of the territories. East Jerusalem and the Golan Heights were annexed by Israel in 1967 and 1981, respectively. The Sinai Peninsula was returned to Egypt as part of the peace treaty. The focus of the dilemma was restricted to the West Bank and Gaza Strip, the possible fate of which from a Zionist perspective has become the central political issue in Israeli society. This has especially been the case since 1974, with the onset of activities by Gush Emunim, which has strongly advocated the annexation of these territories to Israel. The dilemma further intensified with the rise to political power of the right-wing Likud party in 1977. The old debate between Left and Right on territorial minimalism-maximalism surfaced once again (Zur, 1982, p. 108). The focus of the geographical implementation of Zionism now moved from settlement forms to settlement regions. Nevertheless, a new settlement form was created—the community settlement (a form of exurb), which was later imported into Israel proper.

The new accent on territory has found expression in the policy outlines of all Israeli governments since 1967. For example, in 1970, immigration and social integration were still mentioned first, followed in order by peace and security, settlement (including urban), the construction of Jerusalem, and the development of the economy. In 1975, the government, for the first time, put peace and security first, rather than immigration, which dropped considerably in priority. Second came Jerusalem, followed by settlement ("action will be taken for continued settlement, according to decisions to be made by the State of Israel"—without details), the need for a constitution, the Diaspora, then immigration, and last social and economic issues. These were also the first governmental policy outlines in which the development towns were mentioned explicitly. The order of priorities reflected the change from a population to a territorial accent.

In Likud governments from 1977–1981, the order of objectives has been this: the unified destiny of the Jewish people, the right to the land, rural and urban settlements, immigration (in 1977), and peace (in 1981, following the peace treaty with Egypt; it appeared immediately after the right to the land). Agriculture, which began to be ranked lower in Labor governments from 1967, appeared in the 1977 policy outlines of the first Likud government only in the twentieth paragraph. In 1981, immigration was mentioned only in a late paragraph, even after agriculture and together with the issue of out-migration.

That year, development towns were referred to only indirectly, in a clause dealing with extended school hours. The unity (Labor and Likud) government established in 1984 displayed a priority order that went from consensus issues to those in disagreement: the Jewish people, social integration, immigration, peace, security, Jerusalem, restricted settlement activity (in the occupied territories), and economic issues. The development towns were treated in only one clause in chapter 17, and agriculture was left for chapter 19.

The settlement project in Judea and Samaria had started in 1967, immediately following the Six Day War, with the territorial objective providing the prime catalyst for this activity. In contrast to the rural and development town projects, it was the first time that a settlement project had started with territory constituting the primary objective. The cooperative villages had been set up in their time with a new mode of life as a leading objective, and the development towns had been established foremost to provide absorption for an immigrant population (Table 2.2). These differences among the leading objectives at the beginning of each settlement ideal reflect the changing problems confronting Zionism in each period. Following the 1967 war the central problem was the attitude to the occupied territories. The settlement events in the West Bank following the war were similar in some ways to those at the beginning of the cooperative village era in that the initiative came from below. Early settlement of the territories occurred when children of the original settlers of villages abandoned during the 1948 war rebuilt several ruined kibbutzim (Kfar Etzion, part of the Etzion bloc south of Bethlehem, and Beit Ha'arava, next to the Dead Sea). Only later were initial plans made by governmental authorities to settle the Jordan Valley. The same process of initiative from below happened, too, in the 1968 settlement of Hebron and in the settlement of the mountainous areas of the West Bank in the mid-1970s. In these cases, Gush Emunim acted in conflict with governmental decisions, which were later altered with the transition in the administration in 1977. Still, one may identify differences between the already existing development towns, on the one hand, and the community settlement that typified the settlement efforts in mountainous Judea and Samaria, on the other. The development towns

were meant to operate in a manner somewhat similar to the cooperative village, though this was not eventually accomplished. The
establishment of community settlements in the West Bank, however, was not related to earlier settlement ideals; rather, it served as
city extensions in the form of exurbs. As we shall see in the more
detailed discussion of the community settlements, there was an
attempt by Jewish Agency leaders to propose a moshav-type, cooperative community settlement.

Despite its young age when compared with development
towns and cooperative villages, the West Bank settlement project
requires a division into three temporal phases, and not the two that
were proposed for each of the earlier projects. In all three enterprises, the phases relate to transitions in the priority order of Zionist objectives, but now these have changed both faster and more
intensely than in the past. The proposed phase-division is similar to
that suggested by Benvenisti (1984), though the accent here is on
related transitions in Zionist priorities.

The Alon Plan and the Rabin Plan: 1967–1977

The first phase of settlement in the West Bank was carried
out between 1967 and 1977, under Labor administration. The
return of second-generation settlers to villages abandoned in 1948
was accompanied by calls in favor of the settlement process by
Labor settlement leaders (especially in the Hakibbutz Hameuchad
movement). Thus, Tabenkin declared in 1967:

> There is a place for settlement in Mount Hebron, in Judea and
> Samaria, and in Jerusalem no less than in places where we are set-
> tled currently, and which were settled until the establishment of the
> state. The Arabs lived here—and we founded hundreds of new set-
> tlements, and we absorbed into them exile immigrants from East and
> West and Holocaust refugees. We did not need the expulsion of the
> Arabs to build our settlements and our state! Our conscience is clear
> so far as the return to Gush Etzion, to Beit Ha'arava, to Gush
> Attarot, as much as it is clear concerning our living now in Ein
> Harod and Mishmar Haemeq, in Nahalal and in Hulda, in Dan and
> Shamir and in Eyal. The abrogation of the Arab-military occupation
> releases forces for the settlement of the expanding country. We have
> to state clearly to the world: We return now to continue to build the
> settlements that were stolen from us—to enhance the development of
> the country, for peace. In the state that had arbitrary boundaries,
> there was no security. These boundaries did not stop the Arabs from

becoming armed against us, from nurturing hatred and organizing for a war of anihilation against us. (Tabenkin, 1983, p. 75)

In these sentences it is possible to identify the major assumptions of the Alon plan. Proposed by Yigal Alon, then foreign minister and reared the same Labor movement as Tabenkin, this plan assumed the following:

1. Security considerations will be taken care of by creating defensible borders; namely, along the Jordan River.

2. There will be a resettlement of pre-1948 Jewish settlements.

3. Arab population and property will remain intact.

The Alon plan, which was discussed by the government in 1967–1968, but never formally approved, called for settlement along the Jordan Valley in a belt 12–15 km wide, later expanded to 20 km to include the eastern slopes of the mountains of Samaria and Judea. This belt was supposed to be annexed to Israel within the context of a peace treaty with the Kingdom of Jordan (Figure 3.2). In addition, the plan permitted settlement activity in Gush Etzion (the Etzion bloc) and in the no-man's land in the Latrun salient, both of which were also to be annexed. These borders were meant to encircle the cores of the Arab population in the West Bank. Interpreted in terms of the priorities of Zionist objectives, the Alon plan intended to continue the order that had prevailed in pre-1967 Israel. First was territorial spread, with primary consideration given to security, so that the Jordan Valley settlement would become classic border-frontier settlements. Second came population, by resettling pre-1948 Jewish areas and communities close to Jerusalem, in addition to the annexation of the greater East Jerusalem area. This annexation permitted the creation of densely built urban Jewish neighborhoods in parts of former East Jerusalem. The settlement map of the Alon plan permitted the territorial use of the West Bank for security purposes without any attachment to the Arab-populated mountainous areas, which were to be returned to Jordan on the basis of "territorial compromise." Third in priority was mode of life. The new villages in the Jordan Valley and in Gush Etzion were of the classic forms; namely, moshavim and kibbutzim. Even the regional organization of these villages was planned along cooperative lines, with two intervillage centers, one for each of the settlement regions.

These principles also served as bases for the "double back-

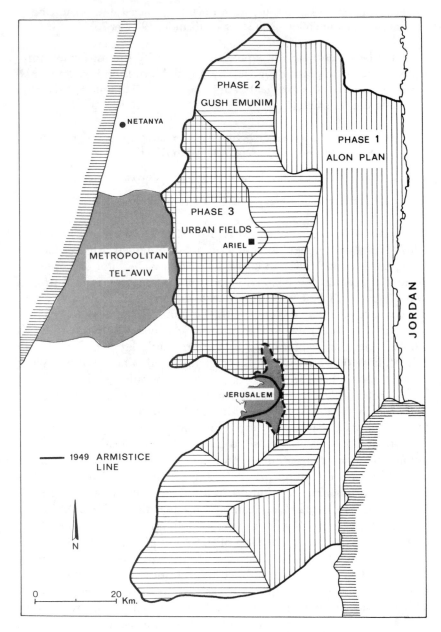

Figure 3.2.   Phases of Jewish Settlement in the West Bank

Source: Following Benvevnisti, 1984.

bone" plan (Wachman, 1977), which proposed to develop an intensive urban as well as rural settlement system along the Jordan Valley as a counterbalance to the coastal plain. The major obstacle to the implementation of this particular plan was the need to develop a new core, separated from the existing one by the West Bank mountains and (Arab) population (Sofer, 1977).

The settlement implementation of the Alon plan was generally modest (Table 3.5). Until 1972, only ten new settlements had been built (three of which were in the Etzion area), with 1200 residents. During 1973–1974, two other settlements were added and the total population increased to 2000.

Simultaneously with the development and public discussion of the Alon plan, the first seeds for the next settlement phase were planted. In Passover 1968, a group of settlers, headed by Rabbi Moshe Levinger, rented a hotel in Hebron and created a de facto settlement there. This event turned into a major dilemma for the Israeli government. The city of Hebron was located outside the security-based territorial spread advocated by the Alon plan. In addition, it was a settlement in the heart of a major Arab town. On the other hand, this settlement fulfilled, at least partially, another criterion; namely, a return to pre-1948 Jewish settlement areas. The 1929 Arab riots had culminated in the murder and expulsion of the ancient Jewish community in Hebron, one of the four "holy cities" in which Jews lived for centuries before the inception of Zionism. In addition, the settlers demonstrated a pioneering spirit, when they lived for a long time in difficult, crowded quarters, first in the hotel and then in the military administration building. The government preferred not to react (Kimmerling, 1983b, pp. 156–157).

The settlers, however, introduced an additional argument for their settlement action—the return to the "land of our forefathers." The town of Hebron was associated with the Patriarchs, especially their burial cave, and the early years of King David's reign as a king of Israel. This argument based the settlement act not just on prior Jewish settlement in the modern era, but also on historical settlements of several millennia past. This historical-religious reasoning became the leading catalyst of the second phase of West Bank settlement. Its geographical implication was an undifferentiating settlement effort all over the West Bank, all of which was considered "our forefathers' land." Rabbi Levinger effectively became the leader of the second wave of settlements, which started in 1974.

It is important to comment briefly on one additional development connected to the first phase, the Rabin plan. This plan, pro-

Table 3.5. Jewish Settlements in the West Bank and Gaza, 1972–1987

	THE WEST BANK							GAZA		TOTALS		
YEAR	TOTAL	NEW SETTLE-MENTS	PERCENT ANNUAL GROWTH	POP. IN THOUS.	PERCENT ANNUAL GROWTH	MEAN POP. PER SETTLE-MENT IN THOU.	PERCENT OF TOTAL WB POP.	NUMBER OF SETTLE-MENTS	POP. IN THOU.	SETTLE-MENTS	POP.	PERCENT OF ISRAELI POP.
1972	10	—	—	1.2	—	0.12	0.2	—	—	10	1.2	0.04
1973	11	1	10.0	1.5	25.0	0.14	0.2	—	—	11	1.5	0.05
1974	12	1	9.1	2.0	33.3	0.17	0.3	—	—	12	2.0	0.07
1975	18	6	50.0	2.6	30.0	0.14	0.4	1	(0.1)	19	(2.7)	(0.09)
1976	21	3	16.7	3.2	23.1	0.17	0.5	2	(0.2)	21	(3.4)	(0.1)
1977	32	11	52.4	5.0	56.3	0.16	0.7	3	(0.4)	35	(5.4)	(0.2)
1978	40	8	25.0	7.4	48.0	0.19	1.1	3	(0.4)	43	(7.8)	(0.2)
1979	43	3	7.5	10.0	35.1	0.23	1.4	3	(0.5)	46	(10.5)	(0.3)
1980	52	9	20.9	12.4	24.0	0.24	1.7	3	0.5	55	12.9	0.4
1981	65	13	25.0	16.1	29.8	0.25	2.2	3	0.5	68	16.6	0.5
1982	73	8	12.3	21.0	30.4	0.29	2.8	5	0.7	78	21.7	0.6
1983	76	3	4.1	23.0	9.5	0.30	3.0	5	0.8	81	23.8	0.7
1984	92	16	21.2	35.3	53.5	0.38	4.4	10	1.6	102	36.9	0.9
1985	105	13	14.1	44.2	25.2	0.42	5.3	11	1.9	116	46.1	1.1
1986	106	1	0.9	51.3	16.1	0.48	5.9	12	2.1	118	53.4	1.5
1987	106	—	—	57.9	12.9	0.55	6.5	12	2.4	118	60.3	1.7

Sources: Number of settlements 1972–1981 (Central Bureau of Statistics, *The List of Settlements*). Number of settlements 1982–1985 and population 1982–1985 (Central Bureau of Statistics, 1965–1988). Population 1972–1981 (Benvenisti, 1984, p. 61).

Notes: The number of settlements does not include army (Nahal) settlements. Gaza population data for 1975–1979 are estimates.

posed in 1975, following the first activities by Gush Emunim in 1974, displayed a Gush Emunim imprint in calling for an expansion of the Jordan Valley belt and for a larger settlement area around Jerusalem. It thus represented an expanded Alon plan, taking into account the aspirations of right-wing ideology, even if only very partially (Benvenisti, 1984, p. 52). In 1975 alone, the number of West Bank settlements increased from twelve to eighteen, or by 50 percent.

Gush Emunim: 1974 to Mid-1980s

Gush Emunim (the bloc of the faithful) was established in March 1974 by students and graduates of the "Merkaz Harav" Yeshiva (rabbinical college) in Jerusalem. The spiritual leader of this institution, Rabbi Zvi Yehuda Kook, was the son of Rabbi Avraham Yitzhak Kook, the first chief rabbi of Palestine and founder of this Yeshiva. Gush Emunim, an activist movement, was founded as a result of the traumatic 1973 war, but its basic ideological elements were shaped earlier. The strong attachment to the Land of Israel and the viewing of settlement as an indispensable part of this attachment had been developed by Rabbi A. Y. Kook, whose philosophy was interpreted to imply the inclusion of the establishment of the State of Israel as an early phase in the Messianic redemption process, which itself called for the need to hold onto all parts of the Land of Israel (D. Rubinstein, 1982; Raanan, 1980; Sprinzak, 1981, Lustick, 1988). However, additional ingredients in the mix that created the Gush were relevant to broader strata of the Israeli society and facilitated the attraction of secular groups as well. First was the resurgence of interest in Judaic historical and religious roots following the 1967 war, stemming from Israel's swift victory and the access that was regained to old Jerusalem. Second, a hedonistic, materialist life-style took hold in the major cities, against which the Gush had nothing to say, since its demands related only to land and budgets. This change in life-styles would be used later to settle exurban areas of Tel Aviv and Jerusalem on the West Bank. Third, Gush Emunim employed the pioneering-rural settlement method, a means associated with the Left (Rubinstein, 1980).

These three points are of significant importance for a more complete understanding of Gush Emunim activities. Its reference to historical-religious roots, not merely to security considerations, called for a geographically undifferentiating settlement all over

Judea and Samaria. This desire meant a departure not just from the Alon plan, but also from Zionist policy as a whole since 1936. This policy accepted, willingly or unwillingly, a partition of Palestine between Jews and Arabs (Benvenisti, 1984, p. 53). The urban origin of the Gush made it possible to invent a new settlement form based on the urban values of materialistic symbols, commuting and privatism. Thus, the community settlements could become attractive to many who wished to enhance their quality of life, although formally the Gush has advocated only territorial objectives (Sprinzak, 1981). As we shall see later, the community settlements were not recognized by government and the Jewish Agency until 1977, when the Likud came to power. The new administration, on the other hand, did not relate to settlement form as an ideological issue; it plainly perceived territory as being of central importance (Newman, 1984a).

The third point, the use of settlements to hold onto territories, was perhaps the most important, at least from the perspective of Likud, which adopted this tactic after it became the reigning party. Placing territory as top priority has always been the way of right-wing Zionism ("two banks has the Jordan" was its anthem, to which the slogan, "the integrity of the Land," was added later on). On the other hand, the use of presence through settlements rather than the use of sovereignty as a means of territory attainment and possession had been a Labor-leftist approach. This concept was transferred to the Right by the religious-national settlers of Gush Emunim, who had been educated within a religious-Labor movement, and by Ariel Sharon, then minister of agriculture, who had been reared on settlement ideals (Rubinstein, 1980, pp. 115–116). The Right adopted the presence-settlement tool but for the purpose of an efficient attainment of territorial objectives. The idea of settlements as creating and fostering a cooperative-agricultural mode of life was not adopted; indeed, it was challenged by the new community settlements. In summary, Gush Emunim was an organization that developed from below and outside the then-existing political parties. Its primary objective was territorial, the capture of West Bank areas, while a secondary aim was the establishment of a new settlement form, the community settlement. This form of settlement served, in turn, as a major tool for the achievement of the primary territorial goal. These objectives and means of Gush Emunim were adopted by the Likud party when it became the dominant political power in 1977.

From the perspective of its territorial objective, Gush Emunim attempted to focus operations on the central mountainous areas and, to a lesser extent, the Western slopes of Samaria (Figure 3.2). The early years of its activities, 1975–1977, were a time of struggle, peaking with the establishment of settlements, despite and against governmental decisions, that brought it into confrontation with Israeli military forces (see Harris, 1980; Aronson, 1990). The 1977 change in administration found the Gush with four unauthorized settlements (Elon-Moreh (Kedumim), Ofra, Tekoa, Mishor Adumim), and just one authorized community (Elkana). Between 1977 and 1978, nineteen new settlements were established in the West Bank, all but one of which (a moshav) were community settlements. At the same time, settlement activity in the Gaza region began, as well, and three settlements existed there by 1977. In 1979 only three new settlements were founded in the West Bank, given governmental obligations within the framework of peace negotiations with Egypt and the United States.

All the settlement sites were usually located next to road junctions, major roads, mountain peaks, and water sources, all of them typical locations for territorial capture through settlement dispersion. The original Gush Emunim plan called for the location of Jewish settlements both among and around Arab settlements (Benvenisti, 1984, p. 52); however, severe constraints of land availability did not always permit this plan to materialize. When the change in state political power turned West Bank settlement into a formal Zionist enterprise, this activity received generous support from the World Zionist Organization, in addition to governmental investments. In 1980, permission was given for West Bank land purchases by individuals, another means of land acquisition paralleling and assisting the settlement activity. The involvement of the private sector in land acquisition and settlement development resulted in a series of speculation scandals and financial bankruptcies. Gush Emunim, meanwhile, established its own settlement movement, Amana, which was recognized by the World Zionist Organization; it thus received the same status as veteran Labor cooperative settlement movements. The new settlements also were given the same municipal status enjoyed by Israeli rural and urban settlements. This was accompanied by the creation of a new voluntary organization, Moetzet Yesha (the Council for Judea, Samaria, and Gaza), to oversee the common interests of all settlements in Judea, Samaria and Gaza.

The period of territorial spread ended between 1983 and 1985. In 1983 only three new settlements were established, because of the Lebanon war. In 1984–1985, twenty-nine new settlements were founded, a figure that represented the largest number of settlements established in any two years; sixteen of these came in 1984 alone, the largest amount for any given year (Table 3.5). In the Gaza region, too, the number of settlements more than doubled, from five to eleven, but these were mostly settlements whose construction had started before the 1984 elections. The unity government (Labor + Likud), which was put together following the elections that year, was supposed to build six new settlements, but did so very slowly because of both Labor objection and budgetary constraints. By 1985, the number of existing West Bank settlements, 105, was not only high, but also pointed to the near exhaustion of possible territorial spread, when taking into account the restrictions posed by Arab population density and land availability.

The Community Settlement

In the second phase of settlement in the occupied territories the new settlement form, representing mode of life, was viewed as second in importance, after territory. This ranking constituted an interesting change per se, given that mode of life was usually third in the geographical implementation of Zionism since the 1930s (Table 2.2). The public's view of the new settlements as displaying a specific mode of life has frequently reflected the hot debate over their geographical raison d'être, in which ironic and sarcastic expressions were often employed. Schweitzer (1984, pp. 83–84), for example, made these assertions:

> The kibbutz and the moshav served [therefore] more than one objective: they expanded the geographical territory of the Jewish community, they assisted in its social recuperation (the turning upside down of the occupational pyramid), and they enhanced—or at least they were meant to enhance—the economic self-supporting capacity of the community, and on top of all these they created a pattern for social existence of special character. The Gush Emunim settlements made no such attempts: these are 'community' settlements whose social content is no larger than that of a large city condominium, in a quarter with above average violent crime. It would be better not to say ahead of time that such an attachment is insufficient for long-term coexistence. The probability, however, is smaller than in the 1920s and 1930s settlements, since the residents of the latter were tied to each other with an interwoven string, whereas the community settlements are tied together only with the string of chauvinism.

There were those who tried to argue that a territorial rift of a cultural nature was developing between the West Bank settlements, on the one hand, and Israel proper, on the other. This rift was said to be characterized by an "intensive and speedy intrusion of characteristics of Western culture and the American plenty society on its western side [of the "green separation line" between Israel and the West Bank], against a rejection trend and a separation from these characteristics on its eastern side" (Goldberg and Ben-Zadok, 1983, p. 77). As we shall see, it is doubtful whether such a territorial rift can actually be identified on the basis of these parameters.

The idea of community settlements was not originally developed by Gush Emunim, but rather by the nonpolitical "movement for new urban settlements" in the mid-1970s, and was originally proposed for construction in Israel proper. In practice, however, the community settlement came into being in Judea and Samaria, given the specific regional circumstances and the settlers' characteristics, in light of processes in the Israeli society at large. This settlement form was later adopted in Israel proper, as well. The concept of community settlements broke several consensual golden rules regarding rural settlements in Israel; nonetheless, they have been frequently treated in light of these old rules. One similarity between rural cooperative settlements and community settlements that may still be identified is that both forms of settlement came into being as a result of unique mixtures of political, ideological, and planning processes (Newman, 1984b, p. 140). Generally, the community settlement is based on urban values, even though the settlement usually functions as an organization for the purposes of its establishment, management, and at times the acceptance of new residents.

The community settlement is typified by its size, 50–500 families, though some communities have planned their growth to exceed 1000 families. The community settlement may be homogeneously structured, along one or more political, religious or professional lines, or it may be heterogenous. Several of these settlements in Judea and Samaria were constructed to establish orthodox religious communities. The community settlements are further characterized by individual rather than collective decision making and by informal relationships among members, insofar as employment and domestic life. Communitywide decisions, however, have to be made regarding the nature of the education and social life of the settlement. A third feature is economic freedom. Privately owned industrial or service firms of any kind may be established in or adjacent to the community. Another characteristic is the permission given to the partial or full introduction of status symbols. The very use of single-family dwellings surrounded by private yards constitutes a status symbol, for instance. In West Bank settlements, a more liberal approach has usually prevailed as to the size, design, and number of levels of family houses. In the large communities within Israel proper (Kokhav Yair in the Center; Timrat and Kfar Vradim in the North), on the other hand, stricter construction and design regulations were used to preserve some uniformity. A fifth characteristic of community settlements is the lack of agriculture and the existence of massive commuting by residents to employment centers, especially in metropolitan areas. The settlements are, thus, primarily residential quarters, sometimes functioning just as bedroom communities, so that their economic contribution may be pursued elsewhere in metropolitan areas (see also Newman, 1984b).

The community settlement responded well to some specific challenges presented by the West Bank settlement enterprise in that it did not require agricultural land, which has rarely been available for sale. Hence, it provided for presence, while using small parcels of land. Construction might have been fast if employment for residents were available in metropolitan areas. This point was of special importance in areas in both the West Bank and Galilee that were adjacent to major metropolitan areas. The community villages reflected various interrelated transitions undergone by the Israeli middle class since 1967, in particular in its residential values. These transitions have been expressed in several spheres. In housing, a desire has emerged to reside in larger apartments or in single- or two-family houses. In transportation habits, a sharp rise occurred in private car ownership, coupled with a readiness to commute longer in both time and space. In the employment market, a professional class crystallized in several technical and service fields. These processes, which have evolved in the Western world at large, called for a transition in the attitude to the village as a settlement form, such that it would not be viewed as exclusively agricultural and cooperative. The breakthrough by Gush Emunim in this regard facilitated the third phase of West Bank settlement and also assisted efforts to settle the Galilee.

The community settlement as an exurb constitutes an infrastructure-rich urban habitat, especially relative to its population size. The establishment of single-dwelling community villages both in Israel and in the occupied territories implied a rather generous allocation of land for urban households. In the West Bank, this land usually had no alternative uses. The evolution of this new residential norm poses a question of land availability in Israel proper, however. Another associated problem is the increased traffic volume owing to commuting. Obviously, there exist urban settlement forms requiring lower direct and indirect costs. On the other hand, there is the question of whether a collectivity would be ready to block the desire of individuals to improve their quality of life. This is not just a social problem; it is a geographical one as well, given the low change elasticity of residential land use. It also involves an ideological component, because the very existence of flourishing community villages may influence the socioeconomic structure of cooperative villages. This latter subsector, in fact, has recently started to undergo several changes in this direction. The classic ideological argument was raised by Reichman (1977, p. 18): "Is Zionist implementation that is integrated with the populating of new regions, without the use of agricultural potential, sufficient enough to warrant the significant participation of state capital in the creation of selective residential areas?"

Recognition of the community-settlement idea was granted only gradually. The first community settlement founded as such was Ofra, established in Judea in 1975. (Alon Shvut, in Gush Etzion, which was founded earlier, was originally meant to serve as an intervillage center; it turned later into a community village; Reichman, 1977.) The establishmentarian settlement institutions objected to its foundation because of their opposition to the new settlement form, which deviated from the norms of cooperative and "productive" settlements, and because of their antipathy to mountainous settlements in Judea and Samaria (Newman, 1984a; 1984b). This objection could thus be interpreted as a reflection of the disagreements between Left and Right on the territorial and mode of life objectives of Zionism. By 1977, when the administration changed, five such settlements were already in existence, four of them unauthorized. The Likud's taking over the reigns of government made it possible to recognize this settlement form, again on both the territorial and mode of life levels. The nonsocialist, noncooperative-agricultural character of the Likud permitted the establishment of less-tightened settlements; that is, nonagricultural, noncooperative, and commuting based. From 1977, the construction of community settlements began to be aided by the World Zionist Organization; in 1981, community settlements were recognized as a rural settlement form by the Central Bureau of Statistics and data on them were published retroactively to 1983 (Table 3.6). By 1987, the total number of community settlements had reached ninety-five, constituting 10.1 percent of all Jewish rural settlements in Israel and the territories. In 1987, too, a total of 18,600 persons lived in community villages, or 5.0 percent of the Israeli rural population. The growth in the number and population of community settlements has been largely responsible for the growth in the mid-1980s in the number of villages and in the population of the rural sector as a whole (Tables 2.3–3.1). The gap between the relatively large share of the community villages in the total number of villages and their relatively small share of the rural population is explained by the small size of several settlements in both the West Bank and the Galilee. A slowdown in the addition of new settlements and an expansion of existing ones may close this gap, though not as fast as one would otherwise expect, owing to the uprising (Intifada) in the occupied territories.

Table 3.6.   Community Settlements in Israel, 1983–1987

YEAR	NUMBER	PERCENT ANNUAL GROWTH	PERCENT OF TOTAL VILLAGES	POP. IN THOU.	PERCENT OF JEWISH RURAL POP.
1983	51	—	6.2	7.8	2.4
1984	77	51.0	8.9	10.5	3.0
1985	79	2.6	9.1	12.7	3.6
1986	86	8.9	9.2	14.8	4.1
1987	95	10.5	10.1	18.6	5.0

Source: Central Bureau of Statistics, *Statistical Yearbook for Israel.*

Note: Total villages excludes institutes and intervillage centers.

The demand for exurban communities that evolved in the late 1970s led the Settlement Department of the Jewish Agency to develop several pilot proposals for such communities, which would be organized along the lines of the veteran cooperative rural sector (*The Community Settlement,* 1978; Applebaum and Margolis, 1983). According to these proposals, the only difference between the older settlement forms and the new ones would be the lack of agriculture in the latter. On the other hand, these proposed communities would be cooperative in structure, with employment locally or regionally based in plants owned cooperatively by the residents. The initiative and sponsorship of settlement would remain with national authorities and settlement movements. Employment of outside workers would not be permitted, and capital would be supplied by the national institutions; the settlers, then, would have provided only labor. These proposals have not materialized, given their strict cooperative nature.

Intense populating received only third priority during the second phase of West Bank settlement. (In Gaza, this has been a secondary issue, because of the severe land constraints.) The data, however, reveal fast population growth, though still far short of the grandiose Likud and Gush Emunim pretensions. The annual growth rates ranged from 23 percent to 56 percent, with the exception of 1983 (in the aftermath of the Lebanon war), when it stood at 9.5 percent (Table 3.5). During the first two years of the Likud administration (1977–1978), the Jewish population of the West Bank doubled, and over the whole period until 1987, the percentage population growth was higher than that of the number of settlements. The mean settlement size was low in the beginning and even declined in 1977 because of the accent on fast territorial spread. In 1978, there began an increase in mean settlement size, which was related, at least partially, to the growth of large urban and community settlements (Ma'ale Adumim, Ariel, Qiryat Arba, Emanuel, Efrat, Kedumim, Elkana).

The share of the Jewish population in the general West Bank population increased, too. In 1978, the Jewish population composed for the first time over 1 percent of the population, and this percentage grew at a rate of about 0.5 percent annually until 1983; however, these growth rates were much more modest than the desires of Gush Emunim. The accent throughout the period from 1978–1983 had been on territorial spread. To this end, Gush Emunim tried to organize immigration from North America directly to Judea and Samaria. No data exist on the outcome of this attempt; the absolute numbers are probably small, though one may presume that in terms of both the general immigration from North America and the Jewish population in Judea and Samaria, the percentages are more significant.

Urban Fields in Judea and Samaria: 1984–1989

The data for 1984 on display a new trend in Judea and Samaria (and more modestly also in Gaza): the increase in population (Table 3.5). The large number of settlements established in 1984–1985 reflects construction starts before the 1984 elections, and the formation of the unity government; thereafter, construction of new villages has almost stopped. The Jewish population of the West Bank grew by 53.5 percent in 1984 alone, and by 25.2

percent in 1985. Then in 1986, the growth rate slowed down; further declines were probably registered in 1988–1989 in consequence of the Palestinian uprising, though absolute growth has continued. The average size per settlement rose from 300 to 550 inhabitants over this period. In 1985, the Jewish population in Judea, Samaria, and Gaza as a percentage of the total Jewish population in Israel reached the 1 percent mark, its annual growth rate doubling from 0.1 percent to 0.2 percent. At the same time, the share of the Jewish population in the total West Bank population increased from 3 percent in 1983 to 6.5 percent in 1987. This percentage, however, has to be viewed in light of the data on absolute population growth. Thus, between 1984 and 1985 the Jewish population increased by 8,900, while during the same period the Arab population grew by 21,600 or over twice the Jewish rate.

This population growth has signified a transition in the priority order of objectives for the settlement process. Population has now become the preferred objective, followed by territory and then mode of life. At least three factors may account for this transition: population, territory, and politics, of which the population factor might well be the most important. A politically and religiously more heterogenous population was now attracted to the West Bank, reflecting a change in settlement motivation. Rather than the security motive of phase one and the historical-religious accent of phase two, the emphasis was residential; that is the desire of individuals to enhance their residential life quality. From a right-wing Zionist ideological perspective, this trend assisted in increasing the Jewish population of the West Bank.

West Samaria, which is located just beyond metropolitan Tel Aviv, and the West Bank areas surrounding Jerusalem compose urban fields having a distance of no more than 30 km from the centers of these two primary urban areas of Israel (Figure 3.2). Under circumstances of high motorization levels and convenient roads, these regions became attractive for both young couples looking for apartments and for families looking to purchase single- or two-family houses. The cheap land and the generous governmental mortgages assisted this trend; hence, the growth of several community settlements and towns. Most striking was Ma'ale Adumim, east of Jerusalem, whose 1987 population of 12,000 had grown sharply from 7,600 residents in 1984. Part of this population would have found it financially difficult to realize a "residential dream" within Israel proper.

The second factor, territory, has to do with the fact that when the unity government was established in 1984, the territorial spreading of the settlements had almost run its course. Restrictions on new settlements formed part of the unity agreement between the two major political parties. In addition, a large human resource reservoir with high ideological motivation was not available to settle the mountainous, densely Arab-populated regions of the West Bank. Western Samaria and the environs of Jerusalem were, thus, comfortable settlement areas, especially as urban and community settlements already existed there. Remaining in the mountainous heartland, therefore, was a relatively small but highly motivated Jewish population, living in an area known for its highly motivated Palestinian population.

The third factor involved in the population accent has been political, both domestic and foreign politics. The creation of a powerful Jewish electorate in the occupied territories could assist the Likud in its effort to forestall an Israeli withdrawal (Benvenisti, 1984, p. 55). It could also serve as a bargaining chip in possible peace negotiations.

The settlement process in the West Bank has evolved in reverse geographical order compared with conventional settlement processes. Instead of moving from the center (the coastal plain) to the periphery (the Jordan Valley), the process moved from the periphery (the Jordan Valley) through the mountains (Samaria and Judea) to the center (Western Samaria and the Jerusalem environs). Such a process was possible as long as the settlement motivation was based on territorial acquisition as the highest priority, whether stemming from security considerations (phase one) or from historical-religious motivations (phase two). Once the territorial accent was replaced by population, however, the process became "normal" in the sense that it began moving from the center to the periphery. As part of this "normal" process, there have emerged several urban-field centers, such as Ariel and to a lesser degree Emanuel. These settlements each offer the potential of a stronger functional status, which could create some growth impacts on their surroundings. Such processes take a long time, however, and they require extensive production, residential, and transportation infrastructures.

Summary and Conclusions

Three Zionist objectives were introduced in the beginning of this part: population, territory, and mode of life. These were supposed to be materialized through, respectively, the cooperative villages, the development towns, and the West Bank settlement communities. These objectives will now be reexamined in light of the discussions up to this point; then, several more general aspects and conclusions will be offered.

Populating Ideological Settlements

Ideological settlements are those that were considered as fulfilling the leading Zionist objectives of the time. They would thus include cooperative villages, development towns, and the occupied territories. Figure 3.3 displays the percentage Jewish population in each of these forms of ideological settlements; a summarizing graph represents the total population in ideological settlements. Table 3.7 presents landmarks in the transition of these distributions. Although these settlement forms cannot be considered complementary either ideologically or functionally, and they may reflect in fact ideologies hostile to one another, it is important to examine the general population totals of the ideological settlements, given the centrality of settlements in Zionist ideology in general.

Figure 3.3 shows that the Jewish rural population reached a relative peak in the early 1940s. Its mid-decade decline reflected mobilization for World War II and then the 1948 Israeli War of Independence. The subsequent increase, however, was in lower values. It was not until the early 1980s that a slight increase in the rural population could again be identified, this stemming initially from a slight increase in the kibbutzim and the collective moshavim. Later, this increase was due to the development of community settlements. The development towns, by contrast, grew rapidly in the 1950s and during the first half of the 1960s. Since then, they have increased only slightly. The settlement of the territories occupied in mid-1967 became more intensive only as of the early 1980s. The total population in ideological settlements reached a relative peak in the mid-1960s, then entered a decline that lasted until the mid-1970s, whereupon the percentage began to pick up once again.

These trends may be demonstrated more sharply by the landmark dates shown in Table 3.7. The year 1941 was the peak year for rural population. The wars, the massive immigration, the tendency for an urban life-style, and the limited absorption capacity in agriculture caused this relative peak to appear at an early date (1941), whereas an absolute peak was reached in 1953. Despite later legal and educational efforts, rural settlement seemed fated to decline. The 1950s, the years of massive immigration, were also

Table 3.7.   Jewish Population in Ideological Settlements in the Land of Israel, 1941–1985 (Selected Years)

| | PERCENT OF JEWISH POP. IN | | | | |
YEAR	VILLAGES	DEVELOPMENT TOWNS	OCCUPIED TERRITORIES	TOTAL	LANDMARK
1941	29.0	—	—	29.0	Peak of rural Jewish population
1948	15.4	1.5	—	16.9	Establishment of the state; decline in rural population because of mobilization
1953	23.3	9.7	—	33.0	Peak of Jewish population
1957	22.5	14.4	—	36.9	Peak of population in ideological settlements
1958	17.9	15.1	—	33.0	Change in classification of colonies (moshavot)
1961	15.4	16.5	—	31.9	More population in development towns than in villages
1967	11.4	19.7	—	31.1	Peak population (in %) in development towns
1968	11.4	17.1	—	28.5	Change in classification of development towns
1972	9.6	17.1	0.1	26.7	(1) Lowest total; (2) rural population below 10%; (3) first appearance of population in occupied territories
1975	9.2	17.9	0.2	27.3	(1) Equal values in 1975 and 1976; (2) lowest values for rural population
1976	9.2	17.9	0.2	27.3	
1977	9.2	17.9	0.4	27.5	Continued low rural population
1979	9.5	18.3	0.6	28.4	New growth of rural population
1982	9.8	18.6	0.6	29.0	Annexation of the Golan Heights and its rural population
1984	10.1	18.4	0.9	29.4	Rural population over 10% because of community settlements
1985	10.1	18.4	1.1	29.6	(1) Population in territories over 1%; (2) partial overlap between population in territories and villages; (3) stability in development towns

Sources: See comments to Figure 3.3.

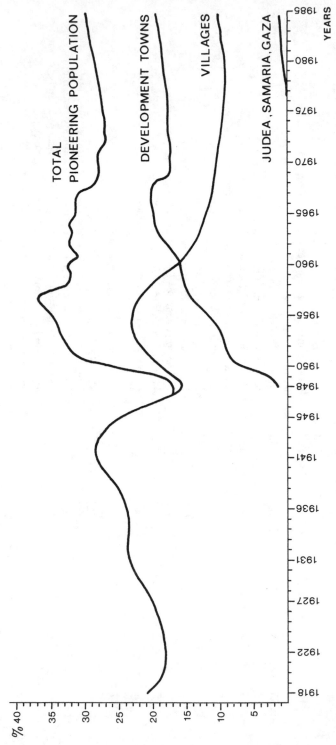

Figure 3.3. Total Jewish Population in Ideological Settlements in the Land of Israel, 1918–1985 (as Percent of Total Jewish Population)

Sources and notes:

Rural population: (1) Source of data until 1948 (Cohen, 1970a, p. 62); 1948–1985 (Central Bureau of Statistics, 1965–1988). (2) "In 1957 a new classification of settlement types was introduced, in order to adjust for standard international definitions. Thus,

Sources and notes (continued):

the current differentiation between urban and rural settlements is based on settlement size and on the percentage of farmers. The term 'Moshavot' does not appear as a settlement type, and they were classified as villages or as urban settlements" (*Statistical Year-book for Israel 9*, 1958, p. 17). (3) Data for 1961 and for 1972 on were adjusted for results of the population census.

Development town population: No standard definition exists for development towns (see a comparative table in Cohen, Peres and Heller, n.d., p. 47). Data up to 1967 are based on Amiran and Shachar (1969) and include development towns according to the governmental definition plus Tirat Carmel, Lod, Or Yehuda, Rosh Ha'ayin, Yehud, and Ramla; they exclude Nahariya and Yoqne'am. Data from 1967 on include the twenty-nine towns classified by the government as development towns. The data for 1967–1971 also include Or Akiva. Data source for 1968–1985 (Central Bureau of Statistics, 1965–1988, and *List of Settlements in Israel;* see also Borukhov and Werczberger, 1980).

West Bank and Gaza population: Data source for 1972–1985 (Central Bureau of Statistics, 1965–1988). As of 1981, the Jew-ish population in the occupied territories is included in the figures for Israeli rural and urban populations. There is, therefore, some overlap between the figures for the rural population and that for the territories for 1981–1987.

the years of the highest percentage of population in ideological settlements, the apex (36.9 percent) coming in 1957. This value was attained despite the flow of most immigrants to the large cities and transit camps. The 1960s presented the decade of the development towns. In 1961, the percentage Jewish population in development towns surpassed the rural proportion. The year 1967 was the peak year for the share of the development towns: close to 20 percent. The early 1970s were years of economic flourishing, and the attraction of the large cities is demonstrated by this period having the lowest value for population in ideological settlements: 26.7 percent, in 1972. That was also the year in which the rural population constituted less than 10 percent of the total Jewish population of Israel. On the other hand, it was also the first year with a significant Jewish population in the occupied territories. The share of the rural population continued to decline, however, and reached a trough point of 9.2 percent during the years 1975–1977. The total population in ideological settlements in the mid-1970s was stable, and for two years remained the same in all subsectors. This phenomenon signifies a special period of self-reflection following the 1973 war. At the end of the 1970s, the rural sector started to grow once again, first in cooperative villages and later in community settlements. At the same time, the share of the development towns stayed stable, while the settlement project in the occupied territories became more significant in size. Thus, in 1985, more than over 1 percent of the Israeli Jewish population lived in the territories and the total share of ideological settlements in the Jewish population reached 29.6 percent. This last value is slightly skewed, as there was some overlap in the statistical data for that year, with community settlements being reported in both the rural sector and in the population residing in Judea, Samaria, and Gaza. The increase of the total population in ideological settlements in the 1980s brings its share back to the values of the late 1960s.

When one looks at the several decades, it is possible to state that the 1940s had a rural accent; the 1950s formed a transitional decade between this accent and the emphasis on development towns that typified the 1960s. The 1970s were again a transitory decade, especially in the first half, "separating" the previous accent on development towns from the evolving focus on the occupied territories.

It seems that, over the years, a population in ideological settlements of around one-third of the total population is a high rate, even if this figure is nowhere near the forecasts, plans, and visions of many kinds. In times of rapid urban metropolitan growth and a loosening of Zionist ideological tension, this level could even be considered a success. In terms of population direction to preferred settlement forms or regions, a different question concerns the trends that may possibly emerge under conditions of mass immigration, given the current concentration of two thirds of the population in metropolitan areas. This issue will be referred to in the concluding chapter of the book.

Population Spread over the National Territory

Cooperative villages created the settlement N, which started to shape itself in the First Aliya and was strengthened after 1936 (Figure 2.1). The establishment of Israel brought about the addition of an arm for this N; namely, from the coastal plain to Jerusalem, the so-called Jerusalem corridor. To a lesser extent, another arm started to develop along the Arava Valley, stretching from the Dead Sea down to Eilat. The West Bank and Galilee settlements in the 1980s have changed this "classical" settlement distribution, but the arms of the N still contain the significantly more densely populated areas. By 1987, Israel could count some 880 Jewish rural settlements (excluding agricultural and educational institutes in the rural sector) (Tables 2.3 and 3.6), which represented a one-third growth over the 1967 figure and more than double the number in 1947 (or a growth of 238.5 percent). The share of kibbutzim declined since 1967 (to 28.6 percent), along with a slight decrease in moshavim (to 43.7 percent). On the other hand, the share of collective moshavim increased to 5.0 percent, though they still constituted the smallest settlement form. The community settlements constituted some 10.1 percent of all rural settlements in 1987.

The spread of development towns took place in two blocks, in the North and in the South, whereas towns in the Center were removed from the list of this settlement form. The towns, too, like the rural settlements, were spread out down to the far South, though just one small town (Mitzpe Ramon) exists in the center of the Negev Desert.

The rural sector together with the development towns were meant to serve as geographical tools for the dispersal of the Jewish population in Israel from the center to the peripheries. This policy of population dispersal has been expressed in several plans over the years; the later the plan, however, the less ambitious it has been (Silberberg, 1973, p. 21). The year 1981 was the target date for the "four million plan," which served as an intermediate step for the Five Million plan (1972). Indeed by 1981, the actual total popula-

Table 3.8. Distribution of the Jewish Population in the Land of Israel: The Four Million Plan and the 1981 Reality

DISTRICT	POP. IN 1970		PLANNED POP. FOR 1981		POP. IN 1981		PERCENT DEVI- ATION
	THOU.	% OF TOTAL JEWISH POP.	THOU.	% OF TOTAL JEWISH POP.	THOU.	% OF TOTAL JEWISH POP.	
Jerusalem	245.1	9.5	388.2	11.4	336.0	10.1	-13.4
North	248.8	9.7	341.5	10.1	322.0	9.7	-5.7
Haifa	391.8	15.3	490.5	14.5	464.7	14.0	-5.2
Central	496.2	19.4	634.4	18.8	743.5	22.4	17.1
Tel Aviv	874.1	34.1	1050.0	31.0	993.5	29.9	-5.4
South	304.4	11.9	443.8	13.1	433.4	13.0	-2.3
Occupied Territories	0.5	0.06	29.6	0.8	27.2	0.8	-8.1
Total	561.4	100.0	3378.0	100.0	320.3	100.0	-1.7

Sources: Planned population: *A Plan for the Geographical Distribution of a Five Million Population in Israel,* 1972. 1981 population: Central Bureau of Statistics, *Statistical Yearbook for Israel,* 1982.

Notes: Percent deviation = [1981 planned pop. in thou. - 1981 actual pop. in thou./1981 planned pop. in thou.] x 100.

See also Kellerman, 1985a.

tion was just 22,000 short of the target, though the Jewish population was 1.7 percent lower than expected. A comparison between the base year of the plan, 1971, and the target year, 1981, in regard to expectations and realities shows, however, that the plan proved only a modest success (Table 3.8; see also Kellerman, 1985a). The population concentrations in the districts of Haifa and Tel Aviv declined relatively, but the Central district, exurban Tel-Aviv, which was supposed to decline as well, increased and very much so. The target regions, therefore, did not gain much. The district of Jerusalem grew less than expected. The Northern peripheral region remained stable rather than displaying an expected growth trend. The Southern peripheral district was the only region that reached the planned population. The goals were modest, but their success has to be assessed against the trend of the attraction of the coastal plain. Here, the Jewish population amounted to 66.3 percent of the total Jewish population in 1981 (the expected share was 64.3 percent), down slightly from 68.8 percent in 1970.

From Zionist Socialism to Social Zionism

The Israeli Left has been characterized since its inception by an accent on mode of life. The idea of cooperative villages was born primarily to establish a productive and cooperative-collective mode of life among Jews in the Land of Israel. The aim of the Labor movement was to turn this ideal into a national idea through consensus. Despite the use of political power and legislation and despite the territorial successes of the rural sector, however, this idea has become a general one only in a limited sense. To some degree, this failure has had to do with the objection of rightist parties and groups; in the main, it stemmed from the high urbanization levels of the Jewish population. To be sure, a large segment of the urban population was supportive of socialism; but it was not ready to accept the ideology as a total mode of life at the level prevailing in the cooperative rural sector.

The general decrease in ideological spirit in Israeli society has been expressed specifically in a lesser emphasis on cooperativeness, equality, and agriculture. This tendency has had a direct, negative impact on the readiness to move to ideological settlements. There are some who ascribe it to more serious defects:

> After 103 years of Zionist settlement in the Land of Israel, after
> huge efforts in this area we reached in the mid-1980s a status quo on

Palestine with our neighbors. We closed a bloody historical cycle, and have found ourselves again at the beginning of the road. This time, however, we are more tired. We lost in this period a precious potential for Jewish immigration, which was annihilated in Europe; we have become more sated and fatter and also more established than in the past, and thus less efficient, less original, and less pioneering. We have "tired out" Western world Jewry: it does not immigrate to Israel, and even its contributions are not enthusiastically given as in the past. (Sofer, 1986, p. 19)

One may identify an exchange or a cycle-closing between Left and Right in contemporary Israeli society. Whereas the Right has explored the idea of geographical implementation through settlement activity, especially for territorial and population objectives, the Left has been integrating into large city life and into contemporary Western culture. This exchange has manifested itself in cultural creation, consumption patterns, and an emphasis on self-fulfillment. The Right has given priority to attempts to implement territorial and population objectives in the occupied territories, integrated into a hedonist mode of life. At the same time the Left has attempted to cope once again with the mode of life issue, but this time in a direction different from socialism: what may be termed *social Zionism*. The emphasis moved to civil rights and to the civic character of the state. From the perspective of "classical" Zionist objectives, the idea has been to nurture Israeli society in line with a specific portion of the Declaration of Independence: "It [Israeli society] will be based on the elements of liberty, justice and peace, in light of the vision of the prophets of Israel; it will maintain complete social and political equality for all its citizens without regard to religion, race, or gender; it will assure freedom of religion, conscience, language, education, and culture." Moral and social values have been listed in the policy outlines of all Israeli governments, but not as first or even as second or third priorities. The exception to this lack of rank was the first government, which put "the citizens' rights" at the top. In 1956 and 1960 the need for "purity of conduct" was mentioned; whereas in 1967 and 1969, the reference was to "social justice values" and the need for basic laws (including one for "citizens' rights"). In 1975, the need for a constitution was cited; and since 1977, all governments have declared the importance of "citizens' rights" and "equal rights," though not as primary objectives.

The fostering of these elements and giving them highest priority constitute a general trend in Western society. Thus similar trends in Israel could attest to the maturing of Israeli society. On the other hand, the emergence of this trend in the Israeli context may also be interpreted as a reaction to the strong territorial accent of the Right and its implications for human and civil rights in general and for Arab citizens and residents in particular. An emphasis on a civic mode of life implies imparting a new meaning to the Zionist mode of life objective. Moreover, it means the creation of both a new priority for Zionist objectives as well as a different significance for the population and territorial objectives. The new priority order is mode of life, population, and territory. As for population, there is a desire to preserve the State of Israel as a country with a Jewish majority, a desire based until recently foremost on the existing population, not on Jewish migration into the country or on a higher and perhaps unwanted natural growth. To assure such a majority, and at the same time to permit full civil rights for both Jews and Arabs, a need was perceived for a limited, or even an extensive, territorial compromise.

> If Israel wants to exist for generations, it has to look for territorial compromises, on the one hand, and to put new emphases on settlement. We have to understand that the Arabs who live here are human beings and citizens (in one variation of another).... The strategy [proposed here] emphasizes coexistence at an inevitable minimal level, on the already created map, while extending mutual respect and equal rights, and the moving of the settlement center of gravity to regions where the separation of Jews from Arabs will be emphasized. In 1985, we attained the *status quo* and maybe the beginning of Jewish settlement withdrawal, and the Jews have to hurry up and to draw conclusions from this. (Sofer, 1986, pp. 19–22)

This "social Zionism" is, geographically, a Zionism of the large, metropolitan city. The modern metropolis is the place that, by its very nature as a large, heterogenous city, has to guarantee individual freedom, pluralism, public tolerance, and individual anonymity. The modern metropolis is also the incubation and evolution source for social innovation. All this stands in contrast to socialist Zionism, which wished to see the cooperative village as the ideological source and focus of society. The large city and its plentiful social-cultural activities can potentially turn into a centripetal factor, preventing settlement diffusion to the periphery. On the other hand, the tremendous metropolitan population growth, coupled with the transition in residential values toward a preference for single- and two-family dwellings, may bring about a more extensive territorial spread of metropolitan areas and of their fields of influence.

Paradoxically, the available regions for such an expansion of metropolitan Tel Aviv and Jerusalem are Judea and Samaria. The Negev is too remote from these two cities. Its capital, Beersheba, is still small in population (a quarter of that of Jerusalem; less than 7 percent of metropolitan Tel Aviv) although it has already expanded into a suburbanlike area, in the form of community settlements (Omer, Meitar, Lehavim). Metropolitan Haifa has several restraints on any possible massive exurbanization in the Galilee, and these will be highlighted in Part 3. The natural expansion areas for Tel Aviv are the coastal plain, lying north and south of the city, and Western Samaria. For Jerusalem it is almost exclusively Judea. The coastal plain has been constrained so far as urban settlement, given both the desire to preserve agricultural land and the plans for population distribution. Thus, the West Bank serves as the major alternative for the development of modern urban fields around two of the three largest cities in Israel. A continued accent on urban consumption values in both the Left and the Right may produce a demand for low-density housing. The political conditions in the West Bank, then, have urban-settlement as well as national-territorial implications. If Israeli settlement activity will be stopped completely, say, as part of a political agreement with the Palestinians, a vast demand will be created for coastal plain lands and for lands in the small hilly area bordering the West Bank (Modi'in). It is unlikely that any government would be able to obviate low density housing, so that current restrictions on coastal plain lands and natural reserves west of Jerusalem will have to be lifted.

The Palestinian uprising (Intifada) that started in December 1987 slowed down Israeli exurban development. Continued political stalemate and long-term, low-key disturbances may renew or even reinforce Israeli exurban developments. This could possibly take one of two possible scenarios. The first is a development of exurbs differentiated by political geographical sectors. Thus, the areas north and south of Tel Aviv along the coastal plain, as well as the areas west of Jerusalem, would house people leaning to the Left, while areas east of Tel Aviv, in Western Samaria, and areas around Jerusalem, other than to its west, will be preferred by people supporting the Right. A second alternative might emerge if the urban fields in the West Bank became more extensive. This would make them attractive to citizens of all political camps; indeed, early signs of this development can be already observed in the larger urban centers of the West Bank.

"Social Zionism" and "territorial Zionism" confront each other in contemporary Israeli society. The civil liberties attempted by the Left may bring about a major change in its own economic and organizational institutions, which are not based on such liberties. Early signs of such a process could be identified in the late 1980s, and their significance will be addressed again in the concluding chapter. Such liberties, though, may put at risk the Jewish-Zionist basis of the State of Israel as such. On the other hand, the accentuated territorialism practiced by the Right has already resulted in disobedience to state authorities in several phases of the West Bank settlement process. Furthermore, it tends to ignore several processes underway in the Arab sector of Israeli society (Sofer, 1986).

General Trends

Each of the three forms of geographical implementation emphasized, in its early phases, another Zionist objective, manifesting particular political and social needs in each period. Thus, the cooperative villages started with an emphasis on mode of life; the development towns originally were meant to solve a population problem; and West Bank settlements began with a territorial objective as first priority. These various forms and emphases have been associated with different political camps. The cooperative sector has been identified with the Left, West Bank settlements mostly with the Right. The development towns, which historically developed between these two, were established by the Left when it was in a position of political power; but the Right has tried hard to associate these settlements politically with its camp, given their accumulation of social, political, and economic hardships over the years of Leftist administration.

The transition from one preferred objective to another within each form of geographical implementation has grown faster with time. The change from a mode of life to a territorial accent in cooperative villages occurred after thirty years of settlement. The move from a population to a territorial accent in development towns took place ten to fifteen years after their initial establishment; the West Bank settlement project has already undergone two priority changes within its twenty years of existence. This speeding up of priority changes may be related to the faster pace of social and political life in Israeli society.

It is interesting to note that the continuous elevation in residential standards following the 1967 war has managed to reduce gaps in the residential landscape among the three forms of ideologi-

cal settlements. Low-density housing has now become the preferred form of residential housing in all areas. Despite this partial
physical similarity, the three types of ideological settlement represent populations of different social milieu and, obviously, of different past and present priority orders of Zionist objectives. The cooperative settlements are the most mature communities. Several
development towns still require much effort to assure their continued development whereas others have but recently reached a take-
off stage. The West Bank project is still in a very early settlement
process. A reexamination of these aspects and their implications
for future developments, the subject of the last chapter, will be
enabled after some light is first shed on the geographical, cultural,
and economic contexts of cores, frontiers, and peripheries in Israel;
those topics will be taken up in the next two parts.

The interrelationship of changing priorities in Zionist objectives and their geographical implementation through ideological
settlements presents one side of each of the three dialetics
described in Chapter 1. This part focused mainly on structures, in
the form of Zionist ideologies and institutions. As shown throughout the last two chapters, human agency has contributed to a different spatial shaping of the country from that prescribed by these
ideologies. The evolution of contemporary urban values received
brief treatment earlier in this section; it remains for the next parts
to outline the evolution of major urban centers in Israel and their
complex sociocultural characteristics.

The relationship between society and space served as a major
axis of this part. The discussions throughout emphasized one side
of the social component; namely, the ideological. All three Zionist
objectives, the territorial one included, have been social objectives.
All, however, have a strong geographical significance in that they
can be implemented through geographical action—by settlement
activity. This part emphasized the settlement record; Part 3 will
highlight some of the regional locations of the first two settlement
ideals and their impact on the shaping of social values. The tension
between ideals, wishes, and visions versus realities has constituted
a major thread of this part, though the emphasis here was more on
ideas. The next parts will place more emphasis on deeds. Nevertheless, the following chapters, too, will show that ideology and
geographical practice are interrerlated.

Part 2

Jerusalem and Tel Aviv:
  Conflict Through Complementarity

Chapter 4

Incubation and Formation of a Capital City and a Core Area

Jerusalem is the city of spirit and Jaffa is also the city of spirit. The spirit of the living God, the holy spirit, hangs over the ancient and sacred city, and the spirit of trade, the spirit of the love for unjust rewards hangs over the city of Jaffa. The residents of Jerusalem fly, hurry, run to every direction and corner, to the Western Wall they will go, to the Tomb of Rachel they will turn, on the Mount of Olives they will pray, on the grave of one who was Godfearing tears will flow, they will beg, pray for themselves, for their children, for their relatives, for their redeemers abroad, those who strengthen and support them, who will pay with their monies for their prayers. And the residents of Jaffa will hurry, leave, go out, fly, go to the beach, run to the place where the camels will come, they will turn to the gardens, where they will collect the land's crops, pick the garden's fruits, make use of the new life-styles, will become the middle-men and will not rest day and night. Who of them is more successful? Who wins, the slave or the lady? (Eliezer Ben-Yehuda, "Jaffa," *Hazvi* 1, no. 37 (1885): 158)

Introduction

The previous part was devoted to an analysis of two basic questions, one concerning the interrelationship of society and space; and the other, ideology and reality. These questions were What (should be built)? and Why (should these be built)? The "what" were the settlement ideals, the "why" the Zionist objectives. The two were shown to be interrelated as the answers changed over time. This part, as well as the next, will also be be devoted to two complementary basic questions: Where (did Zionist activity take place)? and How (were the regions shaped socially and economically)? As such, this part will concentrate on the double core of Israel, consisting of Jerusalem and metropolitan Tel Aviv; the next part will deal with the major frontiers and peripheries.

A discussion of the "where" question, or the locational aspect, implies a presentation of both the areas where decisions have been made, along with the areas where development and growth were supposed to take place, and where the latter eventually occurred. Having portrayed the preferred *sectors*, the discussion now turns to the supposedly disqualified areas for growth and development; namely, the large cities. Since these cities eventually turned into the major population and decision-making centers, the "how" question, in terms of how it occurred and how these areas function, is of no less importance than the "where." The principal locations of the preferred sectors is the subject of Part 3.

Comparing Jerusalem and Tel Aviv–Jaffa amounts to a multi-faceted comparison between the old and the new. It involves histori-cal, functional, and cultural, as well as economic aspects. As we will see, even the Zionist ideological attitude toward these two cities has been complex; thus, the treatment of the role and significance of Tel Aviv and Jerusalem in modern Israeli society cannot focus on just a single set of concepts. On the other hand, these two cities may be viewed together as a double core to be assessed against the rest of the country, which serves as frontier and periphery.

The guiding assumption here is the existence of cumulative activities of human agency in ways that were contrary to Zionist ideological expectations. Although the urban realities of the evolu-tion of Jewish society in Palestine-Israel provide the focus, ideolo-gies and structures will be seen to be evident here, too, and in sev-eral respects. First, Tel Aviv and, before its establishment, Jaffa have played important roles in shaping the Labor movement in both the past and present. Second, Jerusalem has constituted a crucial element in the cultural superstructure of the Jewish people, and this element has been molded into functional, geographical, and cultural structures. Third, Jerusalem and Tel Aviv provide a double core for Israel; but they also present intercity functional and cultural contradictions and conflicts. Fourth, the Israeli net-work of large cities also consists of a third large city, Haifa. Although Haifa served as an integral part of the core area of Palestine during the first half of the twentieth century, it has grad-ually turned into a regional capital with a decreasing number of exclusive national functions. The city, which once possessed a unique social-political character, does not share the cultural and economic dialog and conflict represented by Tel Aviv and Jerusalem throughout most of the twentieth century (the changing role and status of Haifa will be discussed in the next part).

Jerusalem and Tel Aviv each demonstrate changing relations between society and space. Jerusalem has enjoyed a long tradition as a holy city and a capital, serving as the center for the pre-Zionist Jewish population of Palestine. Although the new, twentieth centu-ry Jewish community in the town displayed special qualities, its ongoing activity has contributed to the character of the contemporary city as a spiritual-cultural center. In Jaffa, the forerunner of Tel Aviv–Jaffa, the nineteenth century economic prosperity made its presence before the First Aliya, thus influencing the new settlers' occupations and the general atmosphere in the town. On the other hand, the new Jewish community contributed to an atmosphere of openness and to an economic accent on urban life, both of which turned stronger after Tel Aviv was established and began flourishing. Similar relationships developed between the new Jewish rural sector that grew along the coastal plain and in the valleys, on the one hand, and Tel Aviv, on the other. This kind of core-hinterland relationship was missing in mountainous Jerusalem, which was not surrounded by an extended Jewish rural settlement.

What follows does not amount to an urban geography of Jerusalem and Tel Aviv, separately or jointly—therefore, such aspects as the development of the two cities, various structures of their populations and transitions in these structures will not be discussed. Rather, major attention is given to the status of the two cities and to relations between them. The geographical-historical roots of the evolution of these two cities into the central cities of Israel, our topic, will point to the continuous historical and geographical uniqueness of the two cities and to their emerging inter-relationship. This history will provide the background for a more elaborated examination of three central aspects. First, the status of the two cities as core and capital areas will be discussed from a political perspective; a comparison will be made with similar conditions around the world. Second, a cultural examination will concentrate on past and present cultural frictions between the two cities. Third, the economic dimension will focus on processes of functional specialization and complementarity. In each of these political, cultural and economic discussions, special attention will be given to the geographical perspective, as well as to relevant general and theoretical concepts that have been proposed elsewhere. All these aspects are interrelated. In other words, the political importance of each city is related, to some degree, to its cultural characteristics, and vice versa, and this is also true of their urban economic specializations.

The observations to be presented on the status of Jerusalem and Tel Aviv and on their interrelationship derive from the perspective of the Jewish community. Arab and Christian impacts will be referred to occasionally, but the view from a Palestinian perspective deserves a separate in-depth treatment. Here we will suffice in this regard with brief comments on a few landmarks. Up to the 1948 war, both cities served as economic and cultural centers for the Palestinian Arabs, perhaps even through some competition between them (though the status of such regional centers as Haifa, Nablus, and Hebron was considerably higher). Following the war, two traumatic changes occurred. First, the two cities were completely separated from each other (a situation lasting until the 1967 war). East Jerusalem was under Jordanian control, and Jaffa, the Arab part of Tel Aviv–Jaffa, was in Israel. Second, the status of both cities declined. Most of the Arab population of Jaffa left the city in 1948, and the city lost its independent political status. East Jerusalem, together with the West Bank, was annexed to Jordan, and Jerusalem lost its status as a capital. National Jordanian development efforts were directed to Amman. Following the 1967 war, a paradox emerged. East Jerusalem was reunited with West Jerusalem, but was separated from the West Bank in terms of political status. Nevertheless, the separation from Jordan, the relative political freedom, and the rise of the Palestinian national movement strengthened the status of East Jerusalem as a national center for the Palestinians. For Jaffa, however, the circumstances did not change in 1967, and it fell to Nazareth to serve as the center for Israeli Arabs. Between 1967 and 1988, Jaffa did hold one advantage over Jerusalem: its own Muslim religious court, which also served the Arab population of Jerusalem. In 1988, though, a separate court was established in Jerusalem.

Comparisons between Jerusalem and Tel Aviv are little evident in Israeli scientific literature. A computerized catalog of Hebrew-language articles in 1989 yielded 910 items dealing with Jerusalem and 336 items on Tel Aviv. Crossing the two lists resulted in only seven items! Of these, only four were found relevant; and of the four, only one was published in a geographical outlet (Amiran and Shachar, 1959, who compared Israel's three large cities). The others presented a hot debate on the cultural character of the two cities (Meiron, 1985; Ophir, 1985; Hasson, 1987). One other article briefly discussed architectural aspects (Kiryati, 1986). Since that survey, a collection of articles on Jerusalem and Zionism was published that contains several essays on the relations between Jerusalem and Tel Aviv (Lavsky, 1989).

The same survey produced 155 items on Jaffa, but only 13 of these dealt with both Jaffa and Jerusalem, and of these only 2 were directly relevant to this discussion. One treats the conflict over the hegemony over the Jewish community during the First and Second Aliyas (Kaniel, 1981), whereas the second makes a comparison of the two cities at the end of the Ottoman era (Kark, 1977).

Jerusalem and Tel Aviv together present a complex urban-geographical situation in terms of their status, their interrelationship, and their regional context. Jerusalem is the capital and metropolitan Tel Aviv the primate city. The 65 kilometers separating the two cities constitute the most convenient interurban travel distance in Israel. The Tel Aviv–Jerusalem expressway is connected at one end to the Tel Aviv city expressway (Netivey-Ayalon), and at the other end to several entrance roads to Jerusalem. Thus, the driving time between the two cities is less than one hour. This fast, convenient connection has contributed to specialization and complementarity processes between the two cities. It is therefore possible to view the two cities as the economic, social, administrative, and cultural focus of Israel; as a result, the rest of the country consists of peripheries at various levels.

Tel Aviv is the major city on the coastal plain, which is densely and continuously settled by Jews; 92.3 percent of its population was Jewish in 1986 (Central Bureau of Statistics, 1987). Jerusalem, however, is the major city in a mountainous area (including the West Bank), where a majority of the population (63 percent) was Arab in 1986 (Central Bureau of Statistics, 1987). On the other hand, whereas the Arab population constituted a very high percentage of the West Bank population (94.2 percent), it was only a minority in Jerusalem (28.3 percent). The difference between Tel Aviv and Jerusalem is also striking insofar as their population size and cultural milieu. Metropolitan Tel Aviv, with a population of close to 2 million in 1990, is a medium-sized metropolis in Western standards. The city of Jerusalem, with a population of over half a million in 1990, has no metropolitan definition, as most of its suburbs are located in military-controlled Judea and Samaria. The addition to the city population of those urban entities that are clearly suburban to Jerusalem (such as Arab Ramallah and Bethlehem and Jewish Ma'ale Adumim, Givat Zeev, and Efrat) would increase the population to 650,000–900,000, depending on the geographical definition used (Kimhi, 1988).

Tel Aviv may be portrayed as a mature, Western metropolis in its accent on contemporary culture, pluralism, business, and entertainment. Jerusalem, on the other hand, restricts itself to public bureaucracy, and concentrates on a spiritual-cultural life; it is a focus for study, research, and confrontation among different Jewish groups, and between Jews and Arabs. The following sections will elaborate these aspects of the two cities and will try to reveal their roots and implications.

Geographical-Historical Roots

In exploring the *foundations* of the urban functions of Jerusalem and Tel Aviv–Jaffa, as well as of the shaping of the relations between them in the twentieth century, a historical emphasis will be restricted to ancient Jerusalem and to nineteenth century Jaffa.

Jerusalem

Jerusalem is probably the oldest among current capital cities around the world, having become a capital city for the first time about 3000 years ago. Jerusalem was unique among capital cities even then. Whereas most oriental nations tended to establish their capital cities in plains or valleys or next to rivers and seas, the Israelites established their capital on a mountain (M. Harel, 1987).

The process by which Jerusalem was chosen to serve as the capital and the Temple site for the ancient Israelite kingdom, which was unified by King David, is somehow obscure. David's first capital, Hebron, which served him for 7.5 years, enjoyed at least two advantages: it was sanctified by the Patriarchs' graves, and it was already considered a very ancient city ("Hebron was built seven years before Zoan in Egypt." Numbers 13:22). Neither the Bible nor the Talmud provide direct details on the reasons for the transfer of the capital from Hebron to Jerusalem or on why David wanted to build the Temple in the latter city. Nevertheless, the fulfillment of the divine command "to the sanctuary which the Lord your God chooses out of all your tribes as the seat of His name, to His habitation you must resort, there you must go" (Deuteronomy 12:5), involved interconnected religious and political choices. These choices, which turned Jerusalem into a holy city and the capital for the Israelites, have since marked the function and status of this city.

The Jewish tradition ascribes sacredness to the Temple Mount (Mt. Moriah) all the way back to Adam (see Maimonides, "Laws of the Temple" 2:1–2). In the Bible, Jerusalem probably appears in a sacred context in the early biblical story of the war between the four and the five kings, in which Abraham was involved (one of the four was a "Melchizedek, king of Salem... priest of God Most High"—Genesis 14:18). "The land of Moriah" is mentioned as the place of the binding of Isaac for sacrifice (Genesis 22:2). In the very first settlement process—namely, by the twelve tribes following their Exodus from Egypt—two places with names referring to Jerusalem are mentioned ("there were two Jerusalems"—Talmud, *Arachin* 32b). One was in Judea's lot (Joshua 16: 63), and this was the Upper City of the current Old Jerusalem. The Judeans conquered the city and burned it during the settlement process (Judges 1:8). This part of Jerusalem later served as the major residential quarter of the city. The second Jerusalem is mentioned with regard to the portion of Benjamin and is called *the Jebusite spur*. This, in present-day terminology, was the Lower City and the Offel (citatel) (Joshua 18:16), areas that were to serve as the Temple and palace sites, respectively. The Benjaminites did not conquer their Jerusalem during the settlement process (Judges 1:21).

The events that eventually brought about the transformation of Jerusalem into the capital of Israel and into the Temple site started with the conquering of the Zion citatel (the Offel) during the time of King David, its renaming as "the City of David," and the construction of the king's house there (II Samuel 5:9-11). The second phase involved the elevation of the Ark up the Judean mountains to Jerusalem (II Samuel 6). The third phase was David's wish to build the Temple, rejected by the Prophet Nathan in the name of the Lord (II Samuel 7). The fourth phase, toward the end of David's life, was the purchase of the threshing-floor of Araunah the Jebusite in the Lower City and the establishment of an altar there, following the Prophet Gad's divine order (II Samuel 24). This last event determined the location of King Solomon's Temple although he still offered sacrifices in the "great high place" in Gibeon in the early days of his kingship (I Kings 3:4).

This biblical report of events does not contain a direct explanation for David's transfer of the capital from Hebron to Jerusalem. It is possible to trace the motives only indirectly, and here one finds an integration of the religious and political choices. The religious choice was probably related to the sacredness attached to the place much earlier and enhanced by the Prophets Nathan and Gad. The political choice points to Jerusalem as a location with a federal character. First, Jerusalem is located on the northern edge of the Judean lot, in proximity to the tribes of Joseph and with a joint boundary with Benjamin, as described in Joshua and Judges. Hebron, in contrast, lies in the heart of Judea. Second, it might well be that Jerusalem itself was not allotted to any tribe, and thus was meant as a federal capital, similarly to modern federal capitals (like Washington, D.C., United States; Canberra, ACT,

Australia). The Talmud mentions this idea numerous times ("Jerusalem was not allotted to the tribes"—*Yomma* 12b; *Meggila* 26a; *Zevahim* 53b; 118b; *Sotta* 45b). According to another talmudic tradition, the city and the Temple area were divided among Judea, Benjamin, and Joseph, with preference given to Benjamin in the sacred areas. The federal advantages of Jerusalem have been discussed by several historians (see, e.g., Tadmor, 1969; Ben-Shalush, 1956).

Several topographic merits of Jerusalem were noted by geographers, who also mentioned its superiority over Hebron in this regard (e.g., M. Harel, 1969, pp. 22–24): the natural fortification of the citadel (Offel) hill; its proximity to the national Patriarchs Road, which crossed the country from north to south; its similar adjacency to the east-west road leading from Jaffa to Amman; its nearness to water sources (the Gihon spring); and its closeness to the Judean Desert, which could serve as a shelter area. The two latter qualities pertained, however, to Hebron as well. Striking was the establishment of the Temple in an area that was topographically inferior to its surroundings (only "in the end of the days the mountain of the Lord's house will be established on top of the mountains"—Isaiah 2:2, Micah 4:1). The area suffered from several disadvantages. There was a need for a landfill (the Millo) north of the Offel, and there was a need to bridge the Lower and Upper Cities. Thus, it might well be that the city was chosen *also* from topographical considerations, though it seems that the religious and political considerations were more important (see Ben-Arieh, 1977, p. 440). The foregoing qualities and events have combined to determine the importance of Jerusalem as both a holy and a central city in the Land of Israel throughout almost every historical period. This importance was later transferred to Christian and Muslim nations as well. Retrospectively, the element of sacredness seems to be the crucial one, as the federal consideration lost its significance following the destruction of the First Temple.

Jerusalem has had a long and complex history. Suffice it to note that the city, probably, has been the largest or at least among the largest cities in Palestine from the time of King David until the 1920s, even though it underwent a process of decline with the destruction of the Second Temple (in 70 A.C.E.). This deterioration culminated in the Arab era (in the seventh century), when the Arab-built city of Ramla served as the capital of the country. Jerusalem once again became the capital under the Crusaders (eleventh–twelveth centuries). The status of the city thereafter declined, but in the modern era it has slowly and gradually regained its traditional position. Ben-Arieh (1977) noted that the Ottomans (who ruled the country from the sixteenth century until World War I) viewed the city as important only from a Muslim religious perspective to be able to secure the pilgrimage to both Jerusalem and Mecca.

In the early nineteenth century, the population of Jerusalem reached 8,000–10,000 inhabitants, which was similar in number to Gaza, Acre, and Nablus, and it served as a district city. Several reforms throughout the nineteenth century provided more equality for Christians and Jews, though the Ottoman administration showed poor self-initiative in city development. These reforms, as well as improvements in transportation, assisted the beginning of modernization in Jerusalem, though "the internal and principal motive" for growth was the religious one; namely, the Jewish and Christian yearning for the holy city (Ben-Arieh, 1977, p. 443). In the middle of the nineteenth century, Jerusalem received informal national and international status (Ben-Arieh, 1981), and in 1924 the British declared it the capital city (Bigger, 1976). Bigger (1983) attributed this step to the deep link felt by the British to the Bible and the Crusaders. In his opinion, it was clear to the British that it would have been easier to rule the country from Jaffa, Ramla, or Haifa; despite this, they chose Jerusalem.

Between the years 70 (the destruction of the Second Temple) and 1924 (Britain's declaration of Jerusalem as capital), the city's two functions originally determined by King David, its being a holy city and the political capital, were maintained separately. Though Jerusalem continued to serve throughout this long period as the holy city for the Jews, and gradually also for Christians and Muslims, it did not function as the capital of Palestine (except for the Crusaders). This obviously reflected the country's lack of sovereignty, but this situation did not necessarily reduce the population seniority of Jerusalem among the cities of Palestine.

As for the Jewish community, it is reasonable to assume that in several periods following the destruction of the Second Temple, there were larger Jewish communities in various cities in Judea, in the Galilee, and along the coastal plain. For example, during the sixteenth and seventeenth centuries the Jewish community in Safed was larger than that in Jerusalem (Rosen, 1984). As of the mid-1800s and until the 1920s, however, Jerusalem contained the largest Jewish community in the Land of Israel (see, e.g., Ben-Arieh, 1987).

Jaffa and Tel Aviv

The seniority of Jerusalem in Palestine in general and in the mountainous area in particular was determined in ancient times and has been preserved, one way or another, throughout history. On the other hand, the seniority of Jaffa in Palestine in general and on the coastal plain in particular has been a new phenomenon, only about 100 years old. This is so despite the fact that Jaffa is no less ancient and may be even older than Jerusalem. Generally speaking, urban flourishing along the coastal plain of Palestine was related in the past to a Western commercial orientation (in turn, by the Phoenicians, the Philistines, the Greeks, the Romans, and the Byzantines) or to joint Western commercial and religious orientations in several periods of Christian ascendancy (the Crusaders, the New Era). In times of Muslim rule, urbanization tended to take place in the interior of the country (Kark, 1990).

In times past, other coastal cities enjoyed seniority. During the First Temple era, three cultures dominated the coastal plain: Phoenician-Canaanite domination in the North (Tyre and Sidon and their environs); "the sea nations" in the Center (of which Jaffa was one); and the Philistines in the South ("the five Philistine princes") (see e.g., Kohavi, 1984). During the Second Temple era, Jaffa enjoyed a special status as the only Hasmonean harbor; but in the succeeding Roman era, Caesarea took over as the major coastal focus. By the eighteenth century, the coastal center of gravity had moved to the North, where Acre was the leading city; this shift had to do with France's Near East coastal trade, which was concentrated on the coasts of Lebanon and northern Palestine. The economic stagnation that developed following the end of Egyptian rule in 1840 negatively influenced the status of Acre, nearby Haifa being still a very junior competitor; however, the actual decline of Acre set in as of the 1880s.

Seniority in urban population by the mid-1800s rested undoubtedly with Gaza, the population of which in 1870 was double that of Jaffa (16,500 versus 6,500–8,500) (Ben-Arieh, 1981; Amiran and Shachar, 1959; Bigger, 1986; Kark, 1990). What, then, brought about the flourishing of Jaffa, first as a center for the coastal plain and later for the whole country, even challenging Jerusalem? And when did these transitions occur?

The rise of Jaffa has been discussed extensively by Kark (1976; 1984), Kaniel (1981), and Ram (1982). Although the development of Jaffa in the modern era started in the eighteenth centu-

ry, the repeated destruction of the port city did not permit a continuous process to prevail until after the Napoleon wars in the early
nineteenth century. The urban-economic growth of Jaffa was
related, on the one hand, to general developments in the country:
improved security on roads and in cities; enhanced status for for-
eigners; economic strengthening, financed partially by foreign bodies; the appearance of steamships; the establishment of permanent
travel companies; and the cancellation of domestic customs. On the
other hand, several specific factors also contributed to turning
Jaffa into a central focus first for the coastal plain and then for the
country as a whole. The first of these factors was that the north of
the country, with Acre at its midst, stagnated following the end of
the Egyptian hegemony in 1840. This happened at a time when
coastal cities along the eastern Mediterranean enjoyed Ottoman
development (e.g., Beirut). Economic attention thus moved from
northern Palestine to the center and south of the country. Jaffa
possessed several advantages over other coastal towns because its
anchorage, though small, was protected; it could, then serve as a
more reliable maritime gate for Jerusalem, at a time when the latter was growing. These basic factors caused, in the middle of the
nineteenth century, a quicker construction of Jaffa than of other
coastal towns and the development there of relatively better education, health, transportation, and communications services. Among
the most important changes were the availability in 1865 of a tele-
graph line from Jaffa to Jerusalem, and to Europe; the opening of
the road between Jaffa and Jerusalem in 1869; and the establishment of the municipality of Jaffa in 1871. These improvements
brought about a continuous growth in the *general* population of
Jaffa, which by 1870 was still half that of Gaza. Although the
increased importance of Jaffa in the middle of the nineteenth century was not a result of Jewish activity as such, the general growth
process that the city experienced during the last two decades of
that century was related to the growth of Jerusalem and the First
Aliya; the process, furthermore, was unique in both its volume and
pace. As a result, "Jaffa turned into the economic center of Palestine even before the end of the Ottoman era" (Kark, 1976, p. 360).

Evidence of Jews in Jaffa in the Ottoman period dates back to
the sixteenth and seventeenth centuries, and there was interrupted
Jewish presence during the eighteenth century (Ram, 1982, p. 21).
A Jewish inn was established in the city in the early nineteenth
century. It was not until the 1830s, however, close to the beginning
of growth in the city at large, that the Jewish community in Jaffa
was renewed. By the middle of the century, this community turned

into the most important Jewish community in Palestine outside the "four holy cities" (Jerusalem, Hebron, Safed, and Tiberias) (Ram, 1982, p. 67). "Productivism marked the Jaffa community since its inception" (Kark, 1984, p. 167) in contrast to the old Jewish communities in these holy cities, which survived on imported charities (*halluka*). This situation evolved, ironically, as a result of harassment both from within the city and from the outside, causing poverty, which for its part did not permit the construction of institutes, congregations, and ethnic neighborhoods as was common in the four holy cities (Ram, 1982, p. 128). A flourishing mid-nineteenth-century Jaffa attracted Jews from other cities and abroad, especially because immigrants tend to settle in the port of arrival in their immigration-destination country. Thus, by the end of the nineteenth century, Jaffa was the location most preferred by Jewish immigrants; it was followed by the new colonies; Jerusalem ranked third (Kark, 1984, p. 124). In the 1870s, an "Alliance" school, providing modern Jewish education, was established in Jaffa by the community rabbi, Yehuda Halevi. The Jews in the city integrated into the foreign trade business; initial agricultural experiments also got under way.

This is the background, covering a period lasting from the 1880s until World War I, that provided a unique incubation for the future urban center of Tel Aviv–Jaffa. Its importance for the city parallels David's kingship in Jerusalem. David came to an existing city, one that was partially conquered (and settled?) by the Judeans before his day. He lay the foundations for the functions of Jerusalem as a holy city and a capital. By the same token, foundations were laid in the 1880s for a new Jewish urban center in Jaffa, which developed within an already existing center and Jewish community. When the incubation of their respective central roles took place, neither Jerusalem nor Jaffa was the largest city in the country.

The new urban center on the coastal plain was going to have a business character, mostly secular, pluralistic, enterprise oriented, modern, innovative, and hedonistic. This center emerged from its inception as a contrast to the ancient center in Jerusalem. The time of the kingship of David in Jerusalem and the turn of the last century in Jaffa were two unique periods in that each provided the groundings for the future functions and status of the two major centers in the urban and socioeconomic systems of Israel.

"From 1882 there arose in Jaffa a community that was completely different in character. It absorbed all the immigrants from cities in Palestine and from abroad whose spirit did not suit the ways of thought and mode of life in Jerusalem and the rest of the holy cities and who looked for an atmosphere of modernization, liberty, secularism and economic enterprise" (Kark, 1984, p. 167). The year 1882 marked the beginning of the First Aliya. The Jaffa Jewish community witnessed a blending of immigrants from abroad and immigrants from Jerusalem who had been educated in Jerusalem. This unique social-religious character was accompanied by several other factors: the economic strengthening of the community in the areas of trade, crafts, and services; a convenient geographical location; the proximity of agricultural land on which the colonies were built; and the modernization of the urban landscape, culminating in the physical destruction of the city walls. The influence of the new immigrants was still limited, however, and most of the Jews in Jaffa still adhered to a Jewish traditional mode of life.

Several consequences of these factors followed soon after. The Jewish population of Jaffa enjoyed a fast growth process, turning this city into the center of the new Jewish community in Palestine ("the new Yishuv") in the early 1880s. The builders of Petah Tiqva, the first colony, made Jaffa their transitional residence (Ram, 1982). General community institutes as well as settlement agencies were established in the city. In 1891 a *general* committee for the Yishuv was established in Jaffa, this action constituting a new phenomenon in the multicongregational structure of the old Jewish communities. During the First Aliya, the centers of both the major settlement movement ("Hovvei Zion") and the Zionist financial agency (APC) made Jaffa their headquarters. By the early twentieth century, with the beginning of the Zionist, Second Aliya, the centrality of Jaffa became amplified even further. The Palestine Bureau of the World Zionist Organization, the central committees of the Labor movements, the centers of the Jewish teachers and physicians, and the center of a national sports organization all located in Jaffa. In 1908, Jaffa's significant cumulative advantage led Ruppin to locate the Palestine Bureau there:

I fixed the location of the Palestine Bureau in Jaffa. This choice was almost obvious in those years. Jaffa was then the location of the Anglo-Palestine Bank, and also there was a representative of the Odessa committee of "Hovvei Zion" (Dr. Hissin and M. Sheinkin) and the land-purchase company "Geula," whose representative at that time was M. Diesengoff. Another reason for the choice of Jaffa was its location in the midst of the largest agricultural settlements (Rishon Le'Zion; Rehovot; Petah Tiqva); but more important was the fact that the majority of the new community was concentrated in Jaffa. In Haifa the new community was smaller than in Jaffa, and in

Jerusalem, where most of the Jews were of the old community, it
was but an insignificant minority. (Ruppin, 1968, p. 48)

Jaffa was thus called the *the city of centers* (Kaniel, 1981, p.
188; Kark, 1976, p. 359), the Jewish community in the town being
like a state within a state (Kark, 1984, p. 41). The commerce,
crafts, and manufacturing in Jaffa were a necessary complement of
agriculture in the colonies (Kaniel, 1981; Kark, 1984, p. 168). Jaffa
also served as a social center and as a recreation and entertainment center for the settlers in the colonies, especially during the
summers, thus adding to the social and cultural heterogeneity that
was one of the characteristics of the city. Meanwhile, several cultural institutions, typical of the new community, were established
in Jaffa: library, high school, elementary schools, teachers' semi-
naries, newspapers, publishing houses, a theater, and musical
activities.

By the end of the 1880s, the population of Jaffa surpassed
that of Gaza, the former numbering some 21,364 inhabitants in
1893 and the latter 20,750 (The Vital-Kina data; see Ben-Arieh,
1987). In other words, Jaffa had attained population primacy on
the coastal plain even before the opening of the railway from Jaffa
to Jerusalem in 1892. At that time, Jerusalem still enjoyed the
largest population in Palestine, 51,000. The development of Jaffa
was, thus, rapid in terms of both population concentration and the
creation of a second Jewish cultural-economic pole in Palestine.
This process occurred within one or two decades, at the end of the
nineteenth century.

The Second Aliya, in the beginning of the twentieth century,
was marked by a significant contribution to the development of
modern manufacturing, commerce, agriculture, and construction
(Ram, 1982). The establishment of Tel Aviv in 1909 signified a
geographical shifting of a society and culture that had been developing in Jaffa for almost thirty years before then. Special symbolism, therefore, attached to the transfer of the "Herzliya" high
school (*gymnasium*) from Jaffa to Tel Aviv marking the dedication
of a new suburb, then called *Ahuzat-Bayit*. The crystallization of
the suburban section, Ahuzat-Bayit, into the town of Tel Aviv was
facilitated even more by the maturation of the processes described
with regard to Jewish Jaffa. During the 1920s, Tel Aviv and Jaffa
would, thus, achieve a national Jewish seniority in both urban population size and cultural-economic dominance.

The evolutionary process of Tel Aviv has been described by
Katz (1986). When the "Ahuzat-Bayit" association was established

in 1906, some 7000 Jews lived in Jaffa, double their number in 1886. The run-down residential conditions and the lack of sufficient housing in Jaffa caused, in part, the establishment of "Ahuzat-Bayit." Another reason was the expectation of an immigration of wealthy people, who were supposed to deal with the marketing of Jewish agricultural crops. The most important factor, however, was the intention to maintain this new section of Jaffa as a completely Hebrew community in terms of the language spoken, the culture, and the population. Characteristically, perhaps, was the nonallocation of a central plot for a synagogue, contrary to other new neighborhoods in both Jaffa and Jerusalem. There was another difference: in Jerusalem, the newly built sections formed an integral part of the city; in "Ahuzat Bayit," in contrast, the idea was to build a distinct and separate neighborhood. "Because the Jews constituted a majority in Jerusalem and built most of the area outside the walls, the need to establish a separate city did not rise. In Jaffa, which was mostly Muslim and the Jews were a minority, more need was felt to unify within a separate autonomous framework" (Kark, 1976, p. 363).

On the eve of World War I, five years after its establishment, Tel Aviv could count about 2000 residents. Contrary to the original design, which called for *economic* dependence on Jaffa, it was clear soon enough that a need existed for land allocation for commercial and cultural activities. Tel Aviv turned into a symbol of new Jewish urban construction in Palestine before World War I, during which its population was evacuated by the Ottomans. This symbolism was expressed in its layout as well as in its cultural character. Thus, it became the seat of several central Zionist institutes.

Following World War I, Tel Aviv underwent more rapid development, the Arab riots in 1921 contributing decisively to this process. "The riots turned Tel Aviv overnight into the center of the Jewish community [in Palestine]" (Ram, 1982, p. 497). In 1921, too, immediately following these riots, Tel Aviv was declared a township; it formally became a city in 1934. The British assisted the development of Tel Aviv, even if only indirectly, by separating it from Jaffa, allocating resources for it, enacting planning laws, and by assisting its industrial development (Bigger, 1983). The flourishing of institutions in various sectors of the new Jewish community in Palestine and the commercial development that accompanied the Fourth Aliya (in the 1920s) turned Tel Aviv–Jaffa into the largest city in Palestine during the 1920s. The 1922 census found 62,578 inhabitants in Jerusalem, and 47,709 in Jaffa-Tel Aviv. In the 1931 census, the situation was reversed, so that Tel

Aviv–Jaffa had 101,840 residents, while Jerusalem numbered 90,503 (Amiran and Shachar, 1959).

The population of Tel Aviv proper surpassed that of Jaffa in the mid-1930s in parallel to its declaration as a city, and it finally surpassed that of Jerusalem during the second half of 1930s (Bigger, 1976). Tel Aviv was the location of the "national" (Palestine—later Israel—Philharmonic) orchestra, the national theater (Habima), and the major banks and insurance companies. Not incidently, the "national" university (The Hebrew University), the national library, the Chief Rabbinate, and Zionist headquarters ("the national institutions") were established in Jerusalem following the declaration of the British Mandate over Palestine. The mandate was later to turn Jerusalem into the country's capital. The "national institutions gradually took over the Palestine Bureau, established by Ruppin in Jaffa (first in their capacity as the Zionist Executive, and eventually as the Jewish Agency). In their location in Jerusalem, close to the British authorities, these institutions fulfilled the need for a Jewish representation, as was called for by the League of Nations when mandating Palestine to Britain (S. B. Cohen, 1977).

History of the Relations Between Tel Aviv–Jaffa and Jerusalem

The emergence of the two major urban centers in modern Israel may be summed up through an elaboration of two terms: incubation and formation.

The term *incubation period,* here does not refer to the *foundation* periods of the cities but, rather, to the times when they started to perform central functions that were eventually carried into similar contemporary functions and that constituted, therefore, central components of their geographical profile. The *formative periods* of the two cities do not refer to the formation of each city separately, but to a period during which the relative sizes and functional relations between the two were formed and molded. In the evolution of Jerusalem and Tel Aviv into the two major urban centers of modern Israel, it is possible to identify a separate incubation period for each city and a common formative period.

Jerusalem's incubation period took place at the time of King David, when the initial elements for its functions as a holy city and a capital were laid down. This statement, which relates to an ancient period, has to be evaluated from two interrelated perspectives, the historical and the cultural. From a historical viewpoint, Jerusalem has undergone much since the King David era: several declines in its status at various periods, and continuous and vigorous growth processes since the nineteenth century. On the other hand, it is important to bear in mind that the development of Jerusalem since its incubation period, as well as its rise beginning in the nineteenth century, have been tied to its status and importance as both a capital and a holy city, each of which status was first determined during the reign of King David. In the 3000 years since then, the city has experienced many transitions in size and status.

For a long period, it actually lost one of the two functions that had been originally created in the incubation period; namely, its being a capital city. The very fact that the incubation period of Jerusalem took place very early on, perhaps the earliest among contemporary capital cities, has brought about the accumulation of an extensive and deep religious-cultural loading with regard to the city. On the one hand, there is the unbroken spiritual connection between Jews and Jerusalem, even throughout an extended physical separation from it; on the other hand, there is its status as a holy city, too, for Christianity and Islam. This additional sanctification of the city has not created a new functional dimension; rather, it has extended and expanded a status that was originally determined by David.

This extended holiness and significance has several implications, however. First, the city is holy to several religions simultaneously, not just to one religion as in other cities (e.g., Rome). The city possessed, therefore, an "extraterritorial nature"—belonging to all and none at the same time. Second, the holiness of Jerusalem is shared with other cities in Christianity and Islam, but not in Judaism. Third, its holiness to several religions has led to conflicts with religious motives in several historical periods as well as in modern times; these contributed to both the suffering and the importance of the city.

From a cultural perspective, the significance of Jerusalem has changed throughout the generations. The ritual during the Second Temple era was different from that in the First Commonwealth; and since the destruction of the Second Temple, Jewish ritual in Jerusalem has not been much different than in other parts of the world.

The significance of past and present Jerusalem, from a Jewish secular perspective, may be shown by comparing it to two other similar cities, Rome and Athens. Fischer (1988, p. 194) called the three *museum cities*. All include numerous archaeological sites, which present their glorious pasts. Jerusalem, however, is unique in several respects:

> First the direct connection to the past embodied through a specific site, the Temple Mount, to which and to its immediate surroundings were connected messages of faith, life, and hope, in reality and symbol; on which was focused the concept of a nation's coming into existence; and around the image of which crystallized ambiguous principles (e.g., Earthly Jerusalem and Heavenly Jerusalem) and ambivalent ones (the sacredness of the city to three religions). Second, the uninterrupted continuity of its historical strata, of ruler changes, of destruction and reconstruction, in all of which the spiritual dimension has been stronger than the urban-economic. And more than everything else, perhaps, is the uniqueness of Jerusalem in the strange dialogue between reality and vision that the human imagination has embroidered around it, beyond the consciousness of its physical existence over time.

Retrospectively, the spatial organization of the Land of Israel during the First Temple era consisted of three elements: first, the concentration of the Israelite population along the mountains rather than along the coastal plain; second, the division of the country into tribal lots; third, the making of Jerusalem into a spiritual and political center. Of these three elements, only two remained in effect during the Second Temple era, following the cancellation of the tribal division. The renewed Jewish settlement in the modern era meant the decline of yet another element—the mountainous concentration of the Jewish population. The major focus became coastal rather than mountainous. Still, the centrality of Jerusalem has proved a common geographical element for all periods of Jewish settlement in the Land of Israel.

Tel Aviv's incubation period extended from the 1880s and 1890s to the outbreak of World War I. If one takes into account that the metropolitan area of Tel Aviv has a current population of about 2 million residents, almost all of whom are Jewish, this means the very fast development of an urban focus. As in Jerusalem of 3000 years ago, the functions characterizing the contemporary metropolitan area were determined during the city's incubation period: commerce, business, entertainment, and manufacturing. These functions were accompanied by a cultural atmosphere that emphasized liberty, pluralism, secularism, and a modern Hebrew culture integrated with the external Western culture.

The incubation period for Tel Aviv did not unfold independent of the veteran urban center, Jerusalem. There was a mutual dependency between the two cities. On the one hand, Jaffa served as the gate for Jerusalem, so that the flourishing of Jerusalem at the time composed a central element for economic prosperity in Jaffa. On the other hand, Jaffa developed as a cultural and economic counterpoint to Jerusalem, despite the growth of a new Jewish community in Jerusalem as well. The openness of Jaffa, the nonexistence of the old, heavy, and profoundly present (physically and spiritually) elements of Jerusalem, and the entrepreneurial atmosphere in Jaffa all combined to create a new urban entity.

The 1920s and 1930s, but notably the 1920s, constituted the formative period for the shaping of relations between the two cities in terms of their relative sizes and functions. Jerusalem was declared capital of Palestine by the British in 1924. The Hebrew University of Jerusalem opened its doors the following year to serve as a national center for a mainly secular, Judaic, and general higher education. For the second time since the destruction of the Second Temple (and for the first time since the Crusades), the two ancient functions of the city reunited.

During the 1920s, Jaffa and Tel Aviv achieved both economic and population predominance in Palestine. This involved two major changes. The first involved the emergence of Tel Aviv–Jaffa into an urban entity that was larger than Jerusalem (in the 1920s). This occurred side by side with the population dominance attained by the new Jewish, mostly coastal settlement over the old, mainly mountainous community. The second change made Tel Aviv, originally a suburb of Jaffa, larger than the previous central city, Jaffa. In terms of population, this occurred in the mid-1930s; but in terms of functions and importance to the Jewish community, it had already taken place in the 1920s. Thus, from the perspective of Tel Aviv, its transition from the incubation phase as a new urban center into dominating the urban system in Palestine, was almost continuous. It was temporarily cut off only by World War I. Otherwise, within a mere forty to fifty years, it went through the phases of incubation, crisis, take-off, and dominance. This unprecedented process relates to the emergence of a new society constructing new urban centers in a country where the indigenous population had enjoyed old urban centers. In other new immigrant societies such old urban centers did not exist, and the urbanization process was kindled on by the intruding immigrants.

The formation of the Jewish community on the coastal plain was new in several respects. First was the very Jewish concentration on the plain, and in Jaffa as a principal focus in particular. Second, this coastal focus eventually became almost three times as large as the mountainous center. Third, both urban centers have been settled by the same nation. During several periods in history, the coastal plain and the mountains were settled by different nations. Thus, during the First Temple era, the Philistines settled the coast while the Israelites lived in the mountains. During the Second Temple era, a Greek-Roman area developed along the coast, whereas the Jews and the Samaritans resided in the mountains. In the modern era, the Jews settled mainly the plains, whereas the Arabs remained mostly on the mountains. The two Jewish centers, Tel Aviv and Jerusalem, have developed, then, through intercity conflicts and contradictions, though their specializations presented some complementarity. This theme will be returned to. First, though, the political significance of becoming and being core areas or a capital city will be probed.

An Eternal Capital versus a Young Core

The relevant terminology concerning the political status of Jerusalem and Tel Aviv and the relations between them are *core areas* and *capital cities*. Frequently, but not always, capital cities are core areas and vice versa (Whittlesey, 1939; see also de Blij, 1973, p. 84). This pair of terms has been discussed mainly in the political geography literature, rather than within urban or economic geography. Two issues will be discussed in the following paragraphs. The first is the question of definitions and classifications for core regions and capital cities, and their implication for the Israeli case. The second issue involves the possible separation between core areas or primate cities, on the one hand, and capital cities, on the other. This situation characterizes modern immigrant nation states (United States, Canada, Australia, New Zealand, South Africa), and it will be assessed for the Israeli case.

Core Areas: General Terms and the Israeli Reality

The classic definition of core areas is Whittlesey's (1939, p. 597): "The area in which or about which a state originates." Following this definition, S. B. Cohen (1977, p. 87) proposed a definition for the "political core": "a unique area whose residents influence national political values and mold national political structures and institutions." Using these definitions for the Israeli case would be problematic at best. In past historical periods of Israelite-Jewish sovereignty in the Land of Israel, specifically during the eras of the two Temples, the core area could clearly be identified. First it lay within the Judean lot (Bethlehem, Hebron), then it moved to Jerusalem, as an intertribal center in the mountainous settlement area; later, an additional core evolved in central Samaria. In the modern era, however, things have turned more complex. On the one hand, there was Jerusalem, which was the largest, most important city in Palestine when the new Jewish settlement began in the third quarter of the nineteenth century. The city was also the focus of Jewish yearnings for the Land of Israel throughout the two millennia of physical separation from the country. On the other hand, there was Jaffa, in which the cultural and organizational centers of the new Jewish community located and which was located in the geographical center of the Jewish settlement area on the coastal plain. Whittlesey's definition, therefore, sharpens the difference between the old and the new in the evolution of core areas in modern Palestine. Pounds (1972, p. 187n) put forward an alternative definition for core areas, one that rather emphasizes the economic dimension: "the area within a state that is at present economically dominant." Applying this definition to Tel Aviv would have turned it into the clear core of Israel and left the capital as a large urban entity outside the core. Such a situation could have been true since the 1920s, and perhaps since the beginning of the twentieth century, if the economic dimension is the only criterion taken into account.

This examination of the political core in modern Jewish Palestine has focused on the relations between Jerusalem and Tel Aviv (S. B. Cohen, 1977). As pointed out earlier, the "national institutions" were located and developed in Jerusalem beginning in the 1920s, concomitantly with the declaration of the city as a capital for the British Mandate. The Jewish political center, however, focused on Tel Aviv in the form of the headquarters of the labor union, the defense organization (Hagana), the newspapers, and economic organizations. This concentration came as a result of both push and pull effects. Jerusalem pushed, as it served as the central location for the non-Zionist sectors in Palestine: the foreign-colonial government, the Arab national movement, and the old Jewish community. Tel Aviv pulled because it was located at the center of the new Jewish community and it (i.e., Jaffa) gained a cumulative economic as well as cultural advantage since the nineteenth century.

The political core remained mainly in Tel Aviv even after the establishment of Israel, because Jerusalem was located on the periphery of the state and, furthermore, was almost surrounded by the Jordanian border. "As long as it was peripheral, even as a capital, Jerusalem was less an independent generator and more a recipient of Israeli political ideals" (S. B. Cohen, 1977, p. 82). At the same time, Israel continued to develop West Jerusalem as a frontier capital, though its development was less impressive than that of the coastal plain. Comparable status was not granted to East Jerusalem, as a possible capital for the Palestinians, by the Jordanians. Hence, the unification of Jerusalem by Israel in 1967 found the Western city with a development infrastructure, while the Eastern city was lacking any core or capital functions of its own. Despite the rapid development of Jerusalem since 1967, several central political functions remained based in Tel Aviv, such as the Ministry of Defense, the Histadruth, and newspaper headquarters. The implications of this situation will be highlighted in a later section.

Even modern definitions and descriptions for core areas and capital cities require careful examination when applied to the special case of the Jewish people returning to their land. Burghardt (1969) proposed three types of core areas. First is the *nuclear core*, which refers to a situation in which a small territory grows into a larger entity in the *longue duree*, while absorbing land and people. A second type is the *original core*, which relates to the region of foremost political, and maybe even economic, importance within the context of a larger territorial framework. The third type is the *contemporary core*, which is the present area of highest political or economic importance. The use of Burghardt's terminology assumes the existence of geographical dynamics in the location of cores over time. A core, therefore, might potentially constitute the historical nucleus of the territory, or it might develop following the establishment of the territorial framework. Furthermore, it may change in modern times. Another assumption behind this classification is the use of political or economic importance as a criterion for the characterization of the core. A central problem in all these definitions of core areas is the lack of specific variables that may be quantitatively examined, such as population size or density or industrial concentration.

Applying Burghardt's classification to the case of Tel Aviv and Jerusalem would exclude the option of a nuclear core, because the making of Jerusalem into a capital in the time of King David constitutes a choice process rather than a settlement-expansion process, which would move from the urban core into the periphery. On the other hand, the questions still remain whether Jerusalem and Jaffa were composed of original cores back in the nineteenth century and whether they have served as contemporary cores throughout the twentieth century. If the special conditions of Jerusalem and Tel Aviv, in which the first gradually received more of a political status whereas the second has had more economic power, are considered, then the answers to these questions would seem to go as follows. Jerusalem served as an original core within the existing territory of Palestine (politically undefined in the nineteenth century), and the city's religious, cultural, and political importance have increased in the course of the twentieth century. Tel Aviv is the contemporary core, having a higher economic-social centrality.

Nevertheless, both Tel Aviv and Jerusalem display certain *characteristics* of nuclear cores. The new community in Jaffa developed in parallel with the First Aliya; in other words, the Jewish core on the coastal plain evolved simultaneously in Jaffa and in the colonies. Jaffa served as an urban and cultural center, while the colonies maintained lands and revived Jewish agriculture in the Land of Israel. The development of Jaffa and, later, of Tel Aviv as central urban settlements in Palestine occurred simultaneously with the development of agriculture and a rural society in the rural areas of the coastal core. Jaffa and then Tel Aviv served as direction, coordination, and cultural centers for these rural settlements. Nineteenth century Jerusalem did not enjoy a comparable advantage. The three other holy cities, Hebron, Safed, and Tiberias, were separated from it. The new Yishuv in Jerusalem built new sections within the city area, but very little in its surroundings (Motza to its west, Gush Etzion to the south, Attarot and Neve Ya'akov to the north). One of the objectives of the West Bank settlement project since the 1970s was to provide for Jewish settlements around Jerusalem. This process, however, has not been similar to the one that took place around Jaffa and Tel Aviv in the late nineteenth century. It has not occurred simultaneously with the construction of the city, and for the most part it does not bring a new population to the region. The process presents more of a case of spillover from the large city, in the forms of suburbanization and exurbanization. From the perspective of the Jewish population in Jerusalem, this has meant a wider territorial dispersion of the Jewish population of Jerusalem and a concomitant reduction in its share within the city proper.

De Blij (1973, p. 84) outlined several characteristics of core regions. As he saw it, they tend to develop in the most fertile area of a country or in the most resource-rich area. The core is also the incubation region for ideas and innovations. Crucial international decisions are made there; housing most foreign embassies it is the most cosmopolitan region of the country. In countries once governed by colonial powers, the core region is usually located on the coast; consequently, the area was influenced by the colonial culture more than were other regions.

These features described by de Blij are generally divided between Jerusalem and Tel Aviv, with one exception: the last one was irrelevant in Palestine. Tel Aviv developed indeed in the midst of the most fertile region of the country, and it has served as the focus of innovations and ideas in the Land of Israel since its establishment. On the other hand, the most important political decisions are made in Jerusalem. It is also difficult to point to the more cosmopolitan city between the two, although since its early days Tel Aviv has presented more openness to ideas originating abroad. It also contains most embassies, given the nonrecognition by many countries of Jerusalem as the capital of Israel. On the other hand, Jerusalem had been the focus of international religious interest, especially by Jews and Christians; as a result, it houses many foreign representatives, not necessarily government diplomats. Jerusalem has also enjoyed a varied pilgrimage, which adds to the cosmopolitan character of the city.

A colonial impact coming specifically from the coast was restricted in Palestine. The Ottomans did not care too much either for Jaffa or for Jerusalem. The British, on the contrary, favored mountainous Jerusalem (Bigger, 1983). The coastal preference was reserved mainly to the Jewish immigrants from Europe who favored Tel Aviv–Jaffa because of the religious conservatism and "historical heaviness" of Jerusalem (in addition to the location of the harbor, in Jaffa, and its proximity to new Jewish settlements in the plain).

From D. J. Elazar's (1970a) perspective, Tel Aviv has a special core status arguing for a three-phase development in Zionist frontier settlement of the Land of Israel. The first was the agricultural phase, as of the early 1880s. The second was urban-industrial, starting in the 1920s. The third is the current technological-metropolitan phase, beginning in the 1950s. Although Katz (1986) identified the foundation of Tel Aviv with the urban-industrial phase, all three phases have apparently been connected with Tel Aviv as a source of new ideas and as a control center for their development. In the agricultural phase, it was for Jaffa (and then for Tel Aviv) to serve the pioneers of the several *aliyas* as a location for meeting, recreation, shopping, and above all organizational centers and ideological foci (together with the valleys; see S. B.

Cohen, 1977, and the next part). The urban-industrial phase was shared by Tel Aviv and Haifa as the initial industrial centers (though the first industrial attempts are attributed to the German-Templer colonists in Jaffa). The metropolitan-technological era began in and has been focused on Tel Aviv (though Haifa holds some advantage here).

Capital Cities: International Classifications and Jerusalem

Following the discussion of the term *core area* and its implications for the Israeli case, we now turn to an examination of the term *capital city* and its significance for Jerusalem and this city's competition with Tel Aviv. This analysis is especially important for comparing Jerusalem to capital cities of other modern immigrant societies.

The modern Hebrew term for capital city, *Bira*, probably originated in the title of the Persian city of Shushan in the biblical Book of Esther, though the original meaning there might refer to a castle or a palace rather than a capital city. Biblical references to Jerusalem using this term referred to either the Temple or a castle (see, e.g., I Chronicles 29:1).

The term though, might already have been expanded in biblical times to include the whole city (Nehemia 7:2; see H. Cohen, 1988). This biblical term attested, therefore, to the double function of Jerusalem as the religious and governmental center.

The classic definition of a capital city was proposed by Jefferson (1939): a capital city is always disproportionately larger than other cities in a given country. Henrikson (1983) and Taylor (1985) noted that this definition suits the "European concept" of capital cities, but not the American. Obviously, it is impossible to use Jefferson's definition for the Israeli case, in which the capital city is disproportionately smaller than the primate city.

De Blij (1973, pp. 119–122), using a historical perspective, classified capital cities into three types: permanent, introduced, and divided. The last type relates to the division of capital functions among several cities, not to any physical division. Jerusalem is surely a permanent capital city (and maybe the most permanent one in the world, given its many years of being a capital). When first declared, however, Jerusalem was an introduced capital, since it was not the first capital city of the ancient Israelite kingdom.

Taylor (1985, pp. 102–104), following Henrikson (1983), also proposed three types of capital cities, but from a political-economy viewpoint. The first type are capitals that were created as part of world core regions, such as the European capital cities, which turned into political control centers of the world economy. This is the "European concept" of capital cities. A second type consists of those cities that came into being as a result of world periphery processes. These are usually coastal capitals established by colonial powers for resource exploitation. The third group of capital cities are those located in countries that were semiperipheral at the time, and in which either a previous capital was cancelled (e.g., Brazil, Turkey) or a federal one was created (e.g., the United States, Canada). These cities signified an accent on national rather than world economy. This is the "American concept" of capital cities. It is difficult to apply Taylor's political economy perspective on the domination of resources to the Israeli case. The British were prompted by religious-historical considerations in making Jerusalem the capital city. Tel Aviv became the economically most important city in British Palestine, not by the colonial power but rather by the Jewish immigrants; whereas the British favored another coastal city, Haifa. Nevertheless, there are several elements in Jerusalem as a capital that make it similar to federal capitals of modern immigrant nations.

Jerusalem versus New Federal Capital Cities

The determination of federal capital cities in Anglo-Saxon immigrant societies has not yet been systematically and comparatively studied. Several studies do exist on specific cities; for example, Ottawa (Knight, 1977) and Washington, D.C. (Henrikson, 1983; Fifer, 1976; 1981). In Canada, Australia, and the United States, the capital presents a compromise among large cities or between different cultural regions. In South Africa, the capital functions are divided among three centers (i.e., a divided capital).

Several common lines link Israel and other, federally organized, immigrant nations. First, a separation exists between the primate city and the capital, which is usually much smaller than the former. Second, the capital was chosen from political consideration. Third, the capital area in most countries is federal territory, which was probably the situation in Jerusalem at the time of King David.

There are, however, several differences between Israel and modern federal immigrant societies, and some of these differences relate ironically to the similarities between the two. Anglo-Saxon immigrant societies are not similar to Israeli society in terms of the nature of the geographical destination of the immigrants. In the first case, they went to a "new world"; the Jewish immigrants, in contrast, returned to their ancient fatherland, where there already had existed a territorial center, Jerusalem. The choice of Jerusalem as capital stemmed from religious as well as political considerations; in other modern immigrant nations, only political criteria were relevant. Once again two central elements in the evolution of modern Israeli society and territory surface: the return to an old fatherland and the sacredness of its capital.

The very existence of a potential capital in Palestine with some spiritual-historical "heaviness" led to a cultural struggle over its status. This is not the case when a capital constitutes a federal compromise. In other words, the lack of a federal structure in modern Land of Israel contributed to the struggle between Jerusalem and Jaffa–Tel Aviv. Thus, the locational demerits of Jerusalem— namely, its inner land and mountainous location—became more significant, whereas the choice of federal capitals usually take into account geographical considerations. On the other hand, the holiness and long history of Jerusalem have given a striking identity to the city per se, not merely to active institutions and personalities within it, as normally happens in federal capitals. Another interesting aspect is the convenient transportation connection between Jerusalem and Tel Aviv, which is typical of a connection between a (federal) capital and a primate city. Nevertheless, in several of the modern immigrant countries, this transportation axis has become an integral part of the core regions (e.g., megalopolis in the United States). In Israel, on the other hand, the Judean mountains west of Jerusalem, known as the *Jerusalem corridor,* have constituted mainly a natural reserve and an agricultural region. As a result, Tel Aviv and Jerusalem have expanded in different directions in recent years. Tel Aviv has grown along the coast and, more recently, into West Samaria; Jerusalem extended beyond its pre-1967 borders to the north, east, and south. Political considerations for the possession of territory around Jerusalem as well as topographical restrictions played a role in determining the directions of this residential expansion of Jerusalem.

Jerusalem may be compared to various cities worldwide. One comparable group may consist of other holy cities, mainly in Asia, such as Beijing, Calcutta, and even Tokyo. Another group would include federal nonprimate capital cities enjoying several cultures and built by immigrants (e.g., Washington, D.C.). An intercity comparison of different cultures assumes a priori the existence of the unique and the different. In Jerusalem, the striking element lies in its holiness and importance to people of different religious affiliations on a universal scale. Several years ago, when the cultural-political profile of Washington was drawn, the city was shown to be the most important among federal nonprimate capital cities (Henrikson, 1983). It is possible to point to several similarities between Jerusalem and Washington, D.C., despite differences in incubation periods and in current national administration systems.

Americans preferred to establish small capitals. This trend prevailed not only at the national level but also at the state and county levels. Henrikson termed this propensity *capitallessness*; the small capital cities were actually "countercapitals." He proposed several reasons for this process. It was, primarily, a reaction to the concentration of government by the British. It furthermore reflected agricultural values, which were at the basis of the evolving American society. Third, it displayed some apprehension of a possible tie between government and business. This same phenomenon of moving the capital into a small, relatively unknown location happened in King David's days regarding Jerusalem. The social values that directed such a move in the United States were irrelevant for Jerusalem, except for the federal consideration. Obviously, the religious motive, so strong in the choice of Jerusalem, did not exist for the District of Columbia.

European capitals tend to produce leading national political opinions, and they serve as national symbols in this regard. Washington, on the contrary, is a capital that serves as a center for political activity "reacting" to political activities taking place in other centers across the United States. The Israeli pattern is similar to some degree to the American. Lawmaking as well as the supreme court and the majority of governmental ministries and agencies are located in Jerusalem. Tel Aviv houses the headquarters of the labor federation and the political parties (see Benvenisti, 1981, p. 24). Jerusalem is the location of state TV and radio broadcasting, but almost all newspapers are published in Tel Aviv. Nevertheless, the political interplay in Israel is limited to these two centers, not necessarily because of the small size of the country but because of an inferior role played by the geographical peripheries (Gradus, 1983).

Washington has been typified by the coexistence of several Washingtons: the federal, the black, the wealthy, the old, the violent. The success of the city is an outcome of its ability to maintain a balance among all these sectors, an act that requires more control than solutions to these conflicts. In a primate city, there may be a tendency to make use of the majority rule. In this context, there is some similarity between Washington and Jerusalem. Jerusalem, too, consists of several sectors—the government, the university, the media, the Jewish ultraorthodox, the Arab, and the poor—that tend to engage in conflicts with one another. In Jerusalem, as in Washington, there are several sectors whose share in the urban community is much larger than their shares in the national society, namely the ultraorthodox Jews and the Arabs. In Jerusalem, too, there have been attempts to control evolving conflicts, mainly through the leadership of a long-time mayor (Teddy Kolek). Although the Palestinian uprising known as the Intifada has shaken some of these controls, they have been based on the neighborhood structure of the city (the "mosaic theory"; see Benvenisti, 1981).

In summary, it has turned out to be difficult to examine and assess the development of core areas and the capital city in Israel through definitions relating to simple conditions: the existence of a core area in a region where a nation was created or where current economic activity tends to concentrate. Simple conditions would also turn the capital city into the largest metropolitan site located within the core area. Developments in the Land of Israel have been more complex, requiring, therefore, a careful examination of the changing relations and interrelationship of Tel Aviv and Jerusalem.

Jerusalem has been an original core, created when the national territory in the Land of Israel already existed. This refers to the distant past and, to a much lesser extent, also to the more recent past. Tel Aviv, on the other hand, has constituted the central component in the contemporary core. It has been difficult to examine the two cities on the basis of joint political and economic criteria, because several core characteristics are divided between them. Tel Aviv is located in the most fertile region of the country; it has served as a national source for innovations and as a frontier for urban development. Jerusalem has turned into the political center of the country. For both cities (but particularly for Tel Aviv), the importance of the colonial factor for their development was less than in other countries under colonial regimes.

Jerusalem is a permanent capital separated from the primate city, similar to new federal immigrant countries. Jewish immigrants were returning to a capital with a long-established identity. Despite its uniqueness, Jerusalem presents some resemblance to Washington in its nonexclusive political function, shared with Tel Aviv, and in its social structure, which consists of large minorities.

The significance that Jerusalem holds for Jews is much stronger than the significance offered by capitals of other new-immigrant societies, given the Israeli city's long existence and holiness to both domestic and universal populations. This point is of special importance in analyzing the struggle between Jerusalem and Tel Aviv and in considering the relative strength of Jerusalem in a small nation that has another large primate city.

Chapter 5

Cultural and Economic Characteristics of Jerusalem and Tel Aviv

Jerusalem and Tel Aviv–Jaffa: Differences and Struggle

The evolution of the contemporary core, first in Jaffa and later in Tel Aviv, was in cultural conflict with and in reaction to the character of Jerusalem, even if part of the economic growth of Jaffa in the nineteenth century was related to the growth of Jerusalem. These cultural differences and competition continued well into the twentieth century. Two periods, in particular, deserve to be highlighted: the incubation decades of the new Jewish community in Jaffa; and the more recent years, especially since 1967. This choice of periods stems from the impression, to be elaborated on later, that the cultural conflict revealed between Tel Aviv and Jerusalem since perhaps the 1980s is actually a new version of the original conflict, dating back to the 1880s. The exposition of this hypothesis will begin with a definition of terms and concepts in regard to the cultural symbolism of cities.

The Cultural Symbolism of the City

The meaning of the city, in terms of its being or developing into a cultural symbol, is a topic that has scarcely been touched in the literature of several relevant disciplines. The consequence is that the terminological and conceptual systems are relatively poor in such fields as urban anthropology, cultural geography, and political geography. What, nevertheless, are the implications for the interrelationship of Tel Aviv and Jerusalem of terms and concepts that have been developed?

The cosmological conception of the world in general, and of the city in particular, underwent a transition in Europe in the sixteenth–seventeenth centuries, from a conception of a vertical cosmos to a conception of a horizontal landscape (Tuan, 1974, pp. 129–130). A vertical conception of a cosmos refers to an entity that is more than merely a piece of territory. Such a conception views

147

space as loaded with transcendental meanings (e.g., sacredness) and is further related to a cyclical conception of time. A cyclical conception of time, which relates to time as a collection of events recurring seasonally or annually, is typical of traditional societies. A vertical conception of space is connected, for example, with the system of holidays. In other words, the views of space, or its cultural meaning, change at various holidays. On the other hand, a horizontal conception of space substitutes a vertical and historically-religiously charged cosmos with a flat piece of nature called *landscape*. A secular reference to landscapes is not loaded with transcendental meanings of time and events.

The transition process in the cosmic conception of space by Jews in the Land of Israel occurred during the last quarter of the nineteenth century, with the development of secular Jewish communities and secular Jewish culture in Palestine. This process has been of special relevance for Tel Aviv, which was established as a new quarter, symbolizing newness in Jewish Palestine. The collective Jewish national memory concerning Jaffa has been dim, since the coastal plain in the far past was usually outside the Jewish settlement area. As Tel Aviv was established outside Jaffa, the former could emphasize elements of newness, youth and dynamism in the design of houses and in the layout of the city, which were not related to older domestic patterns. This was true, too, of its mode of life, which accentuated the new Hebrew culture.

Early Tel Aviv was marked by pale colors, mainly white, the result of painting over cement or prefabricated building blocks. No use was made either of the mountainous, heavy, and white chalk and limestone, or of the coastal beige Kurkar coastal rock (the change in building colors in Tel Aviv in later years and its meanings will be referred to later). Building designs were either purely imported (such as the Bauhaus in the 1930s) or presented a mixture of imported with Arab-oriental elements (such as the use of arches in the street fronts of buildings in the early years). The city was built with wide streets compared to Jaffa, and trees were planted along them. Space was allocated for public institutions, and the synagogue was not supposed to be built in its center. All these aspects, as well as the lack of a clear division of the early city into ethnic or other neighborhoods made early Tel Aviv into a new, completely different urban entity, compared to existing towns in Palestine. Furthermore, it was difficult to identify in the city and in its mode of life a transcendental element or any deeply meaningful seasonal cycling. On the other hand, the Tel Aviv summer leisure, in the form of the beaches and coffee houses have become famous.

As for Jerusalem, the story is more complicated. The traditional Jewish cosmological conception of Jerusalem assumes an element of cyclical time in the form of the Biblical command to visit Jerusalem on three distinct holidays every year. On the other hand, the emphasis in Judaism on historical events as central religious motives (such as the Exodus) turned Judaism into the first ancient culture to adopt linear time (see Kellerman, 1989). Linear time refers to time and events as unfolding along a continuous axis rather than by cycles. This linearity has especially chracterized Jerusalem, which was called *the city of eternity*. The title related both to its centrality in the past and to its major future role in the Judaic Messianic concept. The attitude to Jerusalem as an eternal city has found expression even in a secular Jewish conception of Jerusalem. When he proposed to declare Jerusalem as the capital of Israel, Ben-Gurion noted: "The State of Israel had and will have only one capital—Jerusalem the eternal. This is how it was three thousands years ago, and this is how it is going to be, as we believe, until the end of all generations" (H. Cohen, 1988, p. 247).

It is difficult to note clearly a "flattening" of the Jerusalem cosmos in secular Judaism. First, concerning the past, there has been an ongoing eagerness to reveal the archaeological glory of the city, and its history is thoroughly studied. In modern times, poets have struggled with the problem of whether the city is still "God's province" (Karton-Bloom, 1989). As for the future, the consensual desire to see Jerusalem united under any form of an Arab-Israeli peace agreement makes Jerusalem into a symbol of Israeli attachment to the Land of Israel. Transcendentalism, thus, exists in the secular Jewish cosmological conception of Jerusalem, even if only implicitly. The "anchor," though, is not divine, but human; namely, the nation. Thus, the dualism between Heavenly Jerusalem and Earthly Jerusalem is irrelevant in its original connotation. When moving from older to newer sections of the city, however, one may notice a spatial continuation in the design and structure of the city. All buildings in Jerusalem have to be stone covered (a regulation originally instituted by the British architect P. Geddes); in addition, restrictions exist on high-rise construction. The clear separation of the old city into religious-ethnic neighborhoods has been carried over into the new city as well; until the establishment of Israel, this division also held for the construction of narrow and dead-end streets.

Gottmann (1952) noted the existence of a national iconography, which consists of a flag, historical memories and religious principles, social and economic systems, and national heroes and writers. One may add urban symbols to this list. Jerusalem has surely constituted an indispensable part of the iconography of the Jewish people. Jerusalem and even more so its other name, Zion, have become symbols for the attachment of the Jewish people to the Land of Israel, especially during the long years of exile, in which other national symbols, like a flag, social and economic systems, and so on, were unavailable. This situation still applies to Jews in the contemporary Diaspora. In Israel itself Tel Aviv is becoming part of the national iconography, but on a completely informal basis. Whereas Jerusalem serves as a political capital and as a value in the Israeli educational system, Tel Aviv constitutes an informal symbol for the dynamics of modern culture and for an economic-oriented fast pace of life.

The changing cosmology of the city represents the varying conception of the city by its residents, as well as by others. Another aspect relates to the culture actually developing in given cities. An interesting distinction between two city types was proposed years ago by Redfield and Singer (1954), who differentiated between orthogenetic and heterogenetic cities. The orthogenetic cities were defined as those "carrying forward into systematic and reflective dimensions an old culture" (p. 58). Heterogenetic cities were defined as "creating [of] original modes of thought that have authority beyond or in conflict with old cultures and civilizations" (p. 58). An orthogenetic city is not necessarily culturally stagnant. "The orthogenetic city is not static; it is the place where religious, philosophical and literary specialists reflect, sythesize and create out of the traditional material new arrangements and developments that are felt by the people to be outgrowths of the old" (p. 58). At the same time, the heterogenetic city "is a place of differing traditions, a center of heresy, heterodoxy and dissent, of interruption and destruction of ancient tradition, of rootlessness and anomie" (p. 58). The following paragraphs will show that Jerusalem seems to be more of an orthogenetic city, whereas Tel Aviv fits better the definition of the heterogenetic city.

Tel Aviv has been variously described in the literature (Guvrin, 1989). In its beginning (1909–1921), the new city was a source of pride and astonishment, as well as criticism for its non-rural nature. In the middle period (1921–1933), it was described as a place of fast growth, again attracting criticism for its similarity to Jewish urban life in Europe. From 1933, it has been referred to as the big city, earning less criticism and a more romantic view of its early quiet days. Jerusalem, on the other hand, has been described as an unchanging city, despite the historical and political transitions that have left their imprints.

Elements of both city types are found in each of the two cities, though one form is more dominant for each city. Such a possibility was mentioned by Redfield and Singer. Jerusalem has heterogenetic elements in its cultural life, in the form of the Hebrew University, public struggles over the content and meaning of a contemporary Jewish culture, and even the coexistence of several religions, all of which conceive of the city as sacred. Tel Aviv shows orthogenetic cultural elements in the form of the attempt to preserve a new Hebrew culture, which developed in the city and lasted until the 1960s. Nevertheless, a striking element in the Israeli cultural landscape and spatial organization is the very existence of two urban centers, one of which (Jerusalem) is mainly orthogenetic in nature and the other (Tel Aviv) more heterogenetic. As a result, these two centers have actually been engaged in cultural conflict.

Jerusalem and Jaffa

Kaniel (1981) described the spiritual-cultural struggle between Jerusalem and Jaffa at the turn of the nineteenth century. Nineteenth-century Jerusalem was, indeed, a cosmopolitan city, but on a religious level: the city contained a diversified mix of clergy, representing different religious persuasions, and many Jewish religious-ethnic groups. Jewish Jerusalem was then typified by religious conservatism and poverty, its survival dependent on imported charities, and earning it the appelation *the charitable Jerusalem* (Kaniel, 1981, p. 197). It was, however, "old Jewish Jerusalem that built the new Jewish Jerusalem" (Ben-Arieh, 1977, p. 446). This statement originally related to the physical construction of new Jerusalem, which came in response to the high residential density and poor sanitary conditions of the old city. A similar process of the old developing the new was true of the evolution of the new Jewish community in Jerusalem. Many of the new intellectuals of Jerusalem grew up within the old system. There was no mutual intellectual and economic reinforcement between this new urban community and a rural settlement, as was the case with Jaffa.

Furthermore, the new urban community in Jerusalem did not enjoy the mixture of the domestic and the imported that existed in Jaffa, where immigrants led the new community (Kark, 1984). The Jaffa of the late nineteenth century presented a blend of enhanced economic conditions and external cultural influences. The economic independence and the productivity characterizing the Jewish community of Jaffa since its establishment brought about spiritual independence and an open atmosphere (Kaniel, 1981). It is interesting to note in this regard a very early statement by Rabbi Yehuda Alkalai (1876): "Anybody who will wish to act for the settlement of the Land of Israel will do better by starting his activity in Jaffa and not in Jerusalem, in which the Rabbis and the charity administrators dominate and curse everybody who wants settlement."

The differences between Jerusalem and Jaffa were already visible back in 1885. Eliezer Ben-Yehuda, the father of modern Hebrew as a spoken tongue, described these differences from an interesting perspective. The Jerusalem Arabs were dignified and moderate and tended to prefer the Sephardic Jew, who was familiar with domestic customs, for commercial relations. The Jaffa Arabs, on the contrary, were merchants who ran all over and took off their traditional clothing; they preferred the energetic newcomer Ashkenazic Jews over the quiet Sephardic Jews. Similar trends also related to the cultural atmosphere. Jerusalem intellectuals desired a productivization of the Jewish community; in other words, a socioeconomic change. This was never an issue in Jaffa, where the immigrant intellectuals fought for the next cause—secular education and secular culture. The efforts of the Jerusalem intellectuals may be interpreted as an attempt to provide a middle ground between the old Jewish community of Jerusalem, on the one hand, and the new community in Jaffa, on the other. The Jerusalem intellectuals were moderate, rational, and possessed a quiet spirit. They knew that it would be impossible to attain national-intellectual activity in all parts of the Jerusalem public. The Jerusalem intellectuals were divided in their struggle against the old Jewish community. On the other hand, the Jaffa intellectuals were stormy, sparkling, and provocative. They operated within a community that was open to cultural change. A rabbi from Jerusalem who was appointed to the Jaffa community retreated and returned to Jerusalem; thus, the appointment of Rabbi A. Y. Kook as rabbi for Jaffa *and* the colonies in the early twentieth century signified the religious independence of Jaffa (Kaniel, 1981; Kark, 1976, pp. 366–367). Until World War I, Jerusalem kept its seniority in newspaper and journal publication: seventy-six newspapers and journals were published in Jerusalem, whereas only twenty-nine were published in Jaffa–Tel Aviv. The Jerusalem publications were general, Judaic, literary, and scientific. The Jaffa publications were professional, labor, literary, national, and scientific. This distinction became even more pronounced in the 1920s, when most of the Jewish newspapers moved to Tel Aviv.

In general, the new Jewish community in Jerusalem was not

only different from that in Jaffa, it was also slower in its pace of development. The Hebrew Gymnasium (high school) in Jerusalem was founded in 1909, three years after the Herzliya Gymnasium of Jaffa. The modernization movement in Jaffa began with the First Aliya; the massive development of new community institutions in Jerusalem began only in the early twentieth century, with the secular Second Aliya; with it came new construction: the gymnasium, an arts college (Bezalel), a bank, a community center, several organizations, and the printing industry. The rift with the old community emerged, though the latter continued to constitute a majority in the Jewish community until World War I (Ben-Arieh, 1979).

The Jaffa intellectuals saw Jaffa as their activity focus, and some were even ready to give up on Jerusalem as a potential activity center. They belittled the efforts of the Jerusalem intellectuals, who were employed by, and thus depended on, philanthropic educational institutions. On the other hand, the Jerusalem intellectuals begged modern organizations and institutions either to locate or stay in the city. They were also active in the fight to institute Hebrew as the language of the new Jewish community ("the languages war," 1913–1914). The Zionist attitude to Jerusalem was ambivalent at that time. On the one hand, Jerusalem was the historical capital and the largest city in Palestine. On the other hand, it was an old city. Jaffa had gained cultural dominance (see Usishkin's expressions in Ben-Arieh, 1979, pp. 626–627). A proposal was raised to separate the new Jerusalem from the old, similar to the separation of Tel Aviv from Jaffa. Usishkin opposed this division, both because of the symbolism of the city and because Jews constituted a majority in the city as a whole (Ben-Arieh, 1979, pp. 624–625). Nevertheless, the centrality of Jerusalem for the new Zionist movement was expressed in the reference to the Land of Israel in the Zionist anthem as "the land of Zion and Jerusalem."

From the perspective of a central figure in modern cultural Jerusalem, Eliezer Ben-Yehuda, the situation looked like this:

The decisive power of the coastal city against the national sacredness of the ancient mother-city of the nation and the *competition* between these two cities were instantly revealed in their full power since the first step of the founders of the new Jewish community, and it became stronger and stronger from that moment as the new community advanced further. Jaffa became the activity center of the new community; for many years, 'Hovvei Zion' and the Zionists neglected *Zion* completely and almost erased it from their Land of Israel. A few—one was Moshe Leib Lilienblum—deliberately said that we had no need for Jerusalem and we would not miss anything if it would be forever a foreign lot. Only during the last few years before the outbreak of the war did the attitude of the Zionists toward Jerusalem turn slightly better; still, Jaffa stood like a competing wife to Jerusalem, and the *competition and jealousy* between them may not be over even now. (Quoted in Yaari, 1947, pp. 370–372)

It was thus a mixture of several elements that brought about the construction of a second Jewish cultural focus in the Land of Israel: the economic independence and flourishing of Jaffa in the mid-nineteenth century, its ties with the colonies of the First Aliya, and the influx of immigrants and their intellectual-secular ideas. Against these elements stood the conservatism of Jerusalem and its atmosphere and institutions in both religious-cultural and economic life.

Jerusalem and Tel Aviv

The establishment of the first *Hebrew* city was to a large degree an antithesis to *Jewish* Jerusalem. Several of the physical and social characteristics of the two cities have turned into metaphors in modern Hebrew literature: the mountainous city as static, closed, and conservative versus the coastal city as dynamic and open; the stones of Jerusalem as sacred and long standing compared to the Tel Aviv dynamic and secular sands. Similar metaphors apply, as well, to the social structure and to the histori-cal sediments of each city (Guvrin, 1989).

Meiron (1985) compared the cultural anchoring of Jerusalem authors like Agnon and Greenberg with that of Tel Aviv writers like Alterman and Schlonski. Agnon could not find substance in the externally oriented, easy-going atmosphere of Jaffa, whereas in Jerusalem he identified a difficult truth involving both holiness and the absurd. This truth of a renaissance without faith was, in Agnon's opinion, the tragic problematic of the construction genera-tion. Greenberg conceived of moving the accent from Jerusalem to Tel Aviv as treason to the redemption vision. He envisioned the humiliation of the mountainous city versus "Tel Kezar" (a foreign-like place) celebrating in the coast and disconnected from the his-torical continuum since the patriarch Abraham. Schlonski, in con-trast, established the distinction between the Jerusalem and Tel Aviv versions of domestic culture by employing a terminology orig-inally used for different versions of Jewish prayer. The Jerusalem version was typified by being static and sober; the Tel Aviv version presented dynamics and cheering. Jerusalem signified, in Schlonsky's opinion, the death of wisdom, whereas Tel Aviv marked its revival. Guri (1989) described a more balanced view of Jerusalem and Tel Aviv, in which the latter was dependent on the former. A direct comparison between the atmosphere in socially oppressive Jerusalem and open-minded Tel Aviv in the early twentieth century was portrayed in a short novel by Ben-Zion (Guvrin, 1989).

Schweid (1987) discussed the new connection that had been created between people and the material land, on the one hand, and the physical and political reconstruction of this land by the new Jewish community, on the other. This connection has served as an alternative ideal for the spiritual culture of the nation and the consciousness of the historical continuum. The old is symbolized by Jerusalem, the new by Tel Aviv. Right with the establishment of the "Ahuzat-Bayit" society for the construction of Tel Aviv, the image was raised of the new city as a New York for the Land of Israel. In a brochure prepared in 1906, A. A. Weiss, one of its founders, described the new city: "As much as the city of New York signifies the central entrance gate to America, so we have to build our city, and it will become one day an [Land of] Israeli New York" (Weiss, 1957, p. 17).

The three main decisions and events that determined the status of Jerusalem in the modern era could not decisively turn things around in its struggle with Tel Aviv. The declaration of Jerusalem as capital by the British in 1924 occurred when Tel Aviv already had a status of its own, functioned separately from Jaffa, and (jointly with Jaffa) was larger than Jerusalem. The second decision was the declaration of Jerusalem as capital of the newly born State of Israel in May 1948. The previous year, the Zionist leadership had agreed to an internationalization of Jerusalem as part of a partition plan for Palestine, a decision that was in contradiction to Jewish public opinion and, therefore, was changed in 1948 (Bialer, 1985). Following its redeclaration as the capital, Jerusalem found itself located on an isolated edge of the state, almost completely surrounded by West Bank Jordan. At the same time, Tel Aviv prospered as the cultural capital of the new Israel. Mountainous and isolated Jerusalem versus the coastal core even provided some distorted retrospective views. Thus, Ben-Gurion declared in 1948: "King David chose for his capital one of the most difficult places in the country" (Ben-Gurion, 1969, p. 195). As previously noted, circumstances were different when the Jewish core was mountainous.

The third decision was the unification of West and East

Jerusalem, following the war in June 1967. This happened when Tel Aviv was already a metropolitan area. Moreover, processes since 1967 have brought cultural relations between the two cities to a modern version of the starting point in the 1880s. Ben-Arieh (1979, pp. 628–629) viewed the post-1967 status of Jerusalem as a return to its late nineteenth century "Jewish prestigious status." The city turned into a banner of Zionism and became attractive once again, though this time at the historical-national rather than the religious level. A modern version of the late nineteenth century status, however, has also implied a return to the competitve tension between Jerusalem and Tel Aviv.

Several aspects have resurfaced. Jerusalem has again become a large city, though not the largest metropolitan area in the country. It is once again cosmopolitan, in terms of its attraction to pilgrims and visitors of various religions and countries. Then, too, a major transportation change took place, similar to the introduction of the railway and the road in the nineteenth century. The opening of the expressway between Jerusalem and Tel Aviv and its feeder roads has brought the two cities closer to each other in an unprecedented way. The contact between Jews and Arabs that was typical of Jerusalem was renewed, too, both for the better and for the worse. Furthermore, a nearly complete freedom of ritual for all religions was established although the ultraorthodox Jews, continuing the tradition of the old Jewish community, have turned into a large, influential community in several respects. The increased receptiveness of Israeli society to the Western world following the 1967 war has found Tel Aviv as constantly absorbing first waves of imported culture. The city has also turned more and more into a focus of commerce, finance, and modern international business. These aspects illustrate a new version of the late nineteenth century Jerusalem and Jaffa and the struggle between them. Though the struggles over cultural uniqueness this time have not been as fierce and prominent as those 100 years ago, they still can be expressed boldly (see, e.g., Meiron, 1985; Ophir, 1985; Benvenisti, 1981; Ben-Azar, 1989).

It should be noted at this point that several aspects relating to the spatial organization of the two cities reflect their images and their population structure (see also Kiryati, 1986). Tel Aviv has been built on an almost flat topography, so that its spatial presence has been achieved through urban density and high-rise construction. The originally bright colors of most buildings have gradually turned to grey through air pollution generated by cars. The original external painting of many buildings have peeled-off, making several parts of the city look old and faded. On the other hand, the presence of Jerusalem has been attained by its topographical altitude relative to the Jewish core along the coastal plain. The restrictions on high-rise construction and the universal stone covering of both old and new buildings provide some homogeneity to the city, despite its diversification in both population and physical structure. This uniformity has also been responsible for the unique color of the city, ranging from white to gold. The Jerusalem physical landscape has become, for many, an indispensable element of the spirituality of the city and its symbolism, as expressed in the modern almost-anthem, "Jerusalem of Gold." Nevertheless, these landscape and colors were also viewed negatively by a Tel Aviv poet: "In Jerusalem, a city in which there is plenty of dimness and plenty of decoration, it has nothing immediate and direct" (Kalderon, see Meiron, 1985).

Heterogenous Jerusalem enjoys a *symbolic* center, which radiates to the whole city: the old city and its striking walls. The old city was preserved by the British, Jordanians, and Israelis alike (Kruyanker, 1988), except for some destruction suffered during wars. This center has no physical and functional contact with the daily tasks of the city, whether as a capital (government, parliament, supreme court), a spiritual city (The Hebrew University and most rabbinical academies and research institutions), or a central city (modern commercial centers, industrial areas). Tel Aviv lacks such a clear center. The city, rather, has several central business districts (CBDs), none of them predominating. Formally the city has two CBDs (Allenby and Diesengoff), but practically several other foci exist, as well (Haqirya, the diamond center). The city in general has a much more diffused character than does Jerusalem. Both cities have recently undergone major "greening" efforts, in the form of parks, trees, and flowers planted by their respective energetic mayors.

The new city of Jerusalem was built around separate neighborhoods, reflecting its social-religious composition (Kark, 1976, p. 148; Ben-Arieh, 1979). These sections were built in a fingerlike manner along the major ranges. Nevertheless, the character of the city as a condensed polity has been preserved even without any building in the narrow valleys separating the several ranges (Kruyanker, 1988). In Tel Aviv, in contrast, the low, elongated sandstone (Kurkar) hills cannot provide for a directed expansion of the city; consequently, it has developed along major transportation axes, and the areas between them were built later on. Construction was not usually carried out by social organizations as has frequently been the case in Jerusalem but, rather, by private developers on a profit basis (Amiran and Shachar, 1959). Paradoxically, metropolitan Tel Aviv consists of forty-one municipalities; the many sections of Jerusalem, even before the 1967 war, have constituted just one municipality. Following the war, several large sections with heterogenous social structures were built, and transitions in this direction have also developed in more veteran parts of the city (Hasson, 1987). The geographical and social composition of Jerusalem put the family-apartment and the neighborhood at the center of social life, compared to the metropolitan culture of Tel Aviv (Meiron, 1985; Benvenisti, 1981; Hasson, 1987).

Jerusalem and Tel Aviv reflect contemporary cultural conflicts within Israeli society, whose tension presents a more mature, modern version of the late-nineteenth century struggles. Meiron (1985) noted that the four basic conflicts in Israeli society are reflected in Jerusalem: at the religious level, secular Jews against the ultraorthodox; ethnically, Sephardic versus Ashkenazic Jews; in the political arena, the Right contrasting with the Left; and at the national level, Jews confronting Arabs. Meiron thought that these social sections in Jerusalem have fought for the "creation of facts" by using aggressive, ugly methods. Tel Aviv, in contrast, has introduced "the eternal fight for property, status, success, and benefit." "Contemporary Tel Aviv, as against Jerusalem, is a soft and acquiescent city, a coastal city—almost a Riviera." The very fact that the capital city, Jerusalem, displays a magnified microcosmos of national life is not unique; so does Washington, D.C. Nevertheless, Meiron's distinction between Jerusalem and Tel Aviv, as well as its verbal expression, are of deeper significance.

In Tel Aviv competition is mainly interpersonal; in Jerusalem, it has been more intersectoral. Tel Aviv-style interpersonal competition for property, status, success, and benefit is not unique for Israel; thus it has constituted several elements of Western competition. It presents a capitalist struggle for property, capital, and power. It further shows elements of pluralism and individual liberties while preserving an urban anonymity. It might even display some Christian elements in regard to the centrality of individuality. Tel Aviv competition is not expressed politically in demonstrations, public power fights, and media news coverage. On the other hand, it does have striking spatial manifestations. This is a competition for prestigious residences and prominent construction designs, for luxurious stores with status names, for good restaurants and entertainment centers, and so forth. Jerusalem competition, on the other hand, is not only a microcosmos of national differences and sectors; it also has a Jewish character, in that it has emphasized the collectivity and various forms of togetherness. Its expression is, therefore, of a more political-social nature than spatial-exhibitionist. This distinction between the two cities is far from being exclusive, as Tel Aviv presents intersectoral differences between its wealthy, mainly Ashkenazic northern sections and its poorer, mostly Sephardic southern neighborhoods. It has, furthermore, served as the location for several large, decisive political demonstrations.

Tel Aviv presents in its current cultural atmosphere a new Zionist-national priority of objectives, Jerusalem presents an older priority. The Tel Aviv order is the *social Zionism* described at the end of the previous part. It is topped by a new mode of life emphasizing individuals and their rights, cultural and social pluralism, religious freedom, and a consumer culture. This mode of life has been adopted by the Left, which formerly adhered to socialism. The locus of the modern Hebrew culture, which was developed mainly by the Left, has recently turned away from the cooperative village to the large, coastal city; the latter actually has served as a joint locus for this culture since the 1880s.

In Jerusalem, the renewed focus on mode of life had nothing to do with values originating in the rural cooperative sector. It was a reaction to values represented most strongly by the growing ultraorthodox community and that threatened secular Jews. This new version of the struggle of the old versus the new has been reinforced by the increased power of the coastal focus; namely, Tel Aviv. Its most frequent expression has come in the form of repeated debates, demonstrations, and acts concerning the public celebration and observance of the Jewish Sabbath, the focus being placed especially on forms of public entertainment (e.g., cinemas) and on traffic (in ultraorthodox neighborhoods). An even more central issue that has been presented by Jerusalem since 1967 is territorial, in the form of municipal unification. The problems that have accompanied this step, in terms of Jewish-Arab relations as well as in terms of city development and expansion, have become more prominent than any other issue. This was the case long before the outbreak of the Palestinian Intifada. The unification of Jerusalem has been part of the Jewish national consensus; the Palestinians, too, consider the city the capital of the West Bank and their Palestine. Putting territory at the top of the national priority has been a classic Zionist approach. This "territorial Zionism" (which is consensual for Jerusalem, and rightist for the occupied territories in general) points to the major issue on the political agenda of Israel at large: relations with the Palestinians and the future status of the occupied territories.

Tel Aviv presents some of the challenges *contemporary* Israeli society is facing: in the economic sphere, it is international business, information and service economics; culturally, the openness for universal culture and current social trends. Jerusalem, on the other hand, emphasizes the *basic*, deeper facets of Israeli life; namely, the attitude to tradition, social composition, territorial extent, and relations with the Arabs. This difference, coupled with Tel Aviv's emphasis on personal-economic competition as against the more sectoral emphasis in Jerusalem, creates images of pragmatism and softness for Tel Aviv and of stiffness and violence for Jerusalem. In the somewhat coarse language of theater director Omri Nitzan: "[Jerusalem] is like between the fingers of God. Tel Aviv is like the arm-pit of the world" (Bretzki, 1988).

Once again, this distinction between the two cities is not clear cut. Jerusalem houses several powerful institutions of immense importance for the emergence of contemporary culture in Tel Aviv, notably the Knesset, the supreme court, and state radio and television. On the other hand, one of the larger suburbs of Tel Aviv, Bnai-Braq, has become a center of ultraorthodox Jewry, despite its obvious inferiority compared to the holy city, Jerusalem. Both Tel Aviv and Jerusalem have developed into learning centers although those in Jerusalem focus mainly on research and Judaic learning. This tendency intensified following the 1967 war, when Jerusalem became a world center for all branches of Judaism. In Tel Aviv, learning institutions have concentrated more on professional education as well as on modern culture and literature. The cultural centers of Tel Aviv are consumer oriented, whereas in the capital Jerusalem, the state is more prominent in daily life (Fischer, 1988).

Cultural loyalty and devotion to Tel Aviv by writers and poets have led to attempts at its "secular sanctification." Meiron (1985) likened Tel Aviv to the old Jewish community in nineteenth century Palestine, and to one of its later centers, Me'a She'arim in Jerusalem.

> The contemporary "old community" is that veteran Israeli community that still guards most of its pre-1967 ways of thought and conduct. In Jerusalem these ways are like obsolete history; in Tel Aviv, they are characteristic not merely of a large stratum of the adult population...but also of a younger population.... Hence, Tel Aviv is gradually turning into what Me'a She'arim used to be in the past—a socio- historical reserve.

Furthermore, "Israeli literature is the spiritual expression of the Israeli 'old community', and [this community] constitutes for it what the Talmud did for the ultraorthodox old community." Hasson (1987) saw here expressions of a "Tel Aviv hot secular faith," bold and intolerant as a religious faith. He noted the problems involved in an attempt to create a sanctification and mystification of spaces within a humanistic-secular context. It might well be, however, that the spatial element in Zionism is so immense that even an extremely secular writer has to resort to religious terms and images to portray the cultural core.

In summary, Jerusalem is a city that has been conceived of as a vertical cosmos because of its continuous importance over time. It is a city displaying an orthogenetic culture, in the preservation, restoration, and renovation of ancient traditions. As such it is an integral part of the Israeli-Jewish iconography. Tel Aviv, for its part, presents a horizontal spatial conception of new and secular landscapes and symbols. As such it constitutes an informal component of Israeli society. The city parades a heterogenetic culture, of heresy with regard to the old side by side with diversified, innovative facets. Nineteenth century Jerusalem was a cosmopolitan city at the religious level, though of a conservative and an unproductive nature. Opposing it, a secular Jewish focus evolved in Jaffa, influenced by immigrants from Europe and economic prosperity. Jerusalem underwent modernization processes that originated mainly within the city, albeit slower and later than Jaffa. The mutual reinforcement between Jaffa and the new colonies, which did not exist for Jerusalem, brought about a cultural flourishing on the coast and culminated in the separation of Hebrew Tel Aviv from ethnically mixed Jaffa. All three crucial events or decisions affecting Jerusalem in the twentieth century—the declaration of Jerusalem as capital, first by the British and later by Israel, and the unification of the city in 1967—found Tel Aviv in a position of economic and population superiority. Furthermore, the unification of Jerusalem and its subsequent growth led to a repeated version of its struggle with Tel Aviv–Jaffa. The city once again has become a religious cosmopolitan center, and again it was well connected by road with Tel Aviv. It turned once more into a mixed Jewish-Arab city with a growing ultraorthodox population.

The two cities have developed unique features. Physically, they were characterized by color, skyline, and structure. Socially, Tel Aviv has exhibited interpersonal struggles of an economic nature and an accent on the contemporary, the open, the pluralistic, and the global. Jerusalem has projected the deep, the eternal,

and the problematic in Israeli public life and culture. One consequence has been some alienation toward the city, similar to tendencies during the turn of the present century. Tel Aviv-style trends,
however, may be noticed in Jerusalem and vice versa.

As in the late nineteenth century, the current cultural portrait
of Tel Aviv is highly interrelated with its economic status. The
next section will be devoted to processes of economic specialization
in Tel Aviv and Jerusalem and their relationship to cultural
aspects.

Economic Specializations
in Tel Aviv and Jerusalem

The previous sections have described Jaffa and then Tel Aviv
as cities that served as the economic leading edge of, first, Palestine
and, later, Israel. This function emerged with their evolution as the
core for modern Land of Israel in the last quarter of the nineteenth
century. Jerusalem, on the other hand, was shown to be a double-
function city: holy city and capital. As such, it dates back 3000
years. This section will review these functions from the perspective
of economic specializations. Tel Aviv will be described as a "world
city," leading in economic functions typical of the late twentieth
century: high-tech industries (sharing this with Haifa), computers,
telecommunications, and the evolution of a modern service economy. Jerusalem, on the other hand, will be seen to specialize in public services, spiritual life, and international tourism. The direction
of the following discussions will thus be a comparison between the
two cities, and only scant attention will be given to a more general
analysis of modern economic specializations (on this topic see, e.g.,
Kellerman, 1984a; 1985b).

Tel Aviv: Transition Toward a Postindustrial Economy

Metropolitan Tel Aviv has been undergoing post-industrial
processes in several respects. First, its population has expanded into
a number of suburban rings and even into an exurban ring
(Krakover, 1985; Kellerman, 1985c; 1987). Second, the urban economy is based largely on a culture of mass consumption; in other
words, an attachment to contemporary Western culture. Third,
employment in Tel Aviv has moved from a concentration in classic

manufacturing and public services to accents on high-tech industries and producer services in areas such as computers, telecommunications, and business (with consequent commercial and lodging services). The discussion here will focus on employment; but as the elaboration on world cities will show, new employment trends are interrelated with a certain sociocultural atmosphere.

The evolution of a global economy began to be noted in the early 1970s. The term relates to the increasing economic interrelationships among countries all across the globe, but especially in the world cores (North America, Western Europe, and the Pacific Rim) and in newly industrialized countries (NICs; mainly in the Pacific Rim). These increased interrelationships relate not only to commercial ties but also to a new international division of labor for economic activities. Within this framework, multinational companies have grown and distributed their activities, so that their headquarters are located in several major cities; research and development (R&D) activities tend to locate in developed countries, mass production is in NICs (Shachar, 1987). This division has brought about growth in advanced services in the areas of R&D, business, law, advertising, computers, and so on in major cities (Cohen, 1981). The evolution of the global economy has largely been related to technological developments in production, transportation, communications, control and administration.

Activities related to the domination of technology tend to be concentrated in cities in the developed world, which, as a result, specialize in such domination (Knight and Gappert, 1984, p. 67). These activities have contributed greatly to the evolution of postindustrial societies, coupled with a massive development of public (health and education) as well as personal (especially recreation) services (Kellerman, 1985b).

The cities that serve as locations for the headquarters of several multinational corporations are called *world cities*. These cities are marked by their advanced services and a special structure of their service economy (which will be discussed later). World cities enjoy, furthermore, some unique social characteristics: "ideas, people, and products circulate [there] with relative freedom, [where] people from other countries are given respect and a sense of dignity, are seen as individuals, and [where] there is a willingness to bring to that city the best of the world, including what the city itself has, building on the city's own strengths" (Perlmutter, 1979). In other words, a cosmopolitan environment of people, ideas, and products.

Several simple and clear classifications for world cities have been proposed, based on updated data for the largest corporations worldwide. Knight and Gappert (1984) used *Forbes* data, and Tel Aviv was one of their world cities (probably because of the location there of the headquarters of Israel's two largest banks, Bank Leumi and Bank Hapoalim). Harper (1987) used the *Fortune 500* data for 1984, and Tel Aviv was included (again, because of the two leading banks and Koor Corp. conglomerate).

Israel is thus numbered among a relatively small number of countries that contain a city that serves as a focus for multinational activity and permits the evolution of technological and postindustrial activities. As in most world-city countries, Israel has only one world city defined by economic criteria. These observations have several geographical implications for modern trends in the Israeli urban system, as far as high-tech industries, computers, telecommunications, and service economies. We will examine the possibility that Jerusalem is also a world city, but in a different sense. First, however, some attention has to be given to those modern components of the urban system that are heavily concentrated in world cities: high-tech industries, computers, telecommunications, and service economies.

High-tech industries are considered footloose; that is, their location is not tied to inflexible locational factors, such as energy sources, topography, or raw materials. Sometimes it seems as though this quality means that high-tech industries may locate anywhere within or outside the urban system. As several studies have shown, however, high-tech industries have their own locational factors within the context of an urban system, and they even require some siting factors for their locations inside the city. The most crucial locational factor is the availability of professional personnel; followed, in decreasing order of importance, by labor cost, regional taxation level, proximity to academic institutions, living costs, transportation, access to markets, regional control policy, energy costs, cultural opportunities, climate, and access to raw materials (Glasmeier, Hall, and Markusen, 1983; Premus, 1983).

These factors are at play in Israel, as well. Thus, most of the high-tech industries are located in the vicinity of Tel Aviv and Haifa; in Tel Aviv, however, they have also located throughout its urban field. Tel Aviv enjoys some priority in this area, although not a decisive one. In his study of Israeli high-tech industries, Felsenstein (1986) proposed viewing subsectors 20–28 of the standard industrial classification as high-tech branches. These consisted of the following industries: chemical products, mineral products, basic metals, metal products, machinery, electric and electronic equipment, transport vehicles, and miscellaneous. When the percentage employment in these industries was computed for each region in 1982 (Central Bureau of Statistics, 1985), Haifa subdistrict was found to have a high percentage (circa 74 percent), and its adjacent subdistricts had high percentages, as well (Jezreel 50 percent and Acre about 42 percent). An absolutely high number of employees in these industries was found only in Haifa. In the central area, the largest number of workers in these industries, in absolute values, was found in the subdistrict of Tel Aviv. In percentages, however, suburban Ramla had the lead (84 percent), followed by suburban Petah Tiqva (about 52 percent), Tel Aviv (46.5 percent), and suburban Rehovot (44.4 percent). In other parts of the country, including Jerusalem, both the absolute and the relative values were low.

If one isolates electric and electronic industries as the leading high-tech fields it will be seen that Haifa led nationally (with about 29 percent of those employed in these industries), followed by Tel Aviv (circa 22 percent), Petah Tiqva (nearly 17 percent), and Ramla (about 14 percent). In other words, the geographical expansion of these industries around Tel Aviv was much more extensive than around Haifa (the Jezreel and Acre subdistricts each had 1.3 percent of the total national employment in these industries). In Jerusalem, the numbers were small; in Beersheba, there were none at all. As a total, then, some 60 percent of the employment in electronics in Israel is concentrated in metropolitan Tel Aviv; and some additional 30 percent is employed in greater Haifa. The still small, but growing, high-tech industries in Jerusalem were located there with governmental assistance; further, they received producer services (accounting, advertising, marketing, etc.) from Tel Aviv (Felsenstein, 1988). Felsenstein (1986) also showed that this concentration trend has persisted since the early 1970s. Moreover, his findings showed that more scientists were employed in the metropolitan areas; the early phases of the product cycle; namely, R&D, preferred a metropolitan location.

Data on the computer industry (including production, sales, services, etc.) show 502 companies in this area in Israel in 1983; of these, 341, or 68 percent, were located in metropolitan Tel Aviv, 62 (or about 12 percent) in metropolitan Haifa, and just 41 (or about 8 percent), in Jerusalem (Salomon and Razin, 1985). The gap between the percentage of employment in Tel Aviv in the production phase and the number of computer companies located there points to the increased importance of Tel Aviv in computer services rather than in production. This concentration of computer services in Tel Aviv is manifested more prominently when the distribution of computers and computer workers is examined (see Tables 5.1 and 5.2).

Tel Aviv led in all computer sizes in 1980 (the last year for which the Central Bureau of Statistics published data on this subject). As Salomon and Razin (1985) showed, this trend had been a continuous one since 1965. By 1980, about 45 percent of all computers in Israel were to be found in the Tel Aviv district (which in the case of Tel Aviv is the same as the subdistrict of Tel Aviv). An additional 9 percent were located in the Central district. As the size of computers grew, the dominance of Tel Aviv grew, as well: here were to be found over 70 percent of all giant and large computers in the country, more than 50 percent of all medium and small computers, and over 40 percent of all mini computers. Jerusalem was second in the number of giant and large computers, though their number was between a fifth and a quarter of those located in Tel Aviv. In Jerusalem, these computers reflected the city's seniority in governmental administration and university research. Haifa's share was larger than that of Jerusalem in medium, micro, and mini computers, reflecting its leading position in industrial research and development and its higher consumer income level.

The geographical distribution of computer workers (Table 5.2), highlights Tel Aviv's predominance in the industry. About 63 percent of all computer operations employment in 1980 was concentrated in the Tel Aviv district and an additional 4 percent was located in the Central district. In other words, the location of computers and, even more so, the location of employment in computer operations were concentrated in Tel Aviv proper and within the inner ring of the metropolitan area; only a little was dispersed to the external ring. The supremacy of Tel Aviv in computer employment results from the concentration of computer businesses, headquarters of computer companies, and service companies in that city. Furthermore, many companies (such as credit card companies) perform national batching operations in Tel Aviv. Hence, although Tel Aviv's share of all levels of computer workers ranged from 55–59 percent, it reached 70 percent among nonprofessional employees.

The data on computer employment in Jerusalem raises an interesting point. The total number of computers in the Jerusalem district was about half the figure for Haifa (8.9 percent and 17.4 percent, respectively); however, the total number of computer workers was much higher in Jerusalem (16.9 percent versus 10.4 percent for Haifa). Lastly, the total number of computers in

Table 5.1. Geographical Distribution of Computers in Israel, End of 1980

	TOTAL		COMPUTER SIZE					
DISTRICT	NUMBER	PERCENT	GIANT	LARGE	MEDIUM	MINI	MICRO
Jerusalem	136	8.9	3	4	10	35	84
North	185	12.1	—	—	2	19	164
Haifa	266	17.4	1	2	15	48	200
Center	136	8.9	1	1	4	21	109
Tel Aviv	690	45.2	12	20	48	153	457
South	113	7.4	—	—	5	15	93
Total	1526	100.0	17	27	84	291	1107

Source: Central Bureau of Statistics, 1984.

Table 5.2. Geographical Distribution of Employees in Computer Operations in Israel, End of 1980

| DISTRICT | TOTAL | | NON-PROFESSIONALS | MANAGERS AND TEAM HEADS | SYSTEM ANALYSTS AND SCIENTISTS | PROGRAMMERS | OPERATORS |
	NUMBER	PERCENT					
Jerusalem	1742	16.9	776	152	218	310	286
North	234	2.3	77	16	19	36	86
Haifa	1067	10.4	413	90	149	197	218
Center	424	4.1	113	36	46	82	147
Tel Aviv	6457	62.8	3324	412	564	970	1187
South	356	3.5	74	19	33	47	183
Total	10,280	100.0	4777	725	1029	1642	2107

Source: Central Bureau of Statistics, 1984.

Jerusalem and the Center district was equal although the number of workers in Jerusalem was four times that of the Center (16.9 percent as against 4.1 percent). Two factors may shed some light on these differentials. First, there were more giant and large computers in Jerusalem than in either Haifa or the Center district, and these require more workers. This point may also provide some explanation for Tel Aviv's lead in computer employment. An additional factor relates to the fact that most computers in Jerusalem are used by the public sector, in which personnel costs are lower but employment is more extensive.

The area of telecommunications exhibits wide spatial gaps in Israel. In 1982, Isranet started operations as a data communication system for both domestic and international uses. By 1986, the number of lines in the system amounted to 641. At the same time the fax technology was introduced and the subscribers for this service reached 990 in 1986, growing swiftly to 12,000 in 1990. The geographical distribution of these two means of telecommunications was examined in comparison with the distribution of telephone lines, population, and industrial plants (Table 5.3). The share of the Tel Aviv and Central districts of these two services was even larger than their share of telephone lines, reaching 70 percent in fax and 64 percent in computer communications, compared with 56 percent in telephone lines. Striking was the larger share enjoyed by Jerusalem and the South in computer communications, compared to Haifa and the North; in fax communications, the situation was the reverse. This trend might have to do with the larger concentration of computers in Jerusalem, on the one hand, and the larger industrial concentration in Haifa. The city of Tel Aviv alone counted some 44 percent of all Israeli fax subscribers, the percentage climbing to 67 percent in the metropolitan area. Metropolitan Haifa had 9 percent and Jerusalem less than 7 percent of all fax subscribers. Tel Aviv's leadership in the use of these then-innovative technologies of telecommunications was, thus, prominent.

The development of new technologies for production, computing, and communication has been related to the evolution of service economies, based on innovative producer services and enhanced, sophisticated public services, especially in health and education. A comparative study of major European cities, mostly world cities, found a high rate of workers in finance and business, usually around 50–60 percent of those nationally employed in these areas (Illeris, 1987). This study further showed that the concentration of employment in these fields in major cities did not increase during the 1970s and 1980s. Another study, which compared London to

Table 5.3. Distribution of Computer Communications and Fax Lines versus Telephone Lines, Population, and Industrial Plants, 1984–1986

DISTRICTS	FAX SUB-SCRIBERS, 1986	PERCENT	ISRANET SUB-SCRIBERS 1986	PERCENT	TELE-PHONE LINES IN THOU., 1986	PERCENT	POPU-LATION IN THOU., 1985	PERCENT	INDUSTRIAL PLANTS, 1984	PERCENT
Haifa and North	167	16.9	70	10.9	282.4	23.4	1,299.4	30.8	1835	28.2
Tel Aviv and Center	689	69.6	408	63.7	675.5	55.9	1,904.4	45.1	3756	58.1
Jerusalem and South	134	13.5	163	25.4	250.4	20.7	1,016.3	24.1	888	13.7
Total	990	100.0	641	100.0	1208.3	100.0	4,220.1	100.0	6469	100.0

Sources: ISRANET, 1986; Bezek, 1986a, 1986b; Central Bureau of Statistics, 1986.

all other British cities, claimed that the predominance of London in information-related employment will be preserved, for several reasons: (1) The savings gained from a peripheral location are smaller than are the expenses for telecommunications and computers, so that leaving the city is restricted to a radius of about 100 km. (2) Information employment located in the periphery is sensitive to structural changes; for example, the possible higher capacity of central-city management in the furure. (3) The process of the internationalization of information services, especially for multinational corporations and financial services, will prefer the large city. World cities will, thus, amplify their dominance, and the periphery in a national space economy will undergo additional peripherilization. (4) The public sector may also undergo a process of increased center domination through new technologies (Hepworth, Green, and Gillespie, 1987).

Within world cities, both conflicting and parallel processes take place. On the one hand, the CBDs become stronger and more specialized. Noyelle and Stanback (1984) showed that the headquarters of corporations were largely dependent on advanced producer services (in finances, legal services, accounting, management, consulting, and advertising), and these are located mostly in the CBDs. Sassen-Koob (1985) noted that the employment structure in world cities is dichotomic; in other words, a considerable concentration of professional workers are found in management functions, and workers with lower capabilities are concentrated in catering, lodging, tourism, entertainment, and personal services. On the other hand, a suburbanization trend has evolved for activities that used to be located in the CBD, mainly retail and wholesale trade and back offices (Phillips and Vidal, 1983; Kellerman, 1983).

The data for Tel Aviv reveal its character as a world city along the lines described (Figure 5.1). The percentage of employment in the city, of the national totals, in the areas of finance and business reached 57 percent during 1972–1973. This percentage later dropped and amounted to 44.7 by 1986. The figures here relate to Tel Aviv proper rather than to the metropolitan area, so that the concentration rates for Tel Aviv are similar for those in other world cities. Second to business and finance was the lodging industry, of which about one-third of the national employment in this industry was found in Tel Aviv in the early 1970s. In this area, too, the Tel Aviv percentage declined during the 1980s; but even by 1986, the rate was still high, standing at 26.2 percent. Personal as well as public services are less important for a world city than are the first two service areas. Employment in personal services in

Tel Aviv, which was always higher than in public services, amounted to 18.2 percent of the national total in 1986, compared to only 12.5 percent in public services. The decline in employment concentration in Tel Aviv for all service types stems both from suburbanization processes and from the increased importance of Jerusalem in public service employment.

The several parameters relative to technological innovations discussed so far—computers, computer companies, computer communications, fax, finance, and lodging services—have shown Tel Aviv's superiority in most of these areas. In the area of the production of electric and electronic equipment, Tel Aviv shares the lead with Haifa, although the share of metropolitan Tel Aviv was larger than that of Haifa. Tel Aviv dominates Israeli information and service economies. In the past, only the headquarters of the largest banks were located here; the more recent closing of local and regional banks and the development of national financial and business companies have turned Tel Aviv into a much stronger financial center. The growth of national and international industrial companies as well as the increased international activities of Israeli banks, further added to this supremacy enjoyed by Tel Aviv and to its integration into the system of world cities.

The development of Tel Aviv as a world city and as the focus for Israel's modern information economy has been related to the social-cultural characteristics of the city. Perlmutter's (1979) definition of a world city emphasized the cosmopolitan nature of such a city, its cultural openness and pluralism, coupled with its cultural uniqueness. Tel Aviv has grown into such a city in its mode of life.

Jerusalem: Capitalness and Historical Holiness

The economic specialization of Jerusalem is a direct outcome of its double function as capital and holy city of cultural and historical importance. The examination of such an economic specialization requires the use of several types of data. Therefore, employment in public services may reflect the city as a capital; whereas data on domestic and international tourism in the city, on research and study institutes in various cultural and religious directions, and on the number of rabbinical colleges in the city show aspects related to its holiness.

Figure 5.2 presents the shares of Jerusalem and Tel Aviv of the total national employment in public services (suburban Tel Aviv is excluded for lack of data). It might well be that the number

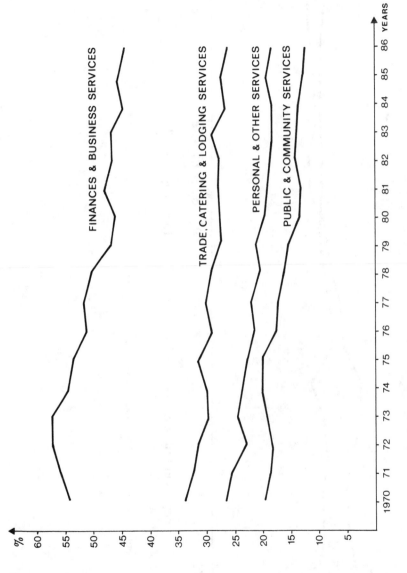

Figure 5.1. Employees in Services in Tel Aviv, 1969–1986 (as Percent of National Totals)

Data source: Central Bureau of Statistics, 1965–1988.

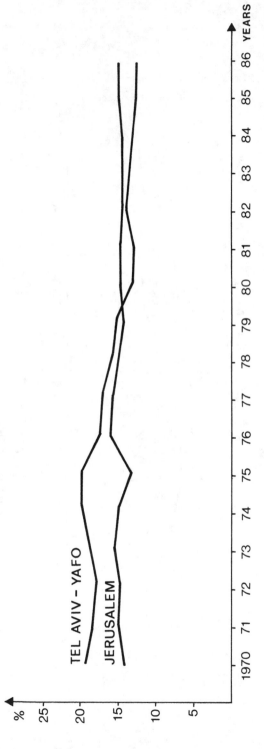

Figure 5.2. Employees in Public Services in Tel Aviv–Jaffa and Jerusalem, 1970–1986 (as Percent of National Totals)

Data source: Central Bureau of Statistics, 1965–1988.

of public service employees in metropolitan Tel Aviv was larger than that in Jerusalem, given the differences in population size; however, the concentration of several governmental offices in Tel Aviv, as well as the labor union, the settlement organizations, the political parties, and so forth, calls for such a comparison.

Only as of 1980 did the share of Jerusalem of the total national service employment become larger than that of Tel Aviv. In 1986, 15 percent of all Israeli public service workers worked in Jerusalem, compared with 12.5 percent in Tel Aviv. As may be noted from Figure 5.1, the concentration of public services in Tel Aviv was the lowest of all service types, and this was so from 1970 on (see Kellerman, 1986a). The popular image of Jerusalem as a city of bureaucracy became meaningful only in the 1980s, when Jerusalem assumed the leading role in public service employment.

Several reasons may be noted for the growth in public service employment in Jerusalem and for its decline in the city of Tel Aviv. First, the city of Tel Aviv has lost population continuously since 1964 (though its metrpolitan area has grown tremendously), whereas Jerusalem has grown continuously, especially since 1967 (and despite a negative migration balance in recent years). Second, the late 1970s marked the opening of the expressway between Jerusalem and Tel Aviv, which more easily permitted one to reside in metropolitan Tel Aviv and work in Jerusalem, as indeed a larger part of the political elite does (Benvenisti, 1981). Third, the Likud administration speeded up the process of moving governmental offices from Tel Aviv to Jerusalem, particularly to East Jerusalem.

Similar to its late specialization in public services, Jerusalem reached national supremacy in international tourism relatively late; namely, in the early 1970s. An analysis of tourism in Jerusalem reveals once again its cultural relations with Tel Aviv, as tourism may reflect a city's attractive power in business, entertainment, and culture. Figure 5.3 presents the number of nights spent by foreign and domestic tourists in tourism hotels in Jerusalem and Tel Aviv from 1969-1986. The general trends of growth and decline are similar in both cities, this phenomenon reflecting both national and international factors, which are beyond the scope of our discussion here. There are, however, two important dates regarding tourism in Jerusalem *per se* and its relation to tourism in Tel Aviv.

In 1971, Jerusalem for the first time attained superiority over Tel Aviv in international tourism, and thus became nationally the leading city in this area; in 1979, it lost its long seniority in domestic tourism in favor of Tel Aviv. This leading role held by Jerusalem

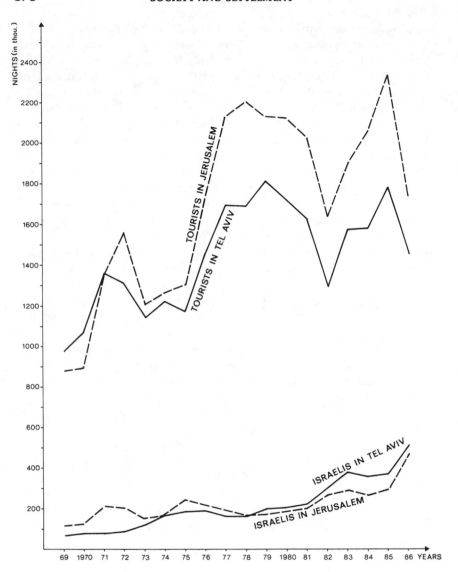

Figure 5.3.   Bed Nights in Tourist Hotels in Jerusalem and
Tel Aviv, 1969–1986 (Israelis and Tourists)

Data source: Central Bureau of Statistics, 1965–1988.

has been a direct result of the 1967 war and the resulting unification of the city. Until 1971, there were more tourist hotel rooms in
East Jerusalem than in the western part of the city. The fast construction of hotels in West Jerusalem after the war made it possible

for the city to surpass Tel Aviv in attracting foreign tourists. In other words, the function of West Jerusalem as the capital of Israel until 1967 did not give it any advantage, either over Tel Aviv or over Jordanian East Jerusalem, so long as it was separated from the historical-religious core in the old city. Opening the old city to Jewish tourists through the unification of the city and the construction of hotels in West Jerusalem not only turned Jerusalem into the leader in international tourism in Israel; it also changed the character of the city. For a while, too, at least until the 1973 war, it increased the gap between Jerusalem and Tel Aviv in domestic tourism in favor of Jerusalem.

By the end of the decade, however, Tel Aviv surpassed Jerusalem in Israeli tourism for the first time, and has since remained as the more preferred touristic city for Israelis. Simultaneously, an increasing gap has evolved between the two cities in attracting foreign visitors. Generally, as foreign tourism has increased in Jerusalem, domestic tourism has grown in Tel Aviv. The loss of Jerusalem's supremacy in domestic tourism may be attributed to several factors. A major reason is the crystallization of the cultural difference between the two cities. Tel Aviv, the worldly city, offers modern entertainment, in form of the beach and its promenade, theaters, high-class shopping, and so on. The rise of a hedonistic life-style in Israeli society has given a higher priority to Tel Aviv as a center of leisure and recreation. On the other hand, contemporary Jerusalem, with its large and constantly increasing variety of reconstructed archaeological sites and museums, offers the Israeli visitor a completely different experience. This difference has been coupled to a growing distinction in the social composition and character of the two cities: Jerusalem has increased its ultraorthodox population and Tel Aviv has become more and more secular.

Despite these differences, Tel Aviv attracts fewer foreign visitors, perhaps because cities like Tel Aviv can be found in their home countries. Historical and religious Jerusalem proves more attractive, a fact manifested not just in general tourism but also in professional tourism, as shown by the data on international conferences in Tel Aviv and Jerusalem (Table 5.4). Tel Aviv, however, is the leader in conducting the travel business through travel agencies, which deal mainly with outgoing tourism and business tourism. Thus, in 1984, there were 450 travel agencies in Israel, 40 percent of which were located in Tel Aviv and less than 15 percent in Jerusalem (with over a half of the latter in East Jerusalem!) (G. Cohen, 1988).

Table 5.4.   International Conferences in Jerusalem
and Tel Aviv, 1976–1986

YEAR	JERUSALEM	PERCENT OF ISRAEL	TEL AVIV	PERCENT OF ISRAEL
1976	56	N/A	23	N/A
1977	38	N/A	30	N/A
1978	73	53.7	23	16.9
1979	55	36.9	29	19.5
1980	52	41.9	27	21.8
1981	63	45.7	36	26.1
1982	28	40.0	N/A	N/A
1983	35	33.3	N/A	N/A
1984	62[a]	45.3	45	32.8
1985	79[b]	51.0	47	30.3
1986	88	60.3	31	21.2

[a]Including six religious conferences.

[b]Including twelve religious conferences.

Sources: Bagelman, 1984–1987; Central Bureau of Statistics, 1987.

   The opening of the expressway between Jerusalem and Tel
Aviv has contributed to the decline in domestic lodging in
Jerusalem, because many of those who come to the city for business or pleasure no longer have to stay overnight. The transition in
the leisure habits of Israelis can also be seen in the national superiority gained by Eilat in 1986, in terms of nights spent in hotels in
the city. Eilat achieved this success because of its popularity among
Israelis, whereas Jerusalem continued to lead in foreign tourism.
As of the 1970s, then, Jerusalem has turned once again into a cosmopolitan city, similar to its status in the late nineteenth century. It
is a world city, but not in the economic sense. Its historical and
religious centrality have been expressed in general, religious, and
professional tourism. This status of Jerusalem, as a capital that is
not a primate city but that serves as an international cultural and
religious center, is unique. Nevertheless, Tel Aviv is the cultural
and entertainment center for many Israelis, again similar to Jaffa
at the end of the nineteenth century.
   Another function through which the different nature of the
two cities is revealed is the number of research, thought, and learning institutes in both cities. As no formal data exist for this aspect,
an indicative examination was made through the telephone directo-

ries of the two cities. All establishments appearing under the term *institute* were classified; excluded were those that were part of a larger organization (i.e., a university). The term *institute* was singled out, rather than the title *center*, because *institute* has been publicly used for a very wide spectrum of establishments ranging from research, learning, and economic services to medical, sport, and automobile services. A comparative examination of Jerusalem and Tel Aviv may indicate whether there is a clear functional division of institutes between the two. For this comparison, the geographical boundaries of the urban areas of each city were those used by the telephone directories. For Jerusalem, this area stretches from Ramallah in the north to Hebron in the south. For Tel Aviv, it includes the metropolitan area, except for the northern suburbs (Herzliya, Ra'anana, and Kfar Sabba) and the southernmost ones (Ramla, Lod, Rehovot), all of which belong to different area codes. This telephone boundary covers most of the metropolitan area of Tel Aviv and includes a population about twice as large as that in the equivalent Jerusalem area.

The functional distribution of institutes in 1987 showed a relative quantitative superiority for Jerusalem, and a clear specialization by the two cities (Table 5.5). Greater Jerusalem counted ninety-one institutes. An equivalent number in metropolitan Tel Aviv should have been about 180, but the actual number was only 129. The number of research institutes in Jerusalem was forty-nine, or about 54 percent of the institutes in that city, compared with just twenty-seven in Tel Aviv. Only five of the research institutes located in Tel Aviv dealt with Jewish subjects in one way or another, whereas thirty of the Jerusalem research institutes dealt with Jewish issues and nine were devoted to Christian studies. Jerusalem also enjoyed a quantitative lead in learning institutes specializing in Judaic studies: in 1987 there were twenty-seven such institutes, comprising some 30 percent of all institutes in Jerusalem; about one half of these (thirteen) had a Jewish religious character (no matter the direction) and one was Christian. Metropolitan Tel Aviv contained no such institutes at all. Altogether, about 84 percent of the institutes located in Jerusalem dealt with research and learning; the equivalent percentage in Tel Aviv was 34 percent. On the other hand, the number of institutes in Tel Aviv that provided economic services was the same as the number of learning institutes in Jerusalem, twenty-seven, whereas the number of economic institutes in Jerusalem was only nine. The largest number of institutes in Tel Aviv was devoted to providing medical services, and their number amounted to thirty-eight, or 29.5 percent of all institutes in the city. Jerusalem had only five such establishments. The share of these medical, and therefore prestigious, establishments among institutes in Tel Aviv was lower than the share of research institutes in Jerusalem, which were the leading ones there. Hence, quantitative predominance in Jerusalem was held by research and learning institutes dealing mainly with Jewish (religious and secular) and Christian issues. In Tel Aviv, no one type predominated, the majority being shared among medical, economic, and general research institutes.

Two other types of institutes compared, those dealing with automobile services and sports, also revealed a big difference between the two cities. In Jerusalem there was one sport institute; whereas Tel Aviv contained eight. Tel Aviv had twelve "car institutes" (providing car testing services), Jerusalem none. These differences reflect variations in leisure habits and motorization levels. The overall difference between the two cities in regard to the types of establishments calling themselves institutes, however, might attest to the evolution of secondary linguistic cultures, with distinct connotations attached to words and terms in accordance with the nature of each of the two cities.

As with institutes, no formal data were available on the number and geographical distribution of rabbinical colleges (*yeshivot*). For comparative and indicative purposes, data collected and published by the Yeshivot Committee for 1987 (The Yeshivot Committee in the Land of Israel, 1987) were used. This body represents most of the *yeshivot* of almost all orthodox groups in Israel. In 1987, some 213 *yeshivot* were affiliated with the committee; of these, 85, or about 40 percent, were located in Jerusalem. An additional 35, or about 16 percent, were located in Bnai Braq, the ultraorthodox suburb of Tel Aviv; and only twelve *yeshivot*, or about 6 percent, were found in Tel Aviv proper. Jerusalem is therefore the dominant center for Torah study in Israel. Tel Aviv, as might be expected from its more secular character, did not even serve as a secondary center, a role undertaken by its religious suburb. Following the 1967 war, Jerusalem became a world center for Judaic studies; about 40 percent of the students in its rabbinical colleges now come from abroad. The roots of this status date back to the second half of the nineteenth century, when major *yeshivot* of the old Jewish community were established there. The first Eastern European-style *yeshivot* were founded in the 1920s; they were later reinforced, following the Holocaust and the establishment of the State of Israel.

In summary, then, the economic specializations of Tel Aviv and Jerusalem fit their historical, political, and cultural status,

Table 5.5. Institutes in Jerusalem and Metropolitan Tel Aviv, 1987

URBAN REGION	TOTAL	RESEARCH		LEARNING		ECONOMIC SERVICES		MEDICAL SERVICES		SPORTS		CARS	
		NUMBER	%	NUMBER	%	NUMBER	%	NUMBER	%	NUMBER	%	NUMBER	%
Greater Jerusalem[a]	91	49[b]	53.8	27[c]	29.7	9	9.9	5	5.5	1	1.1	—	—
Metropolitan Tel Aviv	129	27	20.9	17	13.2	27	20.9	38	29.5	8	6.2	12	9.3

[a]Greater Jerusalem includes the telephone area code 02 ranging from Ramallah in the north to Hebron in the south. Metropolitan Tel Aviv includes the telephone area code 03, which excludes the most northern suburbs (Herzliya, Ra'anana, and Kfar Sava) and the most southern ones (Rehovot, Ramla, and Lod).

[b]Of forty-nine research institutes in greater Jerusalem, thirty dealt with Judaic issues and nine with Christian affairs. In metropolitan Tel Aviv, out of twenty-seven institutes in this classification, five dealt with Judaic issues.

[c]Of twenty-seven learning institutes in greater Jerusalem, thirteen were of a Jewish religious nature and one was Christian. In metropolitan Tel Aviv, there were no such institutes.

Sources: The 1986–87 Jerusalem Telephone Directory, 1986, Golden Pages.
The 1987 Telephone Directory for Tel Aviv and Its Environs, 1987, Golden Pages.

which was patterned along trends that prevailed toward the end of the twentieth century. Tel Aviv is a world city in terms of its financial might. It enjoys additional features of a world city through its specialization in high-tech industries, computers, producer services, and telecommunications. Its open, contemporary cultural atmosphere is integrated with its economic nature as a world city. The status of world city carries with it a rise in personal services and in the lodging industry as part of the leisure and entertainment texture of the new, leading economic-professional sectors.

Jerusalem has presented a growing specialization in its two historical functions, since the 1967 war. Within four years after that war, it turned into the leading Israeli city for foreign tourism. By the end of the 1970s, however, Jerusalem lost its long superiority in domestic tourism in favor of first Tel Aviv and later Eilat. These transitions emphasize the growing cultural attraction of Tel Aviv for most Israelis, and the religious-historical cosmopolitan nature of Jerusalem. From the early 1980s, Jerusalem has led in public service employment, so that its nature as a capital city has been more accentuated. The accompanying decline in public service employment in Tel Aviv was coupled with a rise in other services befitting its status as a world city. Tel Aviv, thus, leads in institutes providing economic, medical, sports, and automobile services. Jerusalem leads in research institutes, particularly those dealing with Judaic issues, as well as in *yeshivot* and Jewish education.

Summary and Conclusions

This part has attempted to examine comparatively from a geographical perspective, the historical, political, cultural, and economic status of Jerusalem and Tel Aviv. The following paragraphs, after summing up this comparison, will attempt to connect these arguments with the previous part. Five aspects will be highlighted: beginnings—new versus old; developmental paces; specialization and complementarity; competition and struggle; and Zionist ideology.

Beginnings—New versus Old

A better formulation of this point would be the *very* old versus the *very* new. Jerusalem's incubation period occurred 3000 years ago, during the reign of King David, when the two functions of the city as a capital city and a holy and spiritual center were first determined. Opposing Jerusalem was new Jaffa–Tel Aviv, whose incubation period took place but 100 years ago. At that time, its functions as a new cultural and economic core in the Land of Israel were first determined. This incubation of the new core was unique, given that the original capital, Jerusalem, had also constituted a permanent capital, despite the waning of the federal rationale following the destruction of the First Temple (and commonwealth). A separation between primate city and capital is typical of modern immigrant societies, but in Jerusalem this consideration was a very old one. Jerusalem has served as a potential or actual capital throughout history mainly because of its function as a holy and spiritual city. This religious and national symbolism was extended to Christianity and Islam and was also carried into the secularization processes that accompanied the Zionist Renaissance in the Land of Israel. The city has served as a cultural-spiritual center in diversified nonreligious manifestations, both Judaic and general. The capitalness and spiritual accent of Jerusalem have continued even when a new population and economic core emerged on the coastal plain.

Tel Aviv is the center of the contemporary core of Jewish Israel. As such, it has served as the focus for urban, technological, economic, and cultural innovations. It was founded within the general framework of economic growth in the center of Palestine in the previous century. The specific factors for its growth were its being a coastal city; the settlement-agricultural activity of the First Aliya settlers on the coastal plain; and most important the concentration of immigrants from abroad who brought with them a desire to develop a national-secular culture, which was difficult to develop in Jerusalem.

The Pace of Development

A central characteristic of the system of relationships between Jerusalem and Tel Aviv–Jaffa was the development of a functional and cultural separation between the two immediately following the birth of the new core in Jaffa. Actually, the very evolution of the new core stemmed from the urgent need for an alternative core; it was not the result of a long geographical process of settlement, such as typifyies the evolution of a nuclear or an original core. The Jaffa–Tel Aviv core was not created *following* the first and second immigration waves but, rather, *simultaneously* with them, with mutual cultural and economic ties between the newly established urban core, on the one hand, and the rural settlements, on the other.

These ties between the new urban and rural entities encouraged the growth of the new core, whereas Jerusalem remained remote, mountainous, and relatively closed. The formation of this interrelationship of Jerusalem and Tel Aviv in terms of population size and the economic specialization of the new cultural core occurred only forty to fifty years after the establishment of the new core; in other words, at a very fast pace. The modern cultural development of Jerusalem came later and was slower and less radical than that of Jaffa, based as it was mainly on indigenous social elements. The declaration of Jerusalem as capital in 1924 and again in 1948 and the reunification of the city in 1967 could no longer turn the trends around anymore in favor of Jerusalem. Hence, Jerusalem has continued to develop as a capital and as a spiritual city, whereas Tel Aviv continued as an innovative cultural and economic urban center. In fact, the functions of Jerusalem as capital and holy-spiritual center were fully expressed in the modern era at a relatively late time, given the partition of the city between Jordan and Israel during the years of massive construction of the State of Israel. Jerusalem attained supremacy in tourism only in the early 1970s, reflecting its spiritual attraction, and gained employment seniority in public services only in the early 1980s, representing its function as a capital.

Specialization and Complementarity

The clear distinctions offered in the literature for a primate city separated from the capital cannot be simply applied to the case of Jerusalem and Tel Aviv, since the latter has not only enjoyed several economic and cultural merits, but it has also constituted a political focus. This was surely the case until the late 1970s, when a large number of governmental ministries were located in Tel Aviv, and even meetings of parliamentary committees took place there. Most party centers, newspaper headquarters, and the labor union and its many organizations are still located in Tel Aviv.

It is possible to identify distinct specializations in each city, stemming from their primary functions. These specializations contribute to an economic-functional complementarity. Tel Aviv has turned into a world city in terms of its concentration of large companies, some of which are multinational corporations, and in terms of the development of innovative sectors characterizing world cities: high-tech industries, computers, telecommunications, and business services. These developments have been accompanied by growth in commerce, lodging, and personal services, and they have been interrelated with the cultural atmosphere that has typified Tel Aviv. In other words, the economic specialization of Tel Aviv, compared to Jerusalem, is connected to its cultural uniqueness, which is different from that of Jerusalem.

The economic specializations of Jerusalem have been tied to its traditional roles as a capital city and a spiritual center. Jerusalem currently leads in the areas of public service employment and learning and research activities. It is also the leading city in foreign tourism. This tourism has consisted mainly of pilgrims, visitors to the historical sites of the city, and convention visitors. One may view Jerusalem as a world city on a historical-religious rather than on an economic basis, given its universal importance and attraction. On the other hand, some of the foreign tourism in Tel Aviv is business related, so that several hotels have specialized in this area. Tourism in Tel Aviv also has a strong entertainment component, expressed by the promenade, old Jaffa, and Disengoff Street.

Competition and Struggle

The competition and struggle between Jerusalem and Tel Aviv have taken place in an area that is informal and even unpolitical in the direct sense of power and resource allocation. Struggle and competition exist on the spectrum of the exchanges of political and cultural messages between the two cities. The competition started in the late nineteenth century, when the new coastal core was established, and was renewed with the massive development of Jerusalem following the June 1967 war.

Jerusalem presents a national microcosmos in terms of the struggles taking place between Jews and Arabs, secular and ultra-religious Jews, Left and Right, and Sephardic and Ashkenazic Jews. Such a concentration of social, political, and cultural struggles in a capital city is typical not only of Jerusalem. On the background of Tel Aviv as an opposing core, a distinction can be made between economic-cultural interpersonal struggles, which typify Tel Aviv, and intersectoral conflicts, which characterize Jerusalem, although social struggles have developed in Tel Aviv as well. This distinction that sharpens the difference between the cultural images of the two cities has contributed to an ambivalent attitude toward Jerusalem and its significance, especially by the secular Jewish Left. Tel Aviv symbolizes the contemporary, not just in the areas of literature, theater, and the arts, but also in consumption and entertainment habits. Jerusalem, in contrast, displays the deeper, historical, and "heavier" elements of culture. The increasing importance of consumer culture in contemporary Israel has accentuated even further the differences between the two cities, as manifested in the preference given by Israeli tourists to Tel Aviv and Eilat over Jerusalem.

Jerusalem, Tel Aviv, and Zionist Ideology

Part 1 of this book has attempted to present the complexities of the changing Zionist ideology and preferred settlement forms. When it comes to Tel Aviv and Jerusalem, the issue is even more complicated still.

One may look at Tel Aviv and Jerusalem from several perspectives as far as Zionist ideology and deeds are concerned. Tel Aviv has served as the major organizational and ideological-cultural center. From an organizational perspective, Tel Aviv was the address where decision making on settlements took place. Until the 1920s Jaffa served as the headquarters location for the Palestine Bureau and the settlement movements. Both then and later on until 1948, the coastal core served as the decision-making locus, with strong feedback from the rural sector, home to many of the decision makers. The initiatives for the several forms of rural settlements as well as for the establishment of several specific villages came from within the rural sector. Tel Aviv, however, was the place where resources were allocated among and within settlement movements and where the provision of goods, marketing, and all other organizational matters occurred.

Following the establishment of the state, a new settlement form was created; namely, development towns. As no central authority was established for development towns and as most governmental offices still remained in Tel Aviv, the responsibility for the development towns project was split between Tel Aviv and Jerusalem. The Ministry of Interior, which eventually was assigned responsibility for national physical planning and which was in charge of municipal governments, was located in Jerusalem, as was the Ministry of Industry and Commerce. On the other hand, the Ministry of Housing, which was responsible for town construction, was based until recently in Tel Aviv. From 1967, the role of Jerusalem as an organizational center began to increase, and then the role of Tel Aviv changed. Thus, several additional governmental functions, including the Ministry of Housing, moved to Jerusalem. Tel Aviv, though, continued to serve as the sole organizational center for the rural sector. This sector, which represented the ideologically new, centered on the new city of Tel Aviv. Development towns, however, depended more and more on Jerusalem as the ever-strengthening bureaucratic center.

The West Bank settlement project was tied even more to Jerusalem. It was not only ideologically rooted in Jerusalem; it also relied heavily on the government for settlement decisions and resources. The importance of Tel Aviv in the West Bank settlement project has increased from a different perspective, however, given the vital role of the private sector in this settlement project, which was not comparable to previous settlement projects. Much of the construction of community settlements was organized and executed by Tel Aviv developers.

From a strict ideological perspective, the attitude of early leftist Zionism to Tel Aviv was a mixed one. On the one hand, city life in general and Tel Aviv as the locus of an evolving Jewish bourgeoisie were declared negative experiences (see E. Cohen, 1970a). Because Tel Aviv served as the organizational center for Labor Zionism, however, the latter has contributed much to its growth, prosperity, and centrality. Tel Aviv also represented a symbol of the modern Jewish settlement of Palestine: it was the first and largest Hebrew city. Furthermore, the creation of a Hebrew secular culture in Palestine originated *simultaneously* in the rural sector and in Jaffa. This important process flourished even further when Tel Aviv took Jaffa's place as the locus of the new Hebrew culture. Thus, Labor newspapers, theater, most book publishers, and so on, located in Tel Aviv. Although members of the pioneering Second and Third Aliyas emphasized a mode of life consisting of communal life and agrarianism, the both condemned and praised big Hebrew city served as their organizational, ideological, and cultural focus. The diminishing of the condemnation of the city by the Left and the emergence of a social Zionism have amplified the cultural strength of Tel Aviv. This development, in turn, may contribute to the process by which previous leftist frontiers turn into peripheries, an issue providing the focus of attention in Part 3.

Zionist attitudes toward Jerusalem have been mixed, as well. During the First Aliya, Jerusalem served more as a symbol than as a settlement target, though this attitude changed slightly in the early twentieth century (Aaronson, 1989; Katz, 1989). During the

Second Aliya, the status of Jerusalem as the most important center for Jews was recognized, even though there was little activity in the city and its surroundings (Shilo, 1989). Prominent Zionist leaders, however, expressed an antagonistic view toward Jerusalem (e.g., Herzl, Ben-Gurion, Bialik, Ahad Ha'am, and Weitzman) because of its location, its ancient Jewish community, and its significance for Christianity and Islam (Elon, 1990; Lorch, 1989; Harel, 1989). When circumstances permitted the flourishing of Jerusalem following the 1967 war, the city developed, at least partially, into a modern version of the city it has been in the late nineteenth and early twentieth centuries; that is, it felt the growing impact of ultra-orthodox Jews and of the Arab population.

It would be in order to conclude with a point originally raised in the introduction to this part. A double duality has developed in Israel concerning the status of Jerusalem and Tel Aviv. On the one hand, the two cities have divided core functions between them, and they jointly serve as the core of Israel, despite the lack of an urban continuum between the two. On the other hand, Tel Aviv is the central element of Jewish Israel, concentrated as it is mainly on the plains; whereas Jerusalem is the central city in the mountains, where most of the population is Arab. The mountains make up the core of the political-geographical Palestinian-Israeli conflict. Jerusalem lies at the heart of this core, because the Palestinians, too, view the city as their capital. On the other hand, Jerusalem is located in the center of the historical core of the Jewish people and has been positioned there since their early history. This duality between new Jewish plains, on the one hand, and mountains that are both Arab and old Jewish, on the other, is not only a geographical duality, but obviously a cultural one as well.

Part 3

Frontiers and Peripheries in Israel

Chapter 6

The North

The previous part was devoted to the double core of Israel, Jerusalem and Tel Aviv. This part will focus on the other side of the Israeli geographical coin, settlement frontiers and peripheries. Although necessarily discussing earlier cores and core margins, this part will focus on the major "objective regions" of the Zionist enterprise. Some of these regions constitute past ideological cores, so that they served as creators of modes of life, settlement forms, and settlement decisions. Overall, however, this part is concerned with the actual geographical-regional setting of these settlement projects, with settlement frontiers eventually turning into national peripheries. The several regions have reflected, in one way or another, Zionist objectives and their priorities; furthermore, they contributed to the evolution of Zionist myths and cultural values, which had specific regional roots and connotations. The cores played a crucial role in the development of frontiers, in the evolution of frontier values, and in the eventual turning of frontiers into peripheries. All these aspects were dependent on a mutuality between the "objective regions" and the cores. This relationship was expressed not only in resource allocation and movement, controlled from the cores, but also in the creation and molding of social values. Hence, the conclusion of this part permits the presentation of a joint perspective for both cores and frontiers-peripheries.

We will begin with several general elaborations of the nature of frontiers and peripheries in general and on those in Israel in particular. These will be followed by an analysis of four specific regions: the valleys, the Galilee, Haifa, and the Negev. The part will conclude with a series of expositions on the territorial and cultural processes involved in the creation of cores, settlement frontiers, and peripheries in Israel.

The major "objective regions" of the Zionist project in this account will not include Judea, Samaria, and Gaza, which were discussed in Part 1, because they served, at least from the mid-1970s, as a settlement ideal in itself. The development of the Negev desert in the 1950s had a similar character, but not to such a degree as the occupied territories and for several reasons. The Negev formed an integral part of the State of Israel when the major efforts for its settlement were made, whereas the occupied territories have presented a special challenge, not least with their being under military control. The Negev project, furthermore, was backed by consensus; the West Bank project, in contrast, has divided the Israeli political spectrum more than any other settlement ideal or project. The West Bank project has a very strong historical connotation, raising basic questions of the degree of geographical and spiritual-cultural continuity to previous Jewish presence in the Land of Israel. The Negev, on the other hand, was supposed to become a leading region for the new modes of life developed in pioneering Palestine, in both its rural and urban settlements.

This and the following chapter will complete the cycle of the three dualities proposed in Chapter 1. The duality between structure and human agency is introduced here once again. Part 1 focused more on the structural-social dimension, here the spatial domain is revealed. The strong, two-way bond between the "objective regions" and the cores will display another aspect of the role of human agency. By the same token, this part provides an additional exposition of the spatial dimension of the duality between society and space, following the earlier more ideological focus in Part 1 and the geographical presentation of the cores in Part 2. The third duality—between ideology and vision, on the one hand, and realities, on the other—will accompany the analysis throughout this part as it moves from cores and frontiers to peripheries. Thus, answers will be provided to the two following questions: What has the classical territorial–modes of life approach to Zionism of the Left achieved? And what happened to these achievements once Labor Zionism adopted social Zionism and settlement-territorial Zionism moved to the Right?

The frontiers, some of which served initially as ideological cores, transmitted social values to the core, which turned these values into cultural and political myths. This process facilitated the allocation of resources for the development of frontier spaces or a spatial expansion of society. The gradual weakening of these values and myths in the core, coupled with a cultural and economic enhancement of the core itself and core values, led to the evolution of core-periphery relations.

Periphery and Frontier

Periphery is the region (or regions) found in an opposite condition to that of the core. Although the core has received several definitions, pertaining to a variety of aspects, only a few definitions of national peripheries exist. Gradus (1983, p. 389) proposed the following:

> Peripheral regions are subsystems of low accessibility to core areas, typified by limited access to markets, means of production, private and public services, cultural facilities, and sources of economic and political power. Core and periphery stand in an asymmetrical relationship of dominance/dependence that is articulated through four major processes: decision-making and control, capital flows, innovation diffusion, and migration.

These processes intensify through the modernization of a state and the increasing centralization of both commercial businesses and governmental agencies. Peripheries are, therefore, regions that have been "left behind," one way or another, while the various facets of the core continue to grow.

The frontier is another relevant term in a discussion of cores and peripheries. *The frontier* has been defined as the "geographical-political region which lies beyond the integrative region of the political unit, and into which expansion can take place" (Glassner and de Blij, 1980, p. 82). Another definition refers to it as "the outer edge of settlement within a given area" (Mikesell, 1960, p. 62). Originally the term was developed by the historian Turner (1928) toward the end of the nineteenth century in dealing with the expansion into the American West. Turner attributed this expansion to free land and several qualities of the American society: a separation from European influence and an intensification of independence, the growth of democracy and a relief from poverty. The people who went west became into innovators, path blazers, and tough people, who learned to cooperate with one another despite their different origins. Turner thus viewed the frontier as a central shaping element in the process of Americanization (Mikesell, 1960). Various objections to these frontier qualities and their implications were raised within both the American and other new-immigrant societies.

Reference to frontiers in the sense used in this book, as settlement frontiers, has mainly typified historical writings within the geography discipline and outside it, too. Political geographers have used the term to define international political *boundaries* or their regions or both. The same term, furthermore, has been used by sociologists to define certain *social* patterns (social frontiers might be different from social boundaries; see Kimmerling, 1989, on the

Jewish Diaspora as the "frontier of Israel"). Interestingly enough in this regard is Kimmerling's (1989) interpretation of Turner, that settlement frontiers refer to an *unlimited space*, whereas boundaries are just the opposite. By the same token, the word *frontier* usually carries a positive connotation of the expansion of individuals' property or societal territory; the term *boundary* may have either negative or positive meanings.

Similarly, a comparison of the definitions of frontier and periphery points to a significant difference between these concepts. The definition of a peripheral region relates to its *inferior* position relative to the core; the definition of a settlement frontier refers to the *superior* condition of a region by virtue of its location in the forefront of a nation-state. The definitions of frontiers and peripheries relate, therefore, to the different *status* of regions and to the activities taking place in each, and not necessarily to different regions in terms of their geographical location. In other words, a frontier region is normally a periphery through its geographical location at the margins of a nation-state and through its current status. At a later stage, the core may possibly expand into the frontier or the frontier may become part of the core. This is not a mutual relation, however, because not every periphery is a frontier, in the sense that not every region geographically located at the margins of a nation-state has the status of a frontier (i.e., being a target region for settlement expansion). This relationship may be true for dynamic developments, as well. Thus, a frontier may turn into a periphery over time if settlement efforts weaken, or a periphery may turn into a frontier if massive settlement activity commences within it.

Frontiers and peripheries, therefore, are not necessarily contradictory terms and processes, nor are they complementary. A region can simultaneously constitute a periphery and a frontier, or it can be just a periphery. By the same token, frontier processes in a region may be developing or retreating, a feature that is also true of its status as a periphery. The status of peripheral or frontier regions may be determined or changed by a national ideological-political conception that directs activities in the entity or by the aggregate activities of human agency and economic companies that move in and out of these regions.

The distinction between primary and secondary frontiers is also important (Prescott, 1978, pp. 33–39). A primary frontier relates to the geographical advancement of settlement before the boundaries of a state are established. This process leaves behind enclaves of unsettled areas. A secondary frontier is the settlement process of these enclaves, following the determination of state boundaries. Settlement waves are accompanied by various levels of population densities and economic activities, and they are not necessarily similar in all countries. In this context, one must also distinguish between two forms of frontier settlements. On the one hand, settlements act as *creators* of boundaries (primary frontiers) or as fillers of *enclaves* (secondary frontiers); on the other hand, *border settlements* are deployed along *existing* borders to act as defensive positions. The last form have been a central part of Israeli security and settlement policies (for elaboration, see, e.g., Efrat, 1981; Newman, 1989). Our main concern here is with primary and secondary frontiers as the main components of frontiers and peripheries.

A different interpretation of the term *frontier* was given by Elazar (1970b; 1987) and mentioned in regard to Tel Aviv in the previous part. According to Elazar, frontiers signify phases in the economic and social development of new societies. In historical order, four such frontiers may be recognized: the agricultural, the industrial, the technological, and the cybernetic. Each of these is connected with the evolution of new settlement forms (the farm and the town, the city, the metropolis, and the citybelt or megalopolis, respectively). Elazar identified the U.S. Northeast as the region where all American frontiers started; but since the emergence and maturing of new frontiers have been nationwide processes, each new frontier has nested within an existing one that had matured. It is intriguing to compare Elazar's notions of frontiers to the more conventional settlement frontiers, though geographically at least they seem to contradict each other. The economic frontiers, as noted by Elazar, nest and evolve first in the core, whereas the settlement frontiers are *usually* on the periphery.

Looking at the two concepts of frontiers from the perspective of the discussion on Israel to follow raises several points. First, large-scale agricultural activity may take place in a settlement frontier at a time when a core may experience only the first phases of industrialization (i.e., the second frontier). Second, conflict may emerge between a process of economic innovation taking place in the core and an existing, more veteran social and economic order located in the periphery. This conflict can be of an economic or ideological nature or both. Third, the uncontrolled evolution of a new economic frontier in the core may cause a settlement frontier to turn into a periphery.

Frontiers and Peripheries in Israel: A General Discussion

It is possible to observe in Israel frontier and periphery processes operating simultaneously. In the past, frontier processes and phenomena were the more important; currently, periphery processes play the more major role. Some comment is necessary on the characteristics and developments of frontier and periphery process in Israel at large.

The Israeli Frontier—Characteristics and Trends

If one looks at the situation in the Land of Israel through Turner's geographical and social frontier notions, then only little frontier activity will be seen to have taken place. Spatially, several aspects differentiated the Israeli experience from the American. Kimmerling (1983b) noted the lack of free land in Palestine. In other words, land was always purchased from one Arab ownership or another. According to Kimmerling, it is possible to measure "frontiering" through land prices, and these have never been zero in Palestine; in contrast, free land was a basic element in the United States. Even in the twentieth century, the price of agricultural land has been higher in Palestine than in the United States. One may attribute this to the nuclear form of Zionist frontiers, compared to the American linear advance. Therefore, where land could be bought, and possibly where water was available (Elazar, 1986, pp. 210–211), Jewish settlements were established, to be later accompanied by additional settlements in the vicinity.

Comparing the Zionist and American frontier settlers from a social perspective yields a more complex picture. The Hebrew word for pioneer, *halutz*, is a biblical term; it has usually been translated into English carrying a different connotation, but one that is meaningful to the analysis here. For example, "We will cross over as picked troops in sight of the Lord" (Numbers 32:32), or "while the picked troops pass on in front of the ark of the Lord" (Joshua 6:7). The pioneers, or in the biblical translation, the "picked troops," considered themselves (and were considered by the rest of the Zionists) as carrying out a *national* task, as messengers of the collectivity. As such, the term *halutz* underwent a secularization process during the Second Aliya, from the "picked troops" of the Lord to those of the people. The American pioneer was more individualistic and exhibited foremost an economic motive in his moving westward. Both the American and the Zionist pioneers saw their lands as "the Promised Land," and both dealt in agriculture. In both countries, the pioneers and frontier settlers were much on the move, and defense was the central motive. In each country, frontier emphases were on the simple mode of life and on toughness. Toughness in the United States, however, often found its expression in drinking, which did not exist at all among Zionist pioneers in the Land of Israel. The attitude of Zionists to the community was much deeper and stronger than that of the American frontier people. Also, the Zionist pioneer was more moderate in his or her attitude to the Arabs compared to the American's relations with the indigenous Indians (Near, 1987). Finally, the collective nature of the Zionist pioneering rural enterprise was unique in history.

Politically, as both Lustick (1987) and Elazar (1986) noted a mixed frontierism characterized Israel in general and the recent phenomenon in the occupied territories in particular. Israel-Zionism adopted the European pattern of moving with vast resources into supposedly empty territories, with the claim of exercising its rights. This initiative, however, has been countered by a Third World pattern of claims for the national rights of minorities and indigenous populations. From 1967, the question of whether the occupied territories are frontiers or boundaries has constituted the central political problem in Israel. The separation line between Israel and the territories (the so-called green line) has, thus, been a relative demarcation, forming a boundary for the Arab population and a land frontier for Jews (Kimmerling, 1989).

A more general definition of settlement frontiers as relating to the expansion into new settlement regions would permit the introduction of an Israeli frontier with its own characteristics. To employ such a definition, the Israeli frontier has to be divided into two periods. The first period is that of the primary frontier, which lasted from the late nineteenth century until the establishment of the State of Israel and which resulted in a de facto determination of its boundaries. The period of secondary frontier includes the time since 1948. The 1967 war, however, reopened primary frontiers on the Golan Heights and in the Jordan Valley, as well as a politically disputed frontier in Judea, Samaria, and Gaza.

The prestate primary frontier was geographically typified by a settlement intrusion into the plains of Palestine and, to a much more modest degree, also into its mountainous areas. During the First Aliya, this activity took place simultaneously in the central coastal plain (e.g., the colonies of Petah Tiqva, Rishon Lezion, and Rehovot) and the northern valleys (e.g., the colonies of Yessod Hama'ala and Rosh Pinna). The move into the South, on the other hand, occurred mainly at a much later stage, in the 1940s.

The penetration of the Zionist settlers into Palestine was from the west, from Europe. Past historical intrusions of Hebrews-Israelites-Jews into the Land of Israel had always come from the east (the patriarch Abraham, the Israelites of the Exodus, and the Jews returning from Babylon). This modern, new intrusion direction has had various implications for the development of a new Jewish locus on the plains, a region that normally was not Jewish in the historical past.

A migration from the east must first reach the mountains because of settlement difficulties in the lower Jordan Valley, an area characterized by water shortages. The ancient battle of Joshua against Jericho was an exception, but that place was a large oasis; thereafter, however, the Israelites continued their way into the mountains. Had the Zionists arrived from the east and attempted their first primary settlement frontier in the Jordan Valley, they probably would have failed, given the water problems. If they had migrated to the mountains, they might have failed owing to the Arabs' likely objection to selling land in that area. On the other hand, at least two other scenarios would have been possible: more money could have been offered for less land, most of which would have been rocky; the Zionists could have fought the Arab peasants for the land, as the Bedouins had done, traditionally attacking from the east.

The Zionists, though, came from the west, so that they perceived the new Land of Israel from west to east rather than from east to west as had their ancestors. This attitude is reflected in several elements. One was the migrants' main settlement efforts in their very port of arrival, Jaffa, and in its environs. Then there were land purchases in a region in which more land was available and at more reasonable prices. There was here, too, the element of an initial coping with water surpluses rather than shortages. Despite all the difficulties involved (e.g., malaria), it was easier and more sensible for an initial primary frontier to cope with water surpluses than with shortages. All these elements permitted a relatively fast consolidation of the settlement project, as well as a good connection with the settlers' countries of origin overseas, similar to frontiers in other new societies (see "The Ben-Gurion Plan," 1963). Consequently, less effort was made to settle in the mountains.

The intrusion from the west into the plains brought about the construction of a new center in Jaffa–Tel Aviv, separate from old Jerusalem. Migration from the east would have strengthened Jerusalem as well as the three other mountainous Jewish communities, but it would also have intensified conflict between the new Jewish community and the old, as well as with the Arabs. This geographical separation between the old and the new was manifested even in regard to the attitude to Jerusalem, as was noticed in the previous part. It contributed to an ambivalent attitude to the mountains in more recent times. The major justification for the Zionist enterprise was the very fact of settlement activity in modern times. Gush Emunim's reference to the historical past with regard to mountainous settlement activity was rejected by the Left, which favored renewed settlement in Jewish mountainous villages that had been deserted in 1948. The settlement phases in Judea and Samaria, which evolved from east to west, were all implemented by settlers who came from the west; that is, from Israel proper.

From the time of the Second Aliya, settlement became part of Zionist action. The frontier in the Land of Israel then received several unique characteristics compared with frontiers in other new societies (see Kark, 1974, pp. 186-187). First was the status of the national organization. Reichman (1984), who compared the Jewish settlement of Palestine to settlement movements in Central Europe noted the revolutionary nature of Zionist action:

> Within the framework of the activities of the Palestine Bureau appeared buds of a revolutionary settlement method, which was unprecedented in the Eastern regions. What is meant by this is settlement based on national capital, including land and production means, given to settlers lacking means of their own, while they enjoy—because of their organization in a cooperative framework—a vast autonomy in their economic decisions. (p. 124)

This national organization replaced the political backing of individual pioneers by governments in other countries, whereas the cooperativeness assisted the newcomers in coping with poor economic circumstances.

The settlement process in Palestine was carried out to some extent on the basis of national planning, in particular that of Arthur Ruppin, head of the Palestine Bureau. He advocated a balancing of new Jewish settlements with Arab settlement regions, the creation of Jewish settlement regions adjacent to existing, old Jewish urban communities, and settling close to transportation routes

(Hasson and Gosenfeld, 1980; see also Chapter 2). From the perspective of the prestatehood period, it is difficult to point to an unequivocal long-range settlement policy, despite all the plans. There were several general programs and specific principles (besides Ruppin's, there was Rochel-Lev's, which will be discussed later). In 1929, the proposal was first advanced to initialize settlement core regions and subsequently to spread from them to other parts of the country. Substantial debate of this issue began in 1936, when several partition plans were proposed for Palestine, and the problem was raised of the ratio between additionally gained territory versus a consequently larger Arab population within the future Jewish state (Reichman, 1979, p. 31).

The Zionist settlement frontier was accompanied by a strong ideological loading. On the one hand, Zionism was a national ideology promulgating settlement per se; on the other hand, socialist ideology advocated cooperation within and among settlements. The socialist accent stemmed from the Eastern European origin of the pioneers, which was an exception among all the Western European originated new societies (Elazar, 1986). America and other new societies emphasized economic motivation and welfare in the frontiering process (Matras, 1973). The socialist ideological power of the early Zionist frontier in Palestine was able to create for a short while an ideological core located in the frontier. This, too, probably constituted an exceptional phenomenon in frontier developments.

The unique profile of the new rural settlements in Jewish Palestine turned the kibbutz into a leading edge in *intrusion* processes into new regions; the moshav, the other cooperative settlement form, served as a means of settlement *basing* (Oren, 1983). Besides these two permanent forms of settlement, four forms of temporary settlements were created in the primary frontier process: a *conquering company*, for land preparation; a *nucleus*, a group that included the initial population of a new settlement; a *settling post*, the first phase of a populated settlement; and an *observation outpost*, an agricultural experimental station for examining settlement potential (Reichman, 1979, p. 41).

The primary Zionist frontier in Palestine has had a special security significance, beyond its importance for local defense and the creation of national boundaries as in other countries. The settlements on the frontier were perceived as providing security for the core. This motive appeared first in the mid-1930s and received additional significance after 1948, with the introduction of border settlements.

Various features of the Israeli frontier are related to several regions. The motive of land holding through settlement as a condition for boundary creation began in the Galilee, first in Tel Hai and later in Hanita and Biriya. The motives of agriculture and cooperation as means for settlement and land possession in the frontier were created in the valleys; and the ideas of "occupying the unsettled" and "blooming of the unsettled" were manifested in both the valleys and the Negev, though in different ways and at different times. There exists, therefore, a two-way relationship between the very going to the frontier, on the one hand, and the frontier as a value creator in Israeli society, on the other. Going to the frontier influenced the development of values in the core, which in turn channeled people, capital, and ideological importance back to the frontier. These processes caused several regions in Israel to receive renewed meaning in the new Israeli society.

Following the establishment of the State of Israel, a secondary frontier has developed, one having double geographical significance. First was the continuation of settlement construction along the borders. The Hebrew term for them was *frontier settlements*, though this referred to the political frontier (i.e., the border) and not to the settlement frontier in the connotation employed here. Second, many settlements were also built in regions that were only sparsely settled during the primary (prestatehood) frontier period. The characteristics of this secondary frontier included those of the primary frontier although now the state shared with the Jewish Agency the obligation of settlement financing and the formulation of settlement plans. The national security issue became prominent in the determination of settlement objectives. Two additional motives have been guiding the settlement process as of 1948. First was population dispersal, which has appeared in all governmental guidelines (Silberberg, 1973) and the plans for which eventually received a legal status (Kellerman, 1985a). The second was the desire to control fertile agricultural land along the coastal plain for possible fast urban expansion (Reichman and Yehudai, 1984); see also Chapter 3.

The Evolution of National Peripheries in Israel

During prestatehood, the regions on the margins of the Jewish settlement areas in Palestine were perceived mainly as *front* regions, based on agriculture. Since the establishment of the state and the beginning of secondary frontier processes, national periphery processes have evolved simultaneously. These latter focused geographically on the frontier regions, the North and the South, side by side with the development of towns and industries in these regions. It is possible to identify four perspectives in the creation of these national peripheries: political, social, economic and demographic.

Politically, as both Elazar (1970a) and Gradus (1983) observed, there is the centralized and aspatial nature of Israeli politics, which originated in the Eastern European political thinking imported to Palestine by the Second and Third Aliyas. The political system provided for a centralized bureaucracy as well as for national parties. These latter served to strengthen the decision-making foci in the cores, but have been responsible for the emergence of national peripheries with low political representation and the lack of regional governments. By the same token, governmental budgets have not reflected in-depth regional considerations.

Socially, an inferior working class of new immigrants was created after 1948; it consisted of those who were sent to the peripheral regions within the context of state ideology by institutional decisions and the spatial manipulation exercised by the governing veteran working class. The new immigrants formed a weak population, consisting mainly of immigrants from Moslem countries; and this population became even weaker after the stronger elements among it migrated to the core. The social gap created between these two classes thus opened a spatial gap, which in turn widened even further the social gaps (Hasson, 1981).

From an economic perspective, the population dispersal policy contained a strong industrialization component during the second half of the 1960s, though few industries actually located in peripheral regions (Gradus and Krakover, 1976). Later, in the 1970s, "intermediate subdistricts," those located between the metropolitan cores and the peripheries, developed (Acre, Jezreel, and Kinneret in the North; the Sharon and Rehovot in the Center). The deep-periphery subdistricts (Safed in the North and Ashqelon and Beersheba in the South) retreated. Industrial diversification in the peripheries has grown, but the high-tech electronics and machinery industries have concentrated in the Center and in Haifa (Gradus and Einy, 1980). A similar trend was also observed for services (Peldi, 1972).

Demographically, negative migration balances could be observed between the core and the peripheries (Shachar and Lifshitz, 1980). The various population dispersal plans were only modestly successful in the aftermath of the end of the huge migration wave in the 1950s (Kellerman, 1985a). In addition to the political, social, and economic factors already mentioned, the discoordination between residential construction and the creation of employment sources in the peripheries has had negative demographic impacts. Important, too, was the attraction of settlers to the large cities, which both typified the Zionist enterprise since its inception and characterized Jewish communities in the Diaspora (see also Chapter 2).

Frontier and Peripheral Regions in Israel

It is possible to draw the frontiers and peripheries in the modern Jewish Land of Israel from at least three perspectives. The first is temporal; namely, an attempt to uncover periods of frontier and periphery creation. The second is regional, or the identification of frontier and periphery regions. The third is conceptual, diagnosing processes and phases of core, frontier, and periphery creation. The classification to be presented in the following sections attempts to show a simple cross cutting along all three perspectives (Table 6.1).

Table 6.1. Transitions in the Status of Peripheral Regions in Israel

REGION	BEFORE 1948	AFTER 1948
Galilee and Golan	Frontier on the periphery	Frontier and periphery
"Width Valleys"	Frontier and core	Semiperiphery
"Length Valleys"	Frontier and core	Frontier and periphery
Haifa	Core	Core fringe
Negev	Frontier and periphery	Frontier and periphery
Judea, Samaria, and Gaza	Periphery	Disputed frontier and periphery

Conceptually, fine definitions have to be used for each region, since a simple notation of *frontier* or *periphery* for each might prove misleading, given the complexities that typify several of the regions. Temporally, a basic distinction will be made between the periods before and following statehood. This distinction overlaps the transition from primary to secondary frontiers, with the obvious exception of Judea, Samaria, and Gaza, and to a lesser extent the Golan Heights, which were eventually annexed to Israel. The distinction denotes periphery creation processes (which were not central ones from a Jewish settlement perspective before 1948). Needless to say, this division into only two periods is a very basic one, and additional processes and events will of necessity be referred to for the various regions. Thus, Hasson and Gosenfeld (1980) found three specific periods of Zionist frontiering in the Land of Israel during the twentieth century. The first period, 1907–1916, marked the beginning of Zionist settlement, so that frontiers were located on the plains and in the valleys, where initial settlement took place. This period was further marked by the beginning of collective agricultural settlement and by the shaping of the nationwide settlement plan drawn up by Ruppin. A second period occurred between 1936 and 1939, the years of the major Arab uprising and the beginning of discussions on a possible partition of Palestine. The "stockade and tower" settlements of those years were meant to determine the future borders of a Jewish state. A third frontier period has unfolded since 1967, as a result of the Six Day War. It has been typified by several settlement forms used to determine the possible future peace boundaries. According to the Hasson and Gosenfeld classification, no distinction is made between primary and secondary frontiers; consequently, the frontier definition relates only to settlements that have determined or may determine a boundary. It seems that these three periods are times of settlement intensification (as described in Part 1), periods of a sharper geographical specification of settlement objective regions. The Zionist settlement process as a whole, however, has to be viewed as a frontier, aimed at determining both the boundaries (through primary frontiers) and the *areas* (through secondary frontiers) of the Jewish state.

The classification in the following sections will use the geographical perspective; that is, it will focus on several regions of the country. The beginning of the new Jewish settlement in the Land of Israel during the First Aliya in the last quarter of the nineteenth century was characterized by the establishment of rural-agricultural settlements around two existing urban centers. One was very old, the two old Galilee communities of Tiberias and Safed; the other was new, Jaffa on the coastal plain (Reichman and Hasson, 1984). When Zionist settlement started during the Second Aliya in the early twentieth century, and when Ruppin put forward his settlement principles, both events were based on these urban foci. The two areas functioned as cores in the early twentieth century; however, whereas the Jaffa–Tel Aviv region turned into a political and economic core, the status of the valleys and the Lower Galilee declined as an ideological-political core.

The following regional classification will concentrate on three regions in the North—the valleys, the Galilee, and Haifa—and will

treat the Negev desert as a single region. The more detailed classification of the North stems from the different status and development of the regions composing it. Each of these regions served as a
core at some time in the past. The Galilee constituted the Jewish
core in the Middle Ages, when Safed was the largest Jewish community in Palestine and the premier town in both spirit (the evolution of the *Kabbala* and the Jewish code of practice) and substance
(the textile industry). Although Safed was to lose its senior position
to Jerusalem, the former still remained one of the two holy communities located in the Galilee. The valleys constituted an ideological
core in the Second Aliya, but lost this status before 1948. Haifa
inherited from Acre the status of the central harbor and became
one of the three largest cities in Mandatory Palestine. It gradually
lost this position when core functions began to be divided between
Jerusalem and Tel Aviv. Compared to all these past-core northern
regions, the Negev never served as a core in the past few centuries,
and its status fluctuated between frontier and periphery. An exception was Gaza, which became the largest city on the coastal plain
during the first half of the nineteenth century (it included a very
small Jewish community) (Kark, 1988). The Lakhish development
region, at the northern edge of the Negev, will not be singled out as
a separate region, because its development was considered part of
the general settlement effort of the desert.

Judea, Samaria, and Gaza will also not be detailed here (they
were analyzed in Chapter 3). However, the political debate concerning their status can be formulated along the lines of the terms
presented here. Those who favor the settlement of these areas per-
ceive them as primary settlement frontiers for the determination of
Israel's borders with Egypt, Jordan, and the Palestinians. At the
same time, Western Samaria and Judea are located on the core
fringe and could potentially turn into an integral part of the core
through massive suburban and community settlement. On the
other hand, those who oppose such a settlement project view these
regions as peripheral from the Jewish settlement perspective. If
they will eventually be turned over to one Arab entity or another,
some of these areas may function as cores for the Palestinians.

The Valleys

The term *valleys* refers jointly to the Jezreel and Harod Valleys that cross the country from west to east as well as to the
Huleh, Kinneret, and Beit-She'an Valleys running from north to

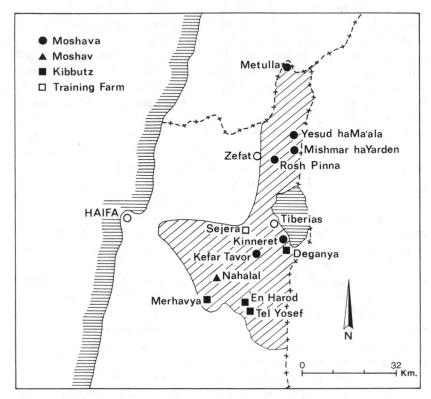

Figure 6.1.   The Ideological Core in the North

Source: Following S. B. Cohen, 1977.

south (Figures 1.1 and 6.1). The growth and decline of these regions as ideological cores occurred from the early twentieth century until close to the establishment of the State of Israel. Later on, some differences in status evolved between the "width valleys" and the "length valleys."

The Ideological Core in the North

The spatial organization of Israeli society in 1948 could be characterized by an extensive core consisting of Tel Aviv and collective (kibbutzim) as well as cooperative villages (moshavim) (Shachar, 1971). Thus the 1948 core was a mixed urban-rural one and included the whole rural sector as one unit. Horowitz and Lissak (1978) commented on the difficulty in using the term *periphery* for the pre-state agricultural sector. This sector even then was far from being backward and traditionally peasantry oriented, but enjoyed special social features: it was charged with European ideologies, and its members were children of the middle class and usually well educated. In these features, the pre-1948 rural class was similar to the immigrant population that developed the urban sector. Moreover, the rural-agrarian sector was then a major source of social value innovation and social entrepreneurship, sometimes even more than the urban centers. These characteristics relate to the whole rural sector as a political-social group. Therefore, during the Second and Third Aliyas, it was possible to identify the northern valleys specifically as a geographical core having a Labor-oriented ideological nature.

Several factors were responsible for the flourishing of the northern valleys as a settlement focus (S. B. Cohen, 1977). The landscape reminded the settlers, to some degree, of grass-covered southern Russia or afforested, humid eastern Russia. "Following Judea, Sejera [a colony in the Lower Galilee] was for me almost what Petah Tiqva meant for me after Plonsk and Warsaw. Here I found the Land of Israel of which I dreamed. The Nature, the people, the work, everything was here so different, more like the Land of Israel of which I dreamed while still residing in Plonsk" (Ben-Gurion, 1971, p. 34). Furthermore, the valleys were located close to the two old Jewish communities of Tiberias and Safed, a fact that Ruppin considered to have merit for settlement activity. In addition, the Zionist movement viewed the inclusion of the sources of the Jordan River and other rivers inside the Jewish settlement areas as an important settlement goal. Indeed, such an objective is of a frontier nature.

Migration to the valleys, in which land was available for purchase, originated geographically in the Lower Galilee colonies, especially the learning farm Sejera, Kfar Tavor, and Yavniel. These colonies were new compared with those in the Judean plain, Sejera being founded in 1899, Yavniel and Kfar Tavor in 1901. These newer colonies exhibited less friction between the farmers and the Second Aliya laborers, thus, providing a comfortable working environment for people like Y. Vitkin, a teacher in Kfar Tavor who was the first advocate of cooperative settlement, and David Ben-Gurion. Nevertheless, laborers desired independence, so that in 1907 the first agricultural cooperative group was established in Sejera. This group was created, too, against the background of the desire for independence in fields guarding; it was also in Sejera that the first such "security" group, Bar-Giora, was formed.

The development of the ideological-settlement core in the North during the Second and Third Aliyas parallels the development of the institutional-settlement core in Jaffa–Tel Aviv (Table 6.2). The establishment of the first of every new type of cooperative settlement took place in the valleys. The first kibbutz (kvutza) was Degania, the first collective settlement was Merhavia, the first moshav was Nahalal, and the first large kibbutz was Ein-Harod. Around each of these firsts, there quickly formed several additional similar settlements. The settlement establishment, however, was organized outside this region. The Palestine Bureau was established in Jaffa in 1908, and Ruppin remarked on its proximity to the colonies on the Judean coastal plain and the concentration of the new Jewish community in Jaffa (see Part 2). At the same time, Jaffa enjoyed the location of the Anglo-Palestine Bank as well as several other settlement organizations. The labor union (Histadruth) and the defense organization (Hagana) were established in Haifa, but they moved soon thereafter to Tel Aviv, in which were also based the large collective organizations for marketing (Tnuva), insurance (Hassneh), and banking (Bank Hapoalim). By the end of the 1920s, numerous cooperative settlements existed on the coastal plain, too, and the settlement establishment was now based in Tel Aviv. In only some twenty years, the institutional and organizational core of the rural labor and union sector emerged in Tel Aviv, as opposed to the ideological core in the valleys, and this city turned into the bureaucratic center of the working class in general despite Labor's criticism of the city and the service class (Kellerman, 1986a). Nevertheless, part of the political leadership operating in Tel Aviv and Jerusalem continued its membership in kibbutzim and moshavim in the North.

The northern valleys were divided during the core period between the Jezreel Valley in the west, which centered on moshav settlements, and the Harod Valley and the lengthwise valleys (Huleh, Jordan, and later on Beit-She'an), which contained mainly kibbutzim. This difference stemmed largely from the different times of land purchase and preparation (and from kibbutz dominance in the Beit She'an settlement project as of 1936). The difference between the two valley groups grew larger after 1948, when development towns began to be established in the valleys. The varying distances of these towns from the coastal plain became crucial.

The northern valleys offered both a core and a frontier throughout the first three decades of the twentieth century. Their frontier was of a double nature. First, from a geographical perspec-

Table 6.2. Selected Events of Ideological Importance to the
Labor Movement, 1907–1930

EVENT	YEAR	PLACE
Second Aliya		
Founding of Bar Giora	1907	Jaffa and Sejera
Founding of the first agricultural		
collective group	1907	Sejera
Establishment of the Palestine Bureau	1908	Jaffa
Establishment of the first Kvutza	1909	Degania Alef
Founding of Hashomer	1909	Kfar Tavor
Establishment of the first collective		
settlement following Oppenheimer	1911	Merhavia
Third Aliya:		
Founding of Ahdut Ha'avoda	1919	Petach Tiqva
First incident of boundary		
determination by settlements	1920	Tel Hai
Founding of the Histadrut	1920	Haifa
Founding of the Hagana	1920	Haifa
Founding of the labor battalion		
(Gdud Ha'avoda)	1920	Tiberias
Establishment of the first moshav	1921	Nahalal
Establishment of the first large kibbutz	1921	Ein Harod
Fourth Aliya:		
Founding of Mapai	1930	Tel Aviv
Establishment of the first kibbutz		
industrial plant	1930	Giv'at Brenner

tive, the frontier developed by the expansion of Jewish settlement areas into the valleys. The first security event in which boundaries were determined through settlements occurred at Tel Hai in 1920 and resulted in the inclusion of the Huleh Valley ("the Galilee Finger") within the British Mandate and, later, the State of Israel. The settlement areas in the valleys further determined the borders of the Jewish state in several partition plans and in the 1949 armistice agreements. A particularly intensified frontier period in this regard were the years 1936–1939, which were typified by "stockade and tower" settlements in the Beit She'an Valley, through which settlement and land possession were extended southward. At the same time, land holdings on the northern edge of the Jordan Valley, the Huleh Valley, were strengthened, as well.

Second, the valleys also served as a frontier in terms of the evolution of the new Israeli society. The emphasis on mode of life in the cooperative and collective settlements, which originated in and centered on the valleys, brought about the creation of certain basic values: equality, simplicity, cooperation, democracy, a superior status for agriculture, defense and security, and self-reliant labor. These values became the ideological hardcore of Labor, whose superior political status from the 1930s turned them into basic values for Israeli society at large, until the change in administration in 1977. These values were brought by the political leadership from the North to Tel Aviv, from which dominant platform they turned into general social values. The agrarian-cooperative frontier that started in the North was thus institutionalized in a city, which then facilitated its distribution nationwide. This same city simultaneously served (jointly with Haifa) as the primary locus for the industrial frontier of Palestine. In the future, these cities provided the primary loci for the technological and cybernetic frontiers. All these developments constituted integral elements of the status of Tel Aviv as a core of the country.

One social value originated in the valleys and was typified by an even more direct geographical loading. This was the desire to "make the unsettled bloom," by way of draining swamps and fighting against the malaria that accompanied them. This value, too, became part of the general national-Zionist myth (Bar-Gal and Shamai, 1983) and, following the establishment the state, transferred to the South for the Negev settlement project, though in a different way.

It is not surprising that the industrialization process in the kibbutz movement began in 1930 in Giv'at Brenner, which is located close to Tel Aviv and its evolving manufacturing sector. By the same token it should not be surprising to learn that the kibbutzim in the Kinneret subdistrict, the cradle region of the kibbutz movement, were the last in this diffusion process, constructing factories only in the 1970s. A correlation of 0.78 was found between the year of industrialization of kibbutzim and their distance from Rehovot subdistrict, where the process originally started. One may, therefore, view the kibbutz industrialization process "as a spatial diffusion of an economic development agent from the developed urban and industrial core to its rural hinterland and to the undeveloped periphery" (Meir, 1980, p. 545). Nevertheless, there was here a conflict between agriculture, which constituted a hardcore value of the new Zionist village, and manufacturing, which was basically considered an urban activity.

The Valleys Since Statehood: Fragmented Peripheries

Several processes caused a decline in the status of the valleys as a core after 1948. First was the continued strengthening of Tel Aviv as a central union-Labor focus. Second was Ben-Gurion's accent on state institutions and less emphasis on sectoral organizations, thus adding more importance to the cores. Third was the fact that ideological and material development resources were directed to the South until the 1960s, then for a short time to the Galilee and later to the West Bank. A fourth factor was the relative decline of the large city of the North, Haifa, as an urban core component, creating a longer distance from the valleys to the cores. Fifth, the kibbutz industries and the kibbutz regional industrial centers created a relatively significant economic power in the more veteran villages; however, this process was not restricted to the North (Kellerman, 1972). The refusal by kibbutzim to establish regional nonagriculturally related industrial plants and their attempt to reduce the use of hired labor restricted their ability to serve as stronger economic boosters for their regions.

From the 1970s, there could be observed an evolving different status for the "width valleys," on the one hand, and the "length valleys," on the other. The west-east stretching Jezreel and Harod Valleys have enjoyed a relatively higher economic development, given their economic status as development regions located close to Haifa. This enabled industrial and residential development of development towns in the region (especially Migdal Ha'emeq, Afula, and Upper Nazareth), assisted by the personnel and service infrastructure of Haifa. The process has been amplified in recent years by the commercial development taking place along the major highway crossing the industrial area of Haifa, which pushed industries into adjacent development towns (Kellerman, 1981). The relative economic development of the Jezreel subdistrict was expressed in manufacturing (Gradus and Einy, 1980), services (Peldi, 1972), and population (Shachar and Lifshitz, 1980). For example, the 1948 Jewish population in Jezreel subdistrict was 1.6 times larger than that in the more remotely located Kinneret subdistrict. This ratio gradually increased, so that by the early 1970s it reached 2.4, or a 50 percent increase in the population gap between the two subdistricts.

The "length valleys" have continued to be considered frontiers, in the political sense of the term, given their proximity to the Jordanian and Lebanese borders and, until 1967, also the Syrian border. The development of manufacturing, population, and services has had the character of a peripheral region, similar to that in the Negev (Beersheba subdistrict). This was true of both the urban sector and the veteran agricultural sector, which could no longer rely on a special status in the political or economic system. Therefore, no population growth could be observed in the Huleh Valley, whether in development towns (Qiryat Shemona and Hatzor) or within the rural regional councils in the region (Upper Galilee and Mevo'ot Hahermon), during the second half of the 1980s.

The Galilee

The status of the Galilee in the Zionist settlement enterprise was somehow pathetic. Two old Jewish communities were located in this region, Safed and Tiberias, which served as the Jewish core in Palestine during the Middle Ages. In the Judean mountains, there were also two old communities, Jerusalem and Hebron. During the 1929 riots Hebron was abandoned by its Jews until 1968, whereas Jerusalem has grown continuously. The two "holy cities" in the Galilee were both left behind in terms of their development and status. Numerous calls for a massive settlement of the Galilee were made prior to and following the establishment of the state. In practice, however, Zionist intrusion into the mountainous Galilee, other than the shaping of the borders around it, was limited. With the establishment of Israel, and even after the diversion of settlement attention to the Galilee in the 1960s, the attitude to the Galilee was that of a "declared frontier"; in actuality, it developed into a periphery. The status of the Galilee has never been as important and exciting as that of the Negev. The latter was awarded a favored ideological status, especially during the 1950s, but also earlier, when Ben-Gurion's slogan of "occupying the unsettled" (kind of a primary frontier for the settling of a human-made desert boundary) was able to draw resources extensively. The Galilee attained this seniority only for a short while during the early 1960s in the form of a settlement campaign led by the then-prime minister Levi Eshkol. This campaign was limited in both its extent and time because of an economic recession in 1965, followed by the 1967 war. It seems as though the mountainous Galilee symbolized for Zionist settlement efforts the old and the foreign, the difficult, the different, and the remote. Recent attempts to take up the challenge of Galilee settlement by way of an extensive construction of observation outposts (*mitzpim*) were encountered by Arab frontierlike activities as we shall see.

The Galilee Prior to Statehood: Frontier on the Periphery

The geographical term *Galilee* has referred since early in the settlement effort to the whole region lying north of the "width valley"; it includes, in other words, the Galilee coastal plain in its west and the Huleh Valley to the east (Figure 1.1). The discussion of Galilee settlement here will refer, however, to the Galilee in its more restrictive sense: the mountainous area. The intrusion of Jewish settlement into this area up to the establishment of Israel was very limited (Oren, 1983). Most of the Galilee did not meet most of the settlement criteria set by Ruppin; consequently, it was left outside settlement *N*. After 1936, however, the concept of the creation of the northern border was stressed, amounting in fact to going beyond settlement *N*.

The battle over Tel Hai, located at the edge of the eastern Galilee, turned the region into a major symbol of the primary frontier idea: "The 'Land of Israel' is the place where we settle, work and cultivate, and out of this—the plough sets the border" (Oren, 1980, p. 24). This line of argument became the ideological basis of the "stockade and tower" settlements as border setters from 1936–1939. The Tel Hai moment was raised, therefore, in all major settlement security events, notably in Hanitta, Biriya, the Negev settlement, the fall of Gush Etzion, and the conquest of Eilat (Oren, 1979a; 1980). Tel Hai, furthermore, has become a symbol of the determination of secondary frontiers, as well: "But it is not enough to locate on the border. This is a too simplistic conception of the tradition, as if you go only to the border. It is true, you would like to settle in Tel Hai, but it is unreasonable that you will be cut off in Mahanayim or in Rosh Pinna. For a boundary settlement there is a need also for a territorial continuum" (Oren, 1980, p. 27). Tel Hai served, too, as a lesson for defense considerations as well as for the formulation of merits offered by the pioneers in collective settlements over farmers in the colonies for frontier settlement. Tel Hai has become a symbol and myth of martyrdom for the Right, which has called its youth movement after the Tel Hai hero, Josef Trumpeldor. Tel Hai commemoration day later was transformed into Hagana day and used for assemblies and hiking tours to encourage volunteerism and settlement. Following the establishment of the State of Israel, this day lost its significance, thus symbolizing the disappearance of the primary frontier, rising statism, and the gradual decaying of values to induce exodus from the city into frontier settlements.

The Tel Hai myth (as well as the myths of Hanitta and Biriya) focused on the importance of *Jewish deeds in the present* in the form of land holding against political and military powers at any human and economic cost. Under such ideological circumstances, political, economic, or demographic realities were of less relevance. Once this ideology weakened or disappeared, however, then the bare reality was revealed, and the peripheral location of the mountainous Galilee became striking. In other words, the difference between frontier and periphery in new Jewish Land of Israel has been like the distance between a utopian reality driven by vision and ideology and actual reality, powered by economic, political, and demographic forces. This gap between frontier and periphery has not necessarily been located within the region itself or even among settlers in the region, but in the nation at large, in its government, and in its values. Hence, only a handful of settlements existed on the eastern edge of the Galilee mountains in the 1920s, and it was still considered a frontier; sixty years later, settlements existed all over the mountainous Galilee (and there was a better demographic ratio with the Arab population than in the 1920s), and the region was largely considered periphery. The evolution of peripheries may be gradual and cumulative, so that a decline in an ideological "frontier tension" would cause a simultaneous intensification in periphery processes.

Up to 1936, only one settlement was located inside the mountainous Galilee, Kfar Hahoresh (1929) in the central Lower Galilee, close to Nazareth. Five other settlements had been built in the area leading from the valleys up to the Eastern Lower Galilee, all of them colonies (Mitzpa, Yavniel, Beit Gan, Sejera, Kfar Tavor). Between 1936 and 1948, one additional settlement was established in the mountainous Galilee, Yehi'am (1946), this time in the Western Upper Galilee. In addition, three other settlements were founded close to the Lebanese border: Hanitta (1938), Eilon (1938), and Matzuba (1940). The elite Haganna-unit Palmach settled the eastern fringe of the Galilee with seven posts (Manara, Misgav Am, Biriya, Ein Zeitim, Ramot Naftali, Ami'ad, and Huqok). During the same period, by comparison, some *eighteen* villages were established in the Huleh Valley alone, not to mention *fourteen* in the Eastern Lower Galilee, where the five colonies had been established at the turn of the nineteenth century (Figure 6.2).

Until 1936, a kind of labor-division prevailed between PICA, the Rothschild-sponsored development fund, and the Zionist Jewish National Fund. The former was in charge of the development of the Galilee; the latter concentrated on the Hulla Valley. With

Figure 6.2. Jewish Settlements in the Mountainous Galilee Prior to Statehood

Source: Following Oren, 1983.

the beginnings of discussions over a possible partition of Palestine, coupled with attempts at the crystallization of a Jewish settlement map of Palestine in 1936, the international boundary in the mountainous Galilee became a primary frontier, at least by declaration: "First of all we have to purchase [land] in the Upper Galilee, close to the Lebanese border, and to put settlers immediately on the land. We have to do everything in order to make it difficult to exclude the Galilee from our possession" (Ben-Gurion, 1982, p. 463). The practical outcome was the settlement of three kibbutzim: Hanitta, Eilon, and Matzuba. Hanitta was compared to Tel Hai by the ideological leader Berl Katzenelson (Avigur, 1978, p. 93), and its settlement was indeed a primary frontier, part of the effort to set the boundaries of the future Jewish state.

In 1943, the Hagana proposed a plan, known as the Rochel-Lev plan, which meant to integrate settlement and security considerations. This plan proposed placing settlements in both primary and secondary frontiers by penetrating into mountainous areas (Galilee, Samaria, and Judea) and by strengthening existing settlement areas. The latter objective should have been achieved through an addition of settlement blocks and the creation of a modified geographical settlement continuum among such blocks (Oren, 1983). The intrusion, or the primary frontier, was supposed to be performed by kibbutzim, whereas the strengthening of existing settlement areas was to be carried out by moshavim. This plan thus provided further evidence of the perception of kibbutzim as being ideologically stronger. In practice, however, an intrusion into the mountainous Galilee in accordance with this plan was implemented only by the establishment of Yehi'am.

Oren (1983) attributed the weak intrusion into the Galilee to the British authorities, who were very strict in prohibiting Jewish land deals in this area. On the other hand, Reichman (1979, p. 61) related the lack of mountainous settlements to the experience gained during the Ottoman era, which showed that modern agricultural settlements would not suit these regions. The difficulties in buying large land parcels in an area settled by Arabs contributed, too, to the near lack of mountainous settlements and the possible isolation of Jewish settlements located in Arab regions.

The Galilee Since Statehood: Frontier and Periphery

The settlement of the Galilee after 1948 has been geographically characterized by three waves of rural settlements, in addition to the construction of urban sites. The first wave, which took place between 1948 and 1967, aimed at the establishment of border settlements along several sections of the Lebanese border (Figure 6.3). By 1967, some 18 moshavim, 5 kibbutzim, and 8 worker villages (most of which turned into moshavim) had been established in the Galilee.

Levi Eshkol, who succeeded Ben-Gurion as prime minister in 1964, wished to divert settlement attention from the Negev, which was preferred by Ben-Gurion, to the Galilee. Early in 1967 the government adopted a comprehensive development plan for the Galilee which was not implemented because of the 1967 war

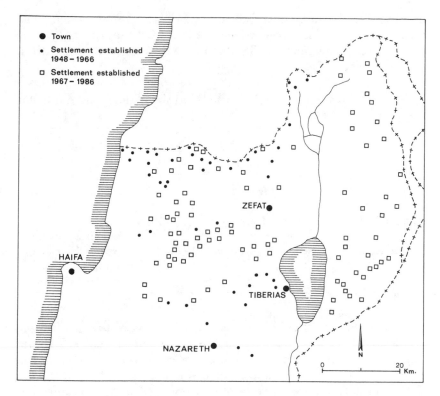

Figure 6.3. Jewish Settlements in the Mountainous Galilee
After 1948

(Rosenman, 1983; Muvhar, 1983). The war brought about a second wave of northern mountainous settlement effort, this time not in the Galilee, but in the neighboring Golan Heights. In the wake of the 1973 war, a third wave of mountainous settlement activity started, this time again in the Galilee, but now in counterpoise to the evolution of nationalist sentiments being expressed by the Arab population in the region. This settlement project was specifically aimed at the heart of the mountainous Galilee, thus creating a truly secondary frontier. It was accompanied by the introduction of some new settlement forms: the observation outpost (*mitzpe*), the mountaintopsite (*mitzpor*), and the industrial village, their names indicating their locations. The outposts have not been of a homogenous nature, so that their name applies more to their location and their mode of establishment as presettlement posts, consisting of a small number of families. Several observation outposts turned into moshavim and a few others into kibbutzim. Some of these moshavim have been based almost exclusively on industry, and have therefore been called industrial villages. Most of the outposts have or will eventually become small community settlements, each with up to fifty families (Table 6.3)).

Table 6.3.　Jewish Rural Settlements in the Galilee and the Golan Heights Since 1948

REGION	OBJECTIVE	PERIOD	SETTLEMENT FORMS
Lebanese border	Defense of a primary frontier	1948–1967	Traditional: Kibbutz, moshav
Golan Heights	Primary frontier	1967–1973	Traditional: Kibbutz, moshav
Galilee Center	Secondary frontier	1974–	New: Observation outpost, industrial village, topsite

The plan for the development of the heart of the Galilee was prepared by 1974 and has been implemented since 1978. Some thirty new rural settlements were established in the context of this plan; they have been organized in three settlement blocks (Segev, Teffen, and Tzalmon). Several of the new settlements are based on high-tech industries, including computer software development. The Galilee settlement project was recently examined for its objectives and achievements (Sofer and Finkel, 1988). The project has had five objectives: First was to hold onto state-owned lands and guard them against a growing expansion of agricultural cultivation or residential construction by the Arab population in the area. This objective has been partially reached, but through the construction of several unneeded settlements, causing Arab opposition.

A second objective was an attempt by the rural Labor-dominated establishment to create an "antithesis" settlement project to the growing right-wing-government-sponsored project in Judea and Samaria. In other words, a secondary frontier was created in the Galilee, not only for its own sake but also in a reaction to the primary frontier in the West Bank.

The supposedly interregional competition between the Galilee and Judea-Samaria may be compared with the earlier competition, in the 1960s, between the Galilee and the Negev. Eshkol's attempt to divert national development attention from the South to the North stemmed formally from the need to attain some balance between frontier-periphery regions. Informally it might well be, though difficult to prove, that this attempt had to do with a desire to create a new regional development image for the new prime minister. The Negev project, after all, was fully associated with Ben-Gurion's vision and deed (he personally moved to a young kibbutz in the center of the Negev). In comparison, the development of the Galilee in the 1980s was motivated by a Zionist development need (virtually continuing the Galilee development plans of the 1960s); at the same time, it attempted to avoid or to reduce development in the West Bank because of a different political approach. Hence, the two attempts at Galilee developments, in the 1960s and in the 1980s, were undertaken in harsh competition with the development of other regions. The recent settlement projects in the Galilee will be compared with those in the West Bank in the following section, but it is important to note at this point that the attempt to divert attention from the West Bank to the Galilee has not succeeded. The number of new settlements in the occupied territories is four times greater than that in the Galilee, and the settlement project in Judea, Samaria, and Gaza has drawn a population twenty times larger than that attracted to the new settlements in the Galilee. These figures attest to the decline in settlement-territorial ideology on the Left and to its adoption by the Right.

A third objective of the Galilee development project was to attract a new population to the Galilee and provide residential and employment options for the second generation of Galilee moshavim within their regional context. Although these goals have been accomplished, the numbers were small. The fourth objective was to establish additional border settlements along the border with Lebanon, and indeed several of the new settlements are just such settlements. The final objective of this project was to create the new settlement forms described.

The Galilee was settled through urban settlement as well. This settlement consisted mainly of an increase in the population of the existing town of Safed and the construction of new development towns. Thus, Upper Nazareth, Ma'alot, Migdal Ha'emeq, and Shlomi were founded in the 1950s; Karmiel was established in the 1960s; and Katzrin on the Golan Heights was settled in the 1970s. In addition to the general objectives of the development towns as service centers and components of population dispersal plans, these towns were supposed to create a Jewish presence in Arab concentrations (Kipnis, 1983). As in other development towns, the emphasis in their development was on industrialization. The lack of massive population growth in the Galilee caused these

Galilee towns to be smaller, for the most part, than those in the Center and the South.

The development of the Galilee following the establishment of the State of Israel suffered from three major problems, which led the region to evolve into a periphery side by side with the existence of frontier processes. The first problem was a national-social one, the second one related to developments on the coastal plain, and the third one was connected with processes in the Arab Galilee.

In the national-social sphere, there has been a decline in a major element of the Israeli frontier since 1948, namely the frontier ideology. The ideology was at least partially connected with agriculture and cooperation, and its decline resulted in the lower availability of a population ready to settle in the Galilee. Under these circumstances, the absence of an ideological or political movement that has turned the settlement of the Galilee into its major objective, as was the case with the Negev or with the occupied territories (by the Right), is not unusual. The effort by Eshkol to create such an ideological consciousness came too late and lasted too short a time. When ideological awareness grows weaker, then other ingredients of the Israeli frontier, especially the accents on national planning, national capital, and security, do not necessarily serve as merits, as their constructive operation depends on frontier ideology. The alternative for ideology-driven growth could have been private enterprise. This would have been difficult to flourish in the Galilee, because of the lack of economic opportunities and resources within the region itself and because of the low level of infrastructure conditions for the operation of the private sector. Pioneering efforts in this regard were initiated by the industrial developer Steff Wertheimer. Another factor involved the simultaneous dispersion of governmental settlement efforts to many regions following the 1967 war, so that it was difficult to facilitate a concentrated effort in the Galilee.

A second factor for the evolution of the Galilee into a periphery was the rapid economic development on the coastal plain. The importance of the distance of the Galilee from the cores added to the negative element. Under such circumstances, the nonexistence of regional governments is striking, because such governments can possibly channel some growth through the contribution of regional processes and powers. The core-periphery gap has caused stronger population elements in the region to leave for the core, making it even more difficult for regional industries. The development of modern telecommunications means would not necessarily close the gap between cores and peripheries, because the major contribution of this technology would be manifested in the core margins (Keller-man, 1986b).

A third central problem is the fast development of the Arab sector in the Galilee, especially since the 1970s. This development has manifested itself in an impressive population growth, so that the Arab majority in the mountainous Galilee grew. It has further been expressed in the evolution of Arab-Palestinian nationalism in the form of Arab frontierlike activities, characterized by illegal residential construction and an illegal use of state-owned lands. The establishment of the outposts, or the modern Jewish frontier, was supposed to cope with these processes; but the Jewish settlement activity has not been large or strong enough to contend with the new Arab frontier activities (Sofer and Finkel, 1988).

The Jewish population in Safed subdistrict in 1987 declined absolutely for the first time, from 63,000 in 1986 to 62,700 in 1987. This decline reflected a drop in the Jewish population in the eastern Upper Galilee, not in the Huleh Valley. It is symbolic that that same year registered a first-time decrease in the Jewish population of Beersheba subdistrict, as well. The two most remotely located subdistricts, in the far North and in the far South, thus experienced population declines, which more than anything else illustrated a transition from a frontier to a peripheral status.

The recent penetration into the mountainous Galilee through the outpost settlement form occurred sixty years after an initial symbol for the frontier had been established in Tel Hai. This new intrusion was performed with a settlement form that was completely different from the collective kibbutz: the new accent was on individualistic values. The later intrusion was much weaker than the earlier one, however, both in its ideological strength and in its population size, and despite, or maybe because of, the use of new technologies.

The Galilee versus Judea and Samaria

The observation outpost settlement project in the Galilee has been similar to settlement in the West Bank in that both projects were established foremost to meet a territorial objective, possessing or guarding lands. In both, new settlement forms were created to fit changing life-styles to the territorial objective. The two were even similar in their emphasis on population objectives, operating in regions with Arab majorities.

There are also, however, numerous differences between the

two projects (see also Newman, 1984a). The Galilee has been continuously settled by Jews since before the modern era. Current settlement efforts there are agreed upon by national consensus,
though there are some who would challenge its rationale (Sofer,
1986). The West Bank project, on the other hand, notably in
Samaria, is new, having started only in 1967. Its second and third
phases, beginning in the mid-1970s, have engendered sharp political debate in Israeli society; and as a result, resource allocation for
and public interest in the Galilee have been smaller. The historical-
religious attachment to Judea and Samaria by several political-
social segments of Israeli society is strong. The settlement process
almost alone provides a Jewish presence, given that the West Bank
is not under Israeli sovereignty. On the other hand, illegal use of
land by Arabs in the Galilee does not abrogate Israeli sovereignty
over the area. The two projects also differ in population objective.
Although settlement was and is intended to create a massive Jewish presence in the West Bank, there was no reasonable expectation that a Jewish majority would be created there. The Galilee, on
the other hand, has long had some Jewish presence; the aim now
was to amplify it to create a Jewish majority in the region.

An important aspect is the location of the two regions relative
to the large urban concentrations. Thus, parts of Judea and
Samaria are close to metropolitan Tel Aviv and to Jerusalem,
whereas the Lower and the Western Galilee are adjacent to Haifa.
Karmiel, the most successful development town in the Galilee,
attracted its population from all over the country as well as many
new immigrants. Only four large community settlements have been
established up to now in the Galilee (Kfar Veradim, next to the
development town of Ma'alot; Timrat, bordering the Jezreel Valley; and Givat Ha'ela and Pi-Ner in the Lower Galilee). This number is small, despite the short distances between the Lower Western Galilee and Haifa.

As will be seen in the following sections, metropolitan Haifa
and its approximately 400,000 inhabitants amount to less than one-
quarter of the population of metropolitan Tel Aviv, and to less than
one-fifth of that of metropolitan Tel Aviv and Jerusalem together.
Thus, the available spillover population for the settling of the
Galilee is much smaller than that available for Judea and Samaria.
Also, metropolitan Haifa has not been as attractive as Tel Aviv
and Jerusalem, the annual population growth of the northern city
in the 1980s being about 1.5 percent, compared to the national rate
of 2.0–2.5 percent. Furthermore, Haifa is built on and around
Mount Carmel, thus offering residential qualities unavailable in flat

Tel Aviv but found in Samaria. In both the Galilee and the West Bank, daily commuting by the previously metropolitan populations means that the areas relevant for urban field settlements are restricted to about 30 km. from the central city. This leaves the higher mountainous areas outside the urban spillover effect. On the other hand, a large-scale liberal land-purchase policy for state-owned land could have brought about increased demand by the Arab population.

Haifa

At the turn of the nineteenth century, Haifa began to grow, to become part of the evolving core in modern Palestine, which took the form of the "three large cities": Tel Aviv, Jerusalem, and Haifa. The city of Haifa reached a peak in this status during the 1930s, when the city constituted simultaneously a core and a frontier. The decline in its status started close to the establishment of the State of Israel and has continued since then. Though Haifa has remained the third largest city in Israel, its former national core functions are for the most part currently divided between Tel Aviv and Jerusalem; furthermore, various port-related functions that had developed in Haifa are now shared with the new port city of Ashdod, located south of Tel Aviv. In its current status as the capital city of the North, Haifa is similar to Beersheba, which serves as the capital of the South. The Haifa meropolitan population, however, is four times as large as that of Beersheba (though it is about 15 percent lower than that of the city of Jerusalem). Its geographical location on the coastal plain and the varied infrastructure that has been developed over the last 100 years have given Haifa the status of a city on the core fringe, which is the reason for its inclusion in the present discussion.

Haifa Prior to Statehood: Core and Frontier

It is customary to identify the beginnings of modern Haifa with the destruction of old Haifa, west of the current downtown, and the construction of a new town in the eastern part. Both actions were performed by the Bedouin governor, Daher-el-Ammar, in 1761. His objective was to build an anchorage that would be more convenient than the then-existing one in Acre (Carmel, 1969). The town grew and developed throughout the nineteenth century with the contribution of several communities. The German Templars arrived in the city in 1869; earlier, the Carmelites had built their monastery in Haifa in 1827. The Jewish community developed in the city mainly from the end of the nineteenth century.

The decline of old Acre and the rise of neighboring new Haifa were speeded up at the turn of the nineteenth century. The process of change in the importance of port towns was not unique for that pair of towns, and not even for Palestine at large, as comparable transformations had occurred all over the eastern coast of the Mediterranean. Thus, Beirut, Alexandria, Port Said, Jaffa, and Haifa emerged as a new coastal trade system, replacing the declining Tripoli, Tyre, Acre, Gaza, Rosetta, and Damietta (Kark, 1990). This process was related to the introduction of steamship technology and growing international trade; consequently, cities located at convenient break of bulk points became more important. This explains the impressive growth in all transportation means in Haifa: in land transportation, railways came in 1906; coach roads at the end of the nineteenth century; automobile roads in the 1920s; in maritime transportation, an anchorage was constructed at the beginning of the twentieth century and a deep-water harbor in the 1930s; in air transportation, an airport was built in 1935. Since Haifa's railways and roads lead to the internal countries of the Middle East (Syria, Jordan, Iraq, Iran), the city enjoyed a unique international status.

Early in the nineteenth century, Acre and Gaza led the coastal towns of Palestine, with about 8000 inhabitants each, whereas only 1000 people then lived in Haifa. Throughout the nineteenth century, Gaza grew more than Acre and overtook it by mid-century. Gaza's leading position was eclipsed by Jaffa toward the end of the century. At that time, Haifa still lagged behind Acre and was still the smallest coastal city. Haifa's leap forward occurred at the turn of the twentieth century; by the eve of World War I, about 20,000 people lived in Haifa, compared to only 8000 in Acre (the population of Acre returned, therefore, to its early nineteenth century size, compared to about 10,000 from 1840–1880). Gaza, however, was still larger than Haifa at that time (25,000); however, by 1922, or just four years after the British occupation, its modern coastal urban ranking was taking shape. Jaffa then led with 47,700 inhabitants, followed by Haifa (24,600), Gaza (17,500) and Acre (6,420) (Kark, 1990). Haifa had climbed to a respected second, but this ranking has remained ever since as Tel Aviv–Jaffa tookover from Jaffa.

The development of Haifa during the second half of the nineteenth century was not only a result of the technological changes in shipping and the advantage of the large Haifa Bay over Acre in this regard. It also had to do with the construction of the German Colony. The Germans—and to a lesser extent also the Carmelites—contributed to the emergence of Haifa as a modern city and as a city with strong connections with a national and international hinterland. This was done by paving roads to Nazareth and the valleys and by the establishment of convenient coach services to these regions as well as to Acre (Carmel, 1969). These services elevated the status of the city over Acre, and a carriage industry developed in Haifa. Its geographical advantages and an already-existing infrastructure brought about the construction in 1900–1905 of an extension of the Damascus–Saudi Arabian railway, which crossed Palestine through the valleys. At the same time, the country's first modern anchorage was inaugurated in Haifa (1908); its first Jewish factory was established there (Atid oil factory, in 1907); a Jewish technological university was founded in this city (Technion, in 1911); and a railway was put into service from Haifa to Acre (1912). Thus, on the eve of World War I, the larger population of Haifa relative to Acre was a result of the international maritime and land transportation advantages possessed by the former. The city achieved superiority over Gaza in the form of a new Jewish population that emphasized modern industries and modern technological education. At this political turning point, however, Jaffa enjoyed two proximities that Haifa did not. It served as the maritime gate for Jerusalem, and it was located in the midst of the numerous new Jewish colonies. Haifa's international transportation advantage, out of which developed a technological-industrial advantage, was envisioned by Herzl, the founder of Zionism. At a later stage, after the State of Israel was established, most of this advantage disappeared when the borders with the neighboring Arab countries were sealed. The technological-industrial infrastructure that had been built during the fifty years prior to statehood, however, made it possible for the city to survive and even to grow, but not significantly to move ahead.

The British Mandate meant for Haifa an intensive development of its natural locational features. The British viewed the city as a military base for securing the Suez Canal and a harbor for oil-producing Middle Eastern countries. Haifa also served as an alternative for the Suez Canal and an air junction between Europe and Africa and the Far East (Bigger, 1989; Stern, 1989). The 1920s saw the construction of infrastructure and of Jewish industry based on raw materials from the indigenous area (Nesher, She-men, and "the Large Mills" for cement, oil, and wheat, respectively). Haifa was declared the district town of the north, replacing Acre. An electric power station was built there, and the Jewish National Fund bought lands and drained in the Haifa Bay area. The 1930s constituted a decade of transportation development by the British, accompanied by industrial and settlement development by the Jews. In maritime transportation, the harbor was built (1933), with a new CBD next to it. In land transportation, roads were opened to Baghdad (1934), Lebanon, and Damascus. Repair shops for the railway system were established (1934). In air transportation, an airfield was built (1935) that served three continents, and thus it became the most important aerodrome in British Palestine (Stern, 1974). Shipping through pipelines was also developed, and an oil pipeline was put into service from Iraq to Haifa (1934). Before the decade was out, the oil refineries opened up (1939). At the same time, suburban Haifa started to emerge north of the industrial Haifa Bay (1932–1937), coupled with the establishment, for security purposes, of a belt of kibbutzim north of the suburban area. The migration of Jews from Nazi Germany during the mid-1930s and the preparations for World War II brought about a massive construction of industries in the bay area, notably consumer and metal industries. This process continued into the early 1940s, by way of the construction of the coastal railway to Lebanon and the integration of Haifa into the war effort (Sofer, 1971).

The 1930s, thus, represented the culmination of the emergence of Haifa as a transportation and industrial focus. It was the only city in Palestine that enjoyed all forms of transportation: land, sea, air, and pipeline. As such, Haifa served as a core not only for Palestine but also for the whole Levant (consisting of Palestine, Jordan, Syria, and Lebanon), a role it shared with Beirut. From an industrial perspective, Haifa constituted a core of heavy industries operating in large plants, while the more general industrial core evolved in Tel Aviv. This difference was apparent in the gap between the low percentage of plants located in the port city against the higher percentage of industrial workers employed (Table 6.4). The share of Tel Aviv in the number of factories, which ranged between 40 and 60 percent of all those in Palestine, was three to five times larger than that of Haifa.

Side by side with the construction of large industrial plants in Haifa the labor union (Histadruth) became even stronger in the city in which it was originally founded. This strength was visible in the organization of unions in factories. The Histadruth, politically

Table 6.4. Industrial Plants and Industrial Workers in the Haifa
Subdistrict, as a Percentage of National Totals, 1925–1985/86

YEAR	PLANTS	WORKERS
1925	11.7	17.5
1929	11.7	17.5
1933	11.8	14.2
1937	16.8	18.5
1943	13.6	15.4
1952	13.8	16.8
1965	12.7	14.8
1975	10.5	12.9
1980–81	11.8	12.8
1985–86	10.9	12.5

Sources: 1925–1943: Sofer, 1971; 1952–1985/86: Central Bureau of Statistics.

dominated by the largest political party (Mapai), developed a total
social autonomy in varied areas of the workers' life, such as
employment, health, absorption, food provision, and so forth. The
particularly strong status of the Histadruth in Haifa may be related
to the existence of a relatively large industrial working-class community and to serious employment problems in the 1920s, which
caused proletariatization (de Fries, 1989). There emerged, therefore, a dissonance between Haifa as an *origin* for workers' power,
on the one hand, and the location of national decision making by
the Histadruth and the political parties in Tel Aviv, on the other.
This gap was especially striking, since Labor had a strong impact
on modes of life in Haifa and enjoyed the political leadership there,
whereas Tel Aviv was governed by middle-class civic parties. Furthermore, Haifa did not serve as an origin for Labor ideological
innovations, a role reserved for the core in the valleys.

The image of Haifa was a mixed one. The city was, on the one
hand, a cosmopolitan commercial city; on the other hand, it was
also a city of the working class, "the red city," as it became known.
These two images tended to balance each other. A similar balancing
also existed in Tel Aviv, where the civic and right-wing sectors were
larger than the Left most of the time, despite the concentration of
the central Labor institutions in the city. Following the establishment of Israel and the subsequent cut-off of much of the international trade to and from Haifa, the cosmopolitan atmosphere disappeared from Haifa and left it with only the "red city" image, hurting
the city in its attempts to attract industries and business.

The massive development of Haifa in the 1930s was not only a result of the British use of the city's natural advantages, but also an outcome of the development efforts by the many Jewish immigrants from Central Europe who were fleeing Nazi Germany. They brought with them property, capital, and technological expertise, and engaged in the establishment of industrial and commercial enterprises. Comparing Haifa with similar European cities that enjoyed a harbor and railway junction, they viewed it as a potentially leading industrial city. They were also influenced by its cosmopolitan atmosphere, which was more dominant than in Jerusalem or Tel Aviv, as well as by the view of the bay from the mountain, the mountainous greenery and the cool summer nights (Stern, 1974, p. 87). Thus, at the start of the Nazi period, investments in construction in Haifa quadrupled in one year, 1932–1933 (Gelber, 1989, p. 95).

Haifa constituted a frontier in addition to its being a core during the 1930s. As a mixed city of Jews and Arabs with an unclear destiny in case of partition, the city was perceived as a most important settlement objective:

> At this time we have to direct all the urban settlement efforts to Haifa. All the urban immigration to Haifa. All the new industry to Haifa.... Tel Aviv will grow and expand—but it is impossible and unnecessary to 'Judaize' Tel Aviv further. One hundred percent is, after all, sufficient, but this is not the case with Haifa. Here is the weak point, *in the city and in the harbor,* and with directed, persistent efforts, with a fast, energetic pace, we have to increase our power, size, weight, economy, holdings—and it is forbidden for us to miss even one minute. (Ben-Gurion, [1938], 1955, pp. 60-61)

Despite its diversified social structure, Haifa was characterized by a Jewish community with an internal stability, openness, unity, and cooperation. This character assisted in security operations, especially concerning the illegal immigration period (Naor, 1989; Ben-Artzi, 1989). On the other hand, the Labor Party's hegemony and its attempts to impose a social homogeneity spoiled the development of Haifa after 1948.

Sofer (1971, 1980) has suggested several reasons why it was impossible for pre-1948 Haifa to become larger than Tel Aviv. First, Tel Aviv was a Jewish city, whereas Haifa was a mixed one (the adjacency of Arab Jaffa to Tel Aviv was of a different nature, given the municipal independence of Tel Aviv). Second, the smaller Jaffa harbor specialized in Jewish immigration, and immigrants tend to settle in their port of arrival. Third, the citrus fruit economy of the Sharon and Judean coastal plains contributed to agricultural developments around Tel Aviv as well as to urban development in the city itself. Fourth, Tel Aviv was based since its beginnings on small businesses, which fit the business mentality of Eastern European immigrants. Fifth, Eastern European immigrants preferred a plain city, which was similar to the urban landscapes of their old countries. Sixth, during World War II there was an apprehension at air raids against the strategically important Haifa. Several other factors relate to financial differences between the two cities (Stern, 1974). The banks were mostly concentrated in Tel Aviv, so that Haifa builders could not provide as high a credit as Tel Aviv builders could. Also, during the 1920s, Tel Aviv was settled by wealthier people, who traded in real estate and investments; Haifa was preferred by laborers and middle class immigrants until the Fifth (German) Aliya in the 1930s.

This rather long list of developmental differences between the two cities may be complemented by an additional factor. The location of Tel Aviv in the center of Palestine gave it an advantage at the national-domestic level. Thus, the emergence of Tel Aviv as a leading center was mainly related to its function as a political, business, and social center for the new Jewish community in Palestine. Haifa, on the other hand, evolved as an international transportation center, a feature, however, that was less important, because the colonial economy of Palestine was not typified by large exports of raw materials, except for citrus fruits, and these were loaded mostly at Jaffa, which was located in the midst of their growing area. The Middle Eastern economy specialized in the export of just one resource, oil, which brought about the construction of oil refineries in Haifa. The *Hebrew* Tel Aviv served as a focus for the development of the Jewish state and of a new Jewish culture and turned into a symbol of these values. The power of attraction of Tel Aviv with these images was probably greater than the attractiveness of Haifa, which represented a restricted international economy, albeit with diversified transportation means.

Haifa Since Statehood: On the Core Margin

The relative decline in the development of Haifa following the founding of the State of Israel has been tied to several local, national, and international processes that affected transportation, manufacturing, the status of the city, and tourism. These processes have caused the merits of Tel Aviv to be more striking and those of Haifa at least partially to be diminished.

During the period of riots shortly before the establishment of Israel the railway line between Haifa and Damascus was closed. Israel's War of Independence in 1948 brought about a full closing of transportation links with all the surrounding Arab countries: roads, railways, and pipelines, including an almost completed pipeline from Saudi Arabia. This total disruption of land contacts led to the cessation of international flights to Haifa by a governmental order in 1950. The sea provided the only outlet, and an auxiliary port was built in Haifa in 1951–1953 (the Kishon Harbor) and the Israel Shipyards in the 1960s. Nevertheless, these projects have not provided enough compensation for the city, neither for its losses in land and air transportation nor for two problems related to international maritime transportation. First was the rise in importance of passenger traffic by air. In 1987 only 22.3 percent of passengers arriving in Haifa by sea used scheduled liner ships, the remainder came on tour ships and ferries; in any event, the total number of sea-passenger traffic amounted to only 8 percent of air passenger traffic. Thus, a passenger terminal and an overpass leading directly from the harbor to downtown have been relatively little in use. The second problem relates to Ashdod port, south of Tel Aviv, which since its opening in 1965 replaced the two rather small ports of Tel Aviv and Jaffa and has gradually become Israel's leading port (Figures 6.4–6.6). It surpassed Haifa in cargo loading in 1968, mainly because Ashdod served the bulk potash and phosphates exports produced in the Negev. By 1981, the total cargo transferred through Ashdod was larger than that through Haifa, and its lead has since increased. Ashdod has become the port of central and southern Israel, which are larger than the northern region, served mainly by Haifa.

A comparative study of industrial sites in the Haifa Bay area found that the port is also losing its importance as a locational factor (Sofer, 1988). In 1968, 36 percent of the large plants in Haifa mentioned the port as a primary locational factor. Since then, however, only chemicals, particularly petrochemical plants, have remained tied to the harbor, whereas food production and textile industries have lost interest. This occurred because of the construction of Ashdod port, the increased use of domestic raw materials, and the concentration of markets in the Center and South. Thus, in 1986, chemical plants contributed some 34.5 percent of the total cargo exported through Haifa, compared to just 12 percent in 1968. Imports of raw materials by all other industries in the

Figure 6.4. Total Cargo in Haifa and Ashdod Ports, 1965–1987

Data source: Central Bureau of Statistics, 1965–1988.

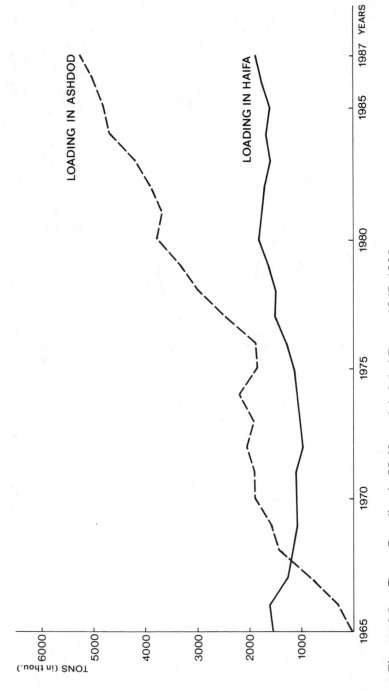

Figure 6.5. Cargo Loading in Haifa and Ashdod Ports, 1965–1987

Data source: Central Bureau of Statistics, 1965–1988.

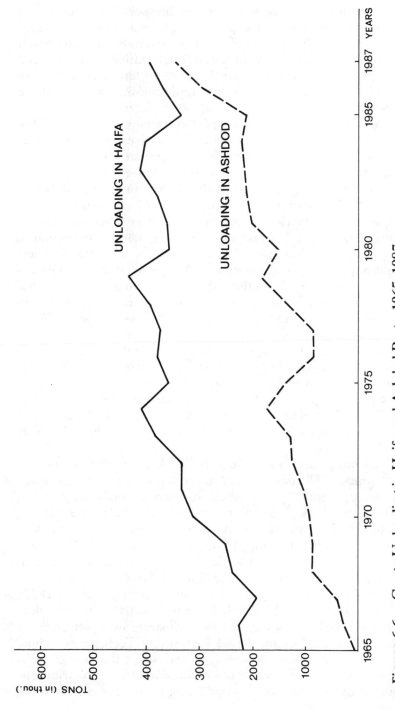

Figure 6.6. Cargo Unloading in Haifa and Ashdod Ports, 1965–1987

Data source: Central Bureau of Statistics, 1965–1988.

bay area amounted to but 9 percent of the port's total unloaded cargo, and their exports were marginal. A large Haifa computer factory noted that 35 percent of its raw materials were domestic, 65 percent were imported by air through Ben-Gurion Airport, and only 5 percent reached it through the port. By the same token, 95 percent of its exports were airborne, and only 5 percent used the Haifa port.

Ben-Gurion international airport, located close to Tel Aviv and Jerusalem and connected to both cities by expressways, symbolizes Israeli air transportation for international traffic of both residents and visitors. This position was once enjoyed by Haifa, which was the city with the most developed international ties in general, and air transportation in particular. Haifa lost, therefore, its uniqueness, its superiority, and to a large degree also its specialization in international transportation. This meant, furthermore, the loss of an important factor for the attraction of new industries; those already existing in the city remained there often out of industrial inertia (the main exception being the petrochemical plants). The vacuum caused by the closure of most international routes to Haifa was filled by a faster development of Tel Aviv (see also Amiran and Shachar, 1959).

The decline in the transportation strength of Haifa was also expressed in the number of those employed in the city in this area compared to Tel Aviv. In 1931, some 7407 people in Haifa were employed in transportation and communications, whereas the figure for Tel Aviv was only 2677. By 1987, some 19,300 workers in Tel Aviv were employed in these areas, compared to just 10,500 in Haifa.

Haifa has always been second to Tel Aviv insofar as industrial concentration. The decline of Haifa in terms of both the percentage of factories and the percentage industrial employment in the city had started back in the early 1940s (Table 6.4). The uniqueness of the Haifa industries was manifested more in plant size than in the number of plants, though both values decreased. Nevertheless, Haifa has continued its leadership in chemical and mineral industries. Therefore, in 1983, one third of Israeli employment in these branches was to be found in Haifa. Throughout the 1970s (with beginnings in the 1960s), high-tech industries, notably electronics, developed in the city. These industries were attracted to Haifa by the Technion, the Israel Institute of Technology. Thus, an early initial advantage possessed by the city in the area of technological education matured in the form of modern industrial production. Although the Technion remains the largest institute for high-level technological education in Israel, this advantage for Haifa has been whittled away somewhat as technological education was began to be provided by other institutions as well (Tel Aviv University, Weitzman Institute, Ben-Gurion University). Thus, although Haifa led nationally in electronics industries, so that 27.9 percent of all employment in this area in 1983 took place in Haifa subdistrict, Greater Tel Aviv (that is including the suburban subdistricts of Petah Tiqva, Ramla, and Rehovot) accounted for 60.4 percent of total national employment in this sector; in contrast, the subdistricts around Haifa (Jezreel and Acre) counted only few employed in electronics industries (Table 6.5).

Table 6.5. Distribution of Employees in the Production of Electrical and Electronic Equipment by Subdistricts, 1983

SUBDISTRICT	NUMBER OF EMPLOYEES IN THE PRODUCTION OF ELECTRIC AND ELECTRONIC EQUIPMENT (IN THOUSANDS)	PERCENT OF NATIONAL TOTAL
Jerusalem	0.6	1.5
Safed	—	—
Kinnereth	—	—
Jezreel	0.5	1.3
Acre	0.6	1.5
Haifa	11.2	27.9
Hadera	—	—
Sharon	0.3	0.7
Petah Tiqva	7.1	17.7
Ramla	5.6	14.0
Rehovot	2.5	6.2
Tel Aviv	9.0	22.5
Ashqelon	2.7	6.7
Beersheba	—	—
Total	40.1	100.0

Source: Central Bureau of Statistics, 1987.

The location of central management is another element of the more general problem of decline in the status of Haifa (Razin, 1984). In 1981, 13.7 percent of the headquarters of the largest industrial companies in Israel were located in Haifa; the share of metropolitan Tel Aviv was 44.3 percent. Further, the highest level of decision making was to be found in only 7.3 percent of the large companies located in Haifa. In a sectoral division, central management located in Haifa was concentrated in electronics, chemicals, rubber, and plastics, and most of these companies were either government or union owned. Geographically, the central management in Haifa served plants located beyond a 30 km. radius from Haifa; ironically, plants sited close to the city were served by the Tel Aviv offices!

The establishment of the state in 1948 hurt the cities of Jerusalem and Haifa, each for different reasons, while it strengthened Tel Aviv. Jerusalem became a capital surrounded by borders, while Haifa was disconnected from its international hinterland. Haifa was turned largely into a regional capital, a trend that has been reinforced since the opening of the port of Ashdod. Under these conditions, the centrally located Tel Aviv became even more advantageous. This caused many maritime service businesses to move from Haifa to Tel Aviv, which is located between the country's two major ports. Jerusalem was able to change and flourish following the 1967 war, though it could not surpass Tel Aviv. Haifa, on the other hand, has not enjoyed either a war or peace event that could improve its status.

The changing status of Israel's three large cities is reflected in their respective population data (Table 6.6). The ratio of population sizes between Tel Aviv–Jaffa and Haifa in 1948 was 1:2.5 in favor of Tel Aviv (98,600 in Haifa compared to 248,500 in Tel Aviv–Jaffa). This ratio grew to 1:4 between the two metropolitan areas by 1983 (391,100 in Haifa and 1,564,000 in Tel Aviv). In 1948, the population of Haifa was slightly larger than that of Jerusalem (84,000 in Jerusalem, compared to 98,600 in Haifa). Until 1967, this gap increased in favor of Haifa, and reached a ratio of 3:2 by 1966 (195,700 in Jerusalem, and 294,800 in metropolitan Haifa). In 1983, however, the 1948 ratio was repeated, but this time in favor of Jerusalem (431,800 in Jerusalem, and 391,100 in Haifa).

At the same time that Haifa's international vitality source largely disappeared, the accent during the first two decades of statehood was placed nationally on the development of the South, which did little to assist Haifa in developing its status as the capital of the North. Moreover, the immense power of the Histadruth in the city deterred potential private capital from investing in Haifa. Particularly harmful in this regard were several large scale strikes in the early 1950s. In subsequent decades, other factors, in addition to the port of Ashdod, chipped away at whatever exclusively Haifa offered: the development of chemical industries in the Negev; the location in Ashdod of an oil refinery, a silo, and a major electric

Table 6.6. Ranking of the Three Largest Cities in Israel, 1922–1983

RANK	1922	1931	1948	1961	1972	1983
1	Jerusalem	Tel Aviv–Jaffa	Tel Aviv–Jaffa	Metropolitan Tel Aviv	Metropolitan Tel Aviv	Metropolitan Tel Aviv
2	Tel Aviv–Jaffa	Jerusalem	Haifa	Haifa	Metropolitan Haifa	Jerusalem
3	Haifa	Haifa	Jerusalem	Jerusalem	Jerusalem	Metropolitan Haifa

power station; the move to Jerusalem of customs headquarters. The handful of big national companies that remained in Haifa often did so only after public pressure (e.g., Zim-Israel Navigation Co., Israel Electric Co., the three major oil companies). The term, *the three large cities,* which was coined during the British Mandate era, had referred not just to the population size of these cities, Jerusalem, Tel Aviv, and Haifa, but also to their specializations and the division of core functions among them. Nowadays, this term holds only as far as population is concerned. The fourth largest city, Beersheba (if one does not take into account larger suburbs in metropolitan Tel Aviv), is still relatively small, its population just one quarter of that of metropolitan Haifa. It is doubtful, however, whether the term is still meaningful from a functional perspective when the core functions are divided between Jerusalem and Tel Aviv. Nevertheless, Haifa is still much larger and stronger than Beersheba, thanks to the port, industrial inertia, and the initial advantages of the Technion and high-tech industries.

Another aspect of the decline in the status of Haifa is tourism. In 1928, Haifa could count some forty-eight hotels, compared to thirty-four in Tel Aviv, twenty-three in Jaffa, and forty-three in Jerusalem. In 1931, 1408 people were employed in hotels, coffee shops, and restaurants in Haifa, compared with just 989 so employed in Tel Aviv (the total number of workers in Haifa that year was 10 percent larger than in Tel Aviv!) (Stern, 1974). Recreation and tourism constituted important elements for the construction of residential sections on Mt. Carmel during the 1930s, when immigrants from Germany brought with them a European culture of recreation and leisure. By 1958 the number of rooms in tourist hotels in Haifa had fallen in percentage terms but still was just a quarter less than in Jerusalem and Tel Aviv (678 in Haifa, compared with 821 in Tel Aviv and 850 in Jerusalem). Thirty years later, the story was altogrther different. Haifa hotel rooms increased by 40 percent (to 951) by 1987. In contrast, their number in Tel Aviv proper alone grew sevenfold (to 5531), and in Jerusalem almost tenfold (to 8065, including East Jerusalem). These comparative figures reflect several factors. The decline in both the domestic and international status of Haifa brought about a drastic decrease in business tourism. This was coupled with the construction of a good road system that permitted business tourists to do business in Haifa and still stay in Tel Aviv. Another factor was the transition in international as well as Israeli recreation habits through the introduction of active recreation. A comparison between Haifa and Tiberias may demonstrate this last point.

The two cities enjoy a similar topography, being located on both a beach and a mountain. Both cities have a veteran hotel infrastructure. The two cities differ from each other in that metropolitan Haifa is thirteen times larger than Tiberias. The latter offers, however, a sweet-water lake and hot springs, and tourism in the two cities over the last three decades has developed in a way that puts Haifa in the shadow of Tiberias (Figure 6.7). In 1958, Haifa had 678 rooms in tourist hotels, Tiberias only 404. By 1987, however, there were 2615 such rooms in Tiberias, compared with just 951 in Haifa. Tiberias has been typified by constant growth in the availability of rooms in tourist hotels, with two particular growth periods, in 1977 and in the mid-1980s, that saw the construction or expansion of large hotels. In the 1980s, this trend reflected a priority for Tiberias by the Ministry of Tourism. It is interesting to note, however, that similar trends characterized both cities, with even some priority for Haifa, until 1971. It was then that Tiberias started to grow, at first slowly and later much faster, its growth pattern representing a change in life-styles in Israel in general, and in recreation patterns in particular. Tiberias drew on the Kinnereth, being the only sweet-water lake in Israel, on the one hand, and on growing incomes and motorization levels, on the other. It could offer a variety of activities for both short and long recreational stays. Haifa has not adjusted itself to these trends; worse, the location of the port on the city front has not made it easier for it to develop its beaches. Nor has it made its docks a tourist or residential center as other cities around the world have done.

The postindustrial era and its accents on extended leisure times, technology, and business services do not necessarily call for a favorable change for the green, beautiful, and infrastructure-rich Haifa. Tel Aviv has become a world city, and the gaps between the two cities may even widen. The lack of a strong international status for Haifa since 1948 has assisted Tel Aviv in attaining this status with the coming of the age of the global economy. The concentration of headquarters of financial services (banking, insurance) in Tel Aviv has increased throughout the years. A possible peace between Israel and the Arab world does not automatically mean Haifa's return to its special international status of the British Mandate period. Israel's neighboring countries have constructed alternative harbors as well as roads to connect these harbors with their respective cores. Then, too, the Ashdod port is closer to the core of Jordan than is Haifa. Nevertheless, Haifa has become a leader in the current trend to the suburbanization of retail trade through modern shopping malls (Kellerman, 1987a). The Haifa area gener-

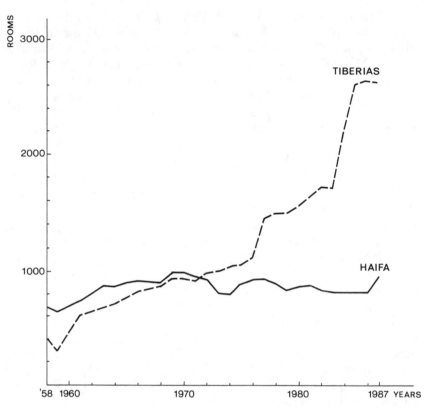

Figure 6.7.   Rooms in Tourist Hotels in Haifa and Tiberias, 1958–1987

Data source: Central Bureau of Statistics, 1959–1987.

ally enjoys a high urban quality of life; an advantage, however, that is threatened by severe air pollution, which may in the long run deter a possible growth in tourism and influence high-tech industries to prefer other regions.

The inferior status and image of Haifa, compared to the cores in Jerusalem and Tel Aviv, have caused it to be almost ignored by the national media and literature. As a result, Haifa became a leader in the development of local press when this medium emerged in Israel in the 1970s. The economic-geographic status of Haifa and its image have been interrelated and mutually reinforcing. As its importance and status have declined, so did its image; and these declines have brought about less attention and attraction by enterprises and population. Perhaps this vicious cycle could have been broken by the reopening of Haifa's international airport, which could potentially have strengthened the city's regional and national status and, therefore, further attracted both tourism and high-tech industries.

Chapter 7

The South

The Negev

A vision or an ideology for a regional frontier in Israel was more striking for the Negev than for any other region. This vision was tied to Ben-Gurion in his capacity as the prime minister of the State of Israel during its pioneering years, in the 1950s. Ben-Gurion's attachment to the Negev had started earlier, however. The myth surrounding the idea of occupying the desert and making it bloom during the first fifteen to twenty years of statehood stands in sharp contrast to the reality of the current decline in the status of the region, which has turned into a periphery. This transition was attested to by a decline in the population of Negev central cities toward the end of the 1980s, and consequently in its relative percentage of the Jewish population of Israel.

The Negev did not have its own Tel Hai in the early pre-state days of settlement. Be'er Tuvia and Ruhama, the two pioneering settlements in the South, did not enjoy a mythical status as did the northern Tel Hai. The settlement project in the South and its accompanying myth were relatively short-lived, though the efforts invested were extensive. The frontier-mythological event in the South that was equivalent to Tel Hai and Hanitta in the North was the establishment of eleven kibbutzim in one night in 1947. This event, which took place just several months before the declaration of Israel's independence, was more powerful than the establishment of Hanitta. It symbolized the tremendous effort that was going to be invested in the settlement of the Negev immediately following the establishment of the state. In the North, the Huleh Valley served the Galilee as an initial target region adjacent to the challenging mountainous target region. In the South, the southern coastal plain (Figure 1.1) offered the initial target region for the Negev. Although penetration into the Negev was highly intense, given the environmental problems of the region, the intrusion into the Galilee was restricted and did not peak until the 1980s. The exchange of the Negev for the Galilee (by Prime Minister Levi Eshkol) as the preferred settlement object in the mid-1960s proved to have been done too early in terms of the maturity of the Negev,

243

as far as population size, available resources, and transportation networks were concerned. It was also, however, too late for the Galilee, for several reasons: the decline of the frontier spirit among the Israeli Left, the growing choice of frontier regions following the 1967 war, and the quantitative and qualitative growth of the Arab population in the Galilee.

The Negev Prior to Statehood: From Periphery to Frontier

It is possible to divide the pre-state settlement activity in the Negev into three subperiods (Kark, 1974, p. 14). The first one took place at the end of the Ottoman rule (1880–1917); the second included most of the British Mandate period (1917–1939), and the third covered the decade prior to the founding of Israel (1939–1947). Though this division is based on major general political events, it reflects the character of settlement at the time. During the first subperiod, settlement in the Negev was mainly to enable ideas and plans to emerge. The second subperiod concentrated on various experiments and on land purchase; the third signaled the beginning of settlement activity per se.

The first period was known for the plans of Hov'vei Zion (First Aliya members), Levontin, and Herzl (Kark, 1974; Orni, 1979; Oren, 1979b). In practice, however there were only two settlement attempts: the colony of Be'er-Tuvia, which was settled twice (in 1887 and 1896) and considered to be in the Negev, though located more precisely in the "South"; and Ruhama (1911). Both settlements were abandoned during the 1929 riots, but were later resettled.

The second period was similar to the first; but with the exception of Kfar Menachem (1937), saw no new settlements established in the South. This period, however, was typified by continued land purchases, especially around Beersheba (Orni, 1979). Hence, the Negev constituted more of a periphery during the first two pre-state settlement subperiods. At that time, there was insufficient consciousness for the determination of the southern boundaries for the evolving Jewish entity; when such awareness did exist, it was translated mainly into limited land purchases rather than into settlements. In the Galilee, things developed differently, as has been seen. The Tel Hai affair created an *awareness* of boundary determination through settlement; though even there, this awareness did not immediately result in settlement activity. The Negev was perceived during these first two subperiods in two seemingly contradicting ways. On the one hand, it was viewed optimistically as a region suitable for settlement activity; on the other hand, it was also seen as a remote region, mainly because of the lack of roads (Kark, 1974, pp. 181–182).

There were three main reasons for the poor settlement activity in the South. First, the North enjoyed an existing nucleus in form of the old communities in Safed and Tiberias, which served as anchors, even if only of a limited nature, for the settlement activity in the Huleh Valley and in the Lower Galilee (this was also advocated by Ruppin's plan). The Negev and the South in general could not count on such anchors. Another factor was the lack of any knowledge on the ways and means of agricultural settlement in the desert. This ignorance was coupled with the feeling that settlement activity in the region was not urgent, because the Arabs, too, did not show much interest in the area. Lastly, the Jewish National Fund had accumulated a sizeable debt from land purchases in the valleys (Orni, 1979).

The third period of prestatehood activity in the Negev was different. It was characterized by the massive beginnings of settlement activity (Figure 7.1). The Negev, as well as the Galilee, turned into active primary frontiers from 1936, with the outbreak of riots and the early deliberations over a possible partition of Palestine. The Zionist slogan *to the Galilee,* was implemented by the pioneering establishment of Hanitta, whereas the call *to the Negev,* was put into practice by the foundation of Negba (1939), (literally meaning "to the Negev"), as well as of Kfar Warburg. These beginnings were related to Ben-Gurion's pre-state vision.

In 1935, Ben-Gurion had visited Eilat, where he attempted unsuccessfully to establish a fishermen's village, connected by air to the centers of the country (Oren, 1979b). In 1939, he ordered the renting of five houses in Beersheba, to be used by people who would engage in large-scale land purchases. At the same time, he continued his efforts for the study of the Eilat area (Orni, 1979). By February 1948, months shy of statehood, Ben-Gurion introduced the Negev as a region constituting simultaneously a territorial and a mode of life frontier: "A Jewish state without the Negev is almost not a Jewish state, and in a double sense: almost not a state and almost not Jewish, because I do not believe that a Jewish Carthage is possible. And without the Negev there will be a kind of Carthage, which will be called Tel Aviv" (Ben-Gurion, 1951, p. 281). In other words, Ben-Gurion conceived of the Negev as pro-

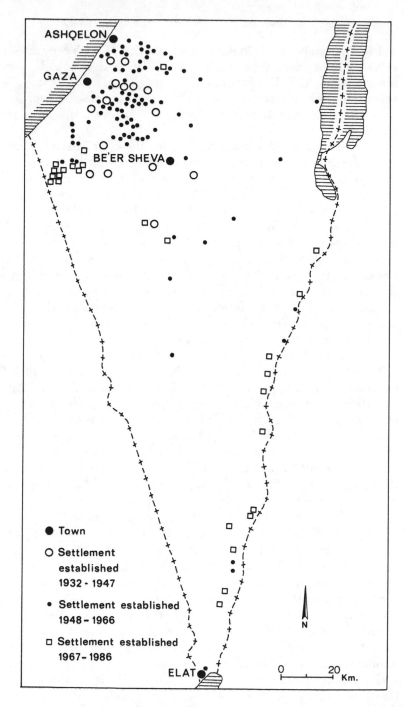

Figure 7.1. Negev Settlements Before and After 1948

viding the Jewish national entity with sufficient territorial base for a state; at the same time he viewed the region as a location that could provide an agrarian-pioneering mode of life, contrasting with bourgeois Tel Aviv. It is important to note here that Ben-Gurion bore two central functions related to the development of the Negev. He was the ideological leader of the Negev vision; he also served as the executive leader of the Zionist movement and, later, as prime minister of the new state during its years of massive development. He was thus able to direct ideological, human, and economic resources to the Negev. In Ben-Gurion's words in 1946: "We shall stand like a fortified wall around the settlement project and the state vision, and both—the project and the vision—are inseparably held and stuck to each other, and we should not fear any wickedness" (1951, p. 113).

Following the intrusion southward in 1939, three settlements were established in the Negev during 1941–1942 (Gat, Dorot, Gvaram), in 1943 six additional ones were founded; in 1944, one settlement was put up (actually a resettled Ruhama); nine settlements came about in 1946; and, excluding the eleven settlements established in one night, five in 1947 (Kark, 1974; Oren, 1979b). Not only did the number of settlements grow, but their expansion into the South did so as well. Two specific, important phenomena have to be singled out in this settlement wave; namely, the observation outposts and the unique affair of the eleven settlements in one night.

The observation outpost settlement in the Negev of the 1940s were not of the same nature as the Galilee presettlements established in the 1980s. The three "look-outs" built in 1943 (Gevulot, Revivim, and Beit Eshel) functioned formally as agricultural research stations, and thus symbolized the agricultural accent in the settlement effort of the Negev at the time. They fulfilled, however, another unspelled mission, that of moving the settlement area further South. This was accomplished, though the future of these stations was unclear at the time; indeed the Haganah's Rochel-Lev settlement plan did not call for such a deep-south intrusion. These look-out settlements constituted, therefore, a primary frontier even relative to the plans for Jewish settlements. The Rochel-Lev plan called for (1) obtaining British concession for Negev settlements; (2) the use of extensive capital for irrigation plans. Thus the Negev was not viewed as a primary settlement objective.

The establishment of eleven settlements in one night in 1947 was a political demonstration, which came in addition to the construction of five other settlements in the Negev that year. The feat marked a large-scale frontier settlement project for those days. These settlements served as an opening for a much larger settlement wave, which was to take place just a short time later, following the establishment of Israel. Ben-Gurion viewed the construction of the eleven settlements and their defense as a repeat of the Tel Hai affair (1951, p. 110). It should be noted that no settlement was built in the mountainous Galilee that year, and in the previous year, 1946, only one settlement was built there, Yehi'am. The Negev was settled in 1946–1947 by twenty-five settlements! Although the number of mountainous settlements in the North was small throughout the British Mandate, they helped determine the borders of the Jewish state in the region. The diversion of the settlement effort to the South, which occurred only as of 1939, yielded the founding of many settlements; however, the secondary frontier that evolved in the Negev after 1948 effectively continued the primary frontier that had emerged between 1939 and 1948. By the same token, the limited settlement attention paid to the Galilee during the critical years prior to 1948 continued well into the years of massive development in Israel, the 1950s. When attention was finally directed to the Galilee, after 1963, it was already too late.

Pre-state Negev settlements, even as frontier, contributed to the setting of the nation's boundaries after bloody battles during the 1948 war (Orni, 1979; Oren, 1979b; Kark, 1974). This settlement expanded southward only up to the central, mountainous Negev, a limit that owed to the lack of water and the ideological conception that agricultural settlements should be preferred even in desert areas. In other words, ideology and its interpretation through resource allocation determined to a large degree the expansion boundary for the primary frontier. The agricultural preference and the water problems made the kibbutz the exclusive settlement form during the pre-state period. This form of settlement, as well as the regional geographical conditions, required a constant resource flow from the core to the frontier (Kark, 1974).

The Negev Since Statehood:
From Frontier to Periphery

Ben-Gurion had argued that the use of the Hebrew phrase, "to go *down* to the Negev," was incorrect; it should, rather, be replaced with, "to go *up* to the Negev," which he also thought was a more biblical idiom. It was in the wake of this expression that the secondary frontier in the Negev developed in the 1950s. Ben-Gurion (1979) demanded that all human and economic resources be directed to the South; and, indeed, this secondary frontier was much more extensive than the pre-state primary one. The myth of "making the desert bloom" was one of the three myths related to Israel during its first three decades of statehood (together with the kibbutz and population dispersal). In practice, however, the idea was more for cities to *settle* the desert than for villages to make it *bloom* (if the Lakhish region is excluded) (Waterman, 1979).

The myth of "occupying the unsettled" originated in the early Zionist project of draining the swamps in the valleys. It originally referred to treating the *surplus* of water. Transferring this myth to the South meant dealing with the *lack* of water. This water problem had been addressed in the Negev before statehood, with the aid of drilled wells and a pipeline from Gvaram. The full evolution of the myth, however, was strongly tied to *statism*, because large-scale settlement and development of the South required national solutions for the water problem. Thus, pipeline systems were constructed to transport water, initially from the Center (the Yarkon Project in the 1950s) and eventually from the far North (the National Water Carrier in the 1960s). The draining of swamps in the valleys was of a rather local or regional nature.

The myth of exploiting the resources of the Negev and Dead Sea also started before 1948, in the form of the Dead Sea Works in Sodom and Beit Ha'arava. Even here, though, large-scale development had to await statehood to obtain the required urban, industrial, and transportation infrastructure. These two myths, of a blooming desert and the use of resources, were created outside the region, by Zionist and state institutions, as well as by Ben-Gurion, who personally moved to a young kibbutz in the Negev, Sde Boker, in 1953.

Another myth concerning the Negev that was created outside the region started to emerge for a short time in the 1970s. It related to the "Seas Canal," which was supposed to connect the Mediterranean and the Dead Sea and to produce ample cheap, electric power. Such a canal had been envisioned by Herzl. The idea was finally abandoned when it became evident that the project would not be profitable. A connection between national projects of mythical value and calculations of economic feasibility, with the latter becoming more important than the former, has become typical since the mid-1970s (another prominent example was the proposed supersonic "Lavi" fighter jet, a project that was of a less geographical nature).

Following the establishment of Israel, all settlement forms "invaded" the Negev. It had become evident by the early 1950s that mass populating of the Negev as well as extensive extraction of its natural resources would require city construction rather than agricultural villages. The realization of the Negev development vision, thus, was tied to an ideological concession so far as settlements were concerned. The towns of Beersheba, Dimona, Yeruham, and Eilat were built shortly after the establishment of the state; following the 1956 war, Mitzpe Ramon was founded. Arad was constructed in the early 1960s as a development town to which new concepts of urban design were applied. By the mid-1960s, the percentage of the urban population in the Negev exceeded 80 percent. In addition to these towns, which were based on natural resources and industries, several service towns were established in the northern Negev (Ofakim, Netivot, and Sderot). These, too, were later turned into industrial towns because of the lack of sufficient contacts with the rural sector surrounding them. During the development period, the rural sector in the Negev grew, too, the number of kibbutzim doubling (from twelve to twenty-four) between 1948 and 1954 and the number of moshavim increasing from two to twenty-eight. The kibbutzim, once again, served as the intrusion settlement form in the 1940s; the moshavim based and expanded the secondary settlement frontier in the 1950s.

The major settlement wave that took place in the 1950s accentuated the northwestern Negev and the northern Negev mountains (Figure 7.1 and Table 7.1). Only 8.6 percent of the immigrants of the huge immigration wave reached the Southern District, however. Since the 1960s, settlement activity also started along the Arava Valley leading to Eilat. This was a time of absolute population growth in the whole of the Negev, at least during the early 1960s. The 1970s were characterized by low population growth, alongside the continued construction of settlements in the southwestern part of the Northern Negev (Table 7.1) (Stern et al., 1986). During this period, there also evolved several special sites that were neither urban nor rural, such as the hotel strip along the Dead Sea and the Sde Boker educational complex (Krakover and Dover, 1987). The 1980s witnessed the development of community settlements around Beersheba (Omer, Meitar, and Lehavim) and the settling of the southern part of Mount Hebron.

The transition process for the Negev, from a secondary frontier of high visionary power to a periphry, started in the mid-1960s. In 1963, the population growth process of Beesheba subdistrict stopped after fifteen consecutive years (Moyal, 1979, p. 719). Even

Table 7.1. Increase in the Number of Jewish Settlements in the Beersheba District, 1948–1987

YEAR	1948	1953	1961	1972	1983	1987
Number of Settlements	15	56	73	80	107	110
Percent Growth	—	273.3	30.3	9.6	33.8	2.8

Sources: Schmaltz, 1979; Central Bureau of Statistics, 1984; 1988.

in the year of the Negev's highest growth, in 1963, only 5 percent of the Israeli population resided there, though its area constituted 60 percent of Israel. That year, the Galilee development project was anounced. The establishment of additional agricultural settlements in the central Negev became questionable, since the quantities of northern water to be transported to this area were limited. A large-scale settlement of the Arava Valley would have required heavy investment for the development of water and land. The textile industry, which served as the industrial base of the development towns, modernized and required fewer workers; several demand crises also took their toll on this sector. Industries based on Negev resources underwent various technological improvements, also cutting the need for personnel. The newly developing high-tech industries produced no offsetting compensation, as they did not diffuse into the South.

These processes brought about a second phase in the population development of the Negev, this time in the form of absolute declines in the urban sector. Dimona and Yeruham recorded losses from the early 1980s, Beersheba and Arad from mid-decade. In 1987, a slight decline was registered for the first time in the share of the Southern District of the total population, from 12 percent in 1986 to 11.9 percent. This drop stemmed from a decline in the Jewish population of Beersheba subdistrict, from 6.9 percent of the total Israeli population in 1986 to 6.8 percent in 1987. Eilat proved an exception to this process, its continued growth tied to its increased popularity as a resort town.

Summary and Conclusions

Because it is possible at this stage to trace the evolution of both cores and peripheries in Israel, the comments to follow will relate to the growth of Jerusalem and Tel Aviv, which was detailed in the preceding part. Highlighting the relationship between the evolution of cores, frontiers, and peripheries, on the one hand, and Zionist ideology on the other, will provide the connecting thread between Parts 1 and 3. The summary will be treated from three viewpoints: first, territorial, the crystallization of core, frontier, and periphry regions in Israel; second, cultural, the evolution of major social values in the frontiers and cores; third, comparative, the two previous aspects will be viewed against changing Zionist objectives and settlement ideals. The first two viewpoints are summarized concisely in Table 7.2.

Territorial Evolution of Cores in Israel

Four major phases may be observed in the territorial evolution of core areas in modern Jewish Land of Israel. The first phase was that of initial deployment, taking place from the last two decades of the nineteenth century until the 1920s. This phase was characterized by the evolution of a new core in Palestine, namely the N core along the coast and in the valleys (see Figure 2.1). The evolution of this core led to a decline of the previous Jewish mountainous core (the "four holy towns"). The exception to this trend was Jerusalem; however, it experienced a relative decline when a new core emerged in Jaffa. Although it is possible to observe some interrelationships between the development of Jaffa and Tel Aviv, on the one hand, and the colonies around them, on the other, settlement activity around Jerusalem was rather limited. The early developments along the coastal plain accentuated both agricultural construction (in the colonies) and urban (in Jaffa, Tel Aviv, and Haifa). Developments in the valleys—the two additional arms of the N core—were also characterized by agriculture (in the colonies and in kibbutzim) and, especially, the evolution of an ideological core emphasizing values that were to become cornerstones of pioneering Israeli society in general and the working class in particular: these were the values of equality, labor, pioneering, and defense.

The second and third phases of core developments amounted to a narrowing or shrinking of the new core. During the second phase, which lasted from the 1920s to the 1940s, a decline occurred in the core status of the valleys in favor of flourishing Tel Aviv, which now housed most of the central institutions of the ruling Labor movement. Ruppin's idea, to establish new settlements adjacent to old Jewish communities (notably Tiberias and Safed in the North) proved itself only modestly. The new settlements in the

Huleh Valley and south of the Kinnereth were indeed assisted by the old communities of Safed and Tiberias during the First and Second Aliyas; in their turn, however, the settlements did not reinforce these towns. Therefore, a new core integrating old urban communities with new rural ones was not created in the North. This was mainly due to major differences in the social and religious cultures of the two community types. The new settlements in the valleys needed the ideological as well as the economic backing of Tel Aviv and to a lesser degree the economic support of Haifa, rather than the support of veteran towns nearby. In the 1920s, a second (and last) Jewish pre-state town was established, Afula, located in the geographical center of the "width valleys." It could not compete, however, with Tel Aviv and its nationally centered location and initial advantage. In 1948, the population of Afula numbered 2,500; that of Tel Aviv a hundred times larger, 244,600. Under such circumstances, the status of Jerusalem should have been even more critical, given that it did not enjoy any mass new settlement activity around it, as Tiberias and Safed did. Jerusalem, however, continued to develop despite its isolation from the new Jewish community. This growth was obviously due to its senior and special religious and national status, which survived the changing geographical and social-cultural circumstances of the evolving new Jewish community.

The third phase in the development of cores in modern Jewish Israel constituted a shrinking and narrowing during the 1950s and 1960s. This process was typified by still another decline in the status of the northern component of the original N core, this time at the northern edge of the coastal arm of the N; namely, the Haifa area. On the other hand, the southern edge of the coastal arm, Ashdod, rose in status. The closing of the international boundaries of Israel in 1948 caused Haifa (and Jerusalem in another way) to suffer more than other regions. Long before 1948, however, it was clear that Tel Aviv–Jaffa enjoyed unequivocal supremacy over Haifa. This status stemmed from the more central location of Tel Aviv and also several crucial initial advantages in the form of the nineteenth century growth of Jaffa and its proximity to both the "old" in Jerusalem and the "new" in the colonies.

The fourth phase in the development of core regions involved a more recent maturing in the 1970s and 1980s. Following the 1967 war, the status of Jerusalem as both a political and spiritual capital began to prosper, while Tel Aviv has turned into a world city. Geographically, then, no change can be observed in the location, expansion, or contraction of the core (if suburban and exurban growth is excluded) in this period. The geographical changes now related

Table 7.2. Geographical and Cultural Evolution of Cores, Frontiers, and Peripheries in the Modern Jewish Land of Israel

PHASE	PERIOD	TERRITORIAL EVOLUTION IN THE CORES	VALUE CREATION IN THE CORES	TERRITORIAL EVOLUTION IN THE FRONTIER-PERIPHERY	VALUE CREATION IN THE FRONTIER
1	1880s–1920s	Spreading the Settlement *N*	*Rural:* Cooperation; equality; labor; pioneering; defense *Urban:* Hebrew language; secular Hebrew culture.	Evolution of a primary frontier, notably in the North.	*The valley myth:* Occupying the unsettled; draining the swamps; agriculture and cooperativeness
2	1920s–1940s	Valleys decline as a core; Tel Aviv becomes the largest city	Autonomy in all spheres and levels; organized Jewish labor (Haifa); the preceding continues	Continued primary frontier: reinforcement of the *N* and its joints; spreading new arms in the North and the South.	*The mountain myth:* Boundary determination through settlement.
3	1950s–1960s	Decline in the status of Haifa	Attempts to integrate the above within state frameworks	*Until 1963:* Diversion of effort to the Negev as a secondary frontier. *1963–1967:* Similar attempts in the Galilee	*The desert myth:* Occupying the unsettled; making the desert bloom; exploitation of Negev resources.

Table 7.2. (Continued)

PHASE	PERIOD	TERRITORIAL EVOLUTION IN THE CORES	VALUE CREATION IN THE CORES	TERRITORIAL EVOLUTION IN THE FRONTIER-PERIPHERY	VALUE CREATION IN THE FRONTIER
4	1970s–1980s	Rise of Jerusalem; Tel Aviv becomes a world city	Social Zionism *versus* territorial Zionism. State and religious centrality in Jerusalem	Evolution of a disputed primary frontier in Judea, Samaria, and Gaza. Additional secondary frontier in the Galilee. The North and the South turn into peripheries in the 1980s.	The mountain myth in Judea, Samaria, and Gaza.

more to transitions in the balance between the two core cities, and between them and the rest of the country. Between the two, the importance of Jerusalem increased and its specializations became more marked, whereas Tel Aviv, for its part, has not declined. On the other hand, the complementary though contradictory developments in the two core cities have accentuated the inferior status of other parts of the country. Furthermore, they have contributed to the growth of modern urban residential values in the core in the form of an increased spatial sprawl of population around the two core cities. The improved, more convenient transportation link btween Jerusalem and Tel Aviv has enhanced ties between the two, thus adding to the evolution of peripheries in Israel.

Territorial Evolution of Frontiers in Israel

The development of a frontier has largely been an outcome of decisions and resource allocations made in the core because frontiering, especially in Israel, has constituted foremost a national or social value. Such a value may develop in the frontier itself; however, without recognition by the core, and in the case of Israel without resource flows from the core, the value could not survive. The first stage in the development of a primary frontier in Palestine was marked by an accent on the North, which frontier developed ideologically from below. In its early stages, it initiated social values, such as the emphases on agrarianism and collectivism, as well as territorial values, in the form of occupying the unsettled. These values were later transmitted to the (other) core in Jaffa–Tel Aviv. At the same time, various ideas were shaped from above, notably Ruppin's program, which also emphasized the North. At a second stage, the Tel Hai affair added a security-defense element to the rural-collectivistic frontier, introducing the importance of settlements for boundary determination. This phase was strengthened following the 1929 riots, and was more concretely expressed after 1936, when early ideas concerning a possible partition of Palestine were raised and coupled with renewed Arab riots.

Toward the establishment of the State of Israel the third stage started, namely the diversion of the frontier effort southward to the Negev. This effort, which continued until 1963, began as a primary frontier and remained as such until 1948, so that following statehood it continued uninterruptedly as a secondary frontier.

As of the mid-1960s, it became more difficult to distinguish between frontier and periphery processes in Israel, as simultaneous emphases have been put on the development of several regions and frontier values have declined in importance in the Israeli Labor movement. In the mid-1970s, the idea of settlement-frontier-ing was adopted by the Right in its attempts to settle the occupied territories. This adoption was geared mainly to the territorial objective of upholding the territories, though a new settlement form was introduced, the community settlement.

Territorial Evolution of Peripheries in Israel

The 1960s witnessed the territorial expansion of settlement frontier regions. Since the mid-1960s, attention has been given to both the Galilee and the Negev, with attempts to emphasize the former a little more. The 1967 war expanded the frontier regions even further, when these two secondary frontiers were accompanied by new primary ones in Sinai, the Lower Jordan Valley, the Golan Heights, and Jerusalem. This territorial expansion of settlement frontiers has caused less direction of resources to the veteran frontiers, and thus their gradual turning into peripheries.

The political struggle around settlement rights in the occupied territories from the mid-1970s has not been accompanied by any widespread countersettlement effort in the Galilee or in the Negev, or by any intensification of settlement activity in the Golan Heights. The 1970s, therefore, presented a political transition that reinforced periphery processes in the Galilee and the Negev, on the one hand, and the creation of a disputed primary frontier in Judea, Samaria, and Gaza. This marked the first time that a primary frontier region in the Land of Israel stood in the center of political life in Israel.

The 1980s saw the deepening of peripheralization processes and probably also their maturing, given the beginning of a structural change in the Israeli economy. Toward the second half of the decade, this process was manifested in a decline in the Jewish population in the remote peripheral subdistricts. The new accents in the Israeli economy on high-tech industries, business services, and international trade in products and services elevated the importance of the cores. Meanwhile, the political debate surrounding the settlement activity in the occupied territories has continued. The Right conceives of this area as a primary frontier, whereas for the Left the areas constitute a periphery. The attempt to establish outpost settlements in the Galilee as a "counterfrontier" has failed in terms of their attracting significant populations.

The settlement processes in the West Bank were generated largely by transitions in residential values in Israeli society that accompanied the general socioeconomic change. The growing middle-class desire for low-density, preferably single-family housing has turned several areas in Western Samaria and around Jerusalem into urban fields of the cores. The "frontier human resource reservoir" of the Right for settlement in the heartland of the West Bank or in Gaza was found to be small. The West Bank, therefore, has served simultaneously as a core fringe (for people of both the Left and the Right), as a frontier (for the Right), and as a periphery (for the Left).

The Emergence of Myth Values in the Frontiers and Cores

Setting frontier myths is not determined or pursued only by frontier settlers. Such activities are joined by a recognition of these values, which is extended by social, political, and economic institutions in the cores. A mutual reinforcement process may thus evolve between myths transmitted from the frontiers to the cores, and resources of all types sent from the cores back to the frontiers. These myths may be tied to circumstances or events that occurred in specific regions. They constitute, therefore, a certain type of spatiality. Specific affairs related to space (such as swamp draining, and settlement defense) create conceptions of space as a frontier and as an element in the process of nation building. These conceptions are later translated into further spatial activity, the construction of settlements. Although the spatial *activity* takes place in the frontier, the changing *conceptions* of space may emerge in both the core and the periphery in both inseparable and interdependent ways.

It is possible to attribute different mythical values to different regions in both the core and the frontiers. The frontier myths may be divided into northern and southern ones. The "northern myth" could be divided again into two parts: the mountains and the valley. The Galilee mountains transmitted basic values of primary frontiering, in the sense of settlements as creators of boundaries and security. This myth started in Tel Hai and was later reinforced in Hanitta and Biria. The valley myth consisted of two elements, one territorial and the other related to mode of life. The former promoted the occupying of the unsettled through draining the valley swamps; the latter called for cooperation-collectivism, equality, labor, and agrarianism.

The southern myth emerged later than did the northern. Whereas the northern myth started to emerge in the early twentieth century, the southern began in the 1940s. The southern myth included northern elements, sometimes in rigid ways, such as the prestatehood attempts to settle the Negev only with agricultural settlements. The northern myth of occupying the unsettled dealt with draining away surplus water. The myth underwent a transition in the South, so that it related there to the lack of water. Another element was added in the South: the exploitation of Negev resources. This new element required an ideological adjustment of the northern myth through the construction of noncooperative resource towns following the establishment of the state (all this unrelated to the problem of service town construction). In the North as well as in the South, the kibbutz was linked to the myth of the primary frontier as a means of intrusion into new territories in prestatehood times. The kibbutz also served as a social frontier, in its adherence to agriculture, collectivism, Hebrew culture, and volunteerism.

In addition to these myths, it is possible to identify additional cultural-mythical elements that originated in the cores. Suffice it here to note that Tel Aviv symbolized the new and secular Hebrew culture; Jerusalem, the connection with the historical past of the nation and its eternity. To a much lesser degree, Haifa symbolized organized Jewish labor. The fast growth of the large Israeli city since 1948 has not brought about an immediate decline in frontier values. This latter process was delayed by the frontier origins of the political leaders in the early years of the state. The declining importance of frontier values in the cores has caused a decrease in the flow of human and economic resources from the cores to the frontiers, thus contributing to their transformation into peripheries. A similar though reverse process has also held true for the rising status of Jerusalem as a religious center. The unification of the city signaled the beginning of a political process of revival and strengthening among the ultraorthodox community, which was fully expressed only in the 1980s.

The Evolution of Cores, Frontiers, and Peripheries and Zionist Ideology

The preceding summary discussion and Table 7.2 lead to several intriguing observations. As the frontiers have expanded territorially, the cores have spatially contracted; and as the cores contracted, the peripheries expanded. The latter of these two observations seems obvious; if a core-periphery dichotomy is assumed, then any region that does not constitute (anymore) a core becomes a periphery (though there might exist "twilight zones" or sectors located between cores and peripheries as we will see in the next chapter). It may also seem clear that whenever additional regions are considered frontiers under stable or declining human, ideological, and economic resources, then some or all of the frontiers may eventually turn into peripheries.

Still open to question, however, is why the cores have *shrunk* (in terms of their *national* spread, not in terms of their *regional*, suburban and exurban, expansion) and whether this process can be related to frontier *expansion*. This question is especially interesting when one compares the Israeli experience to other new societies. In the United States, for example, the western *edge* of the frontier, the Pacific Coast, turned into a secondary national core; thus, the current American periphery lies in the interior of the country, or *between* the original core in the Eastern Seaboard and the new one, formerly a frontier, of the West Coast. Obviously the Pacific Coast enjoyed several advantages that the edge of the Israeli frontier could not offer. These include a sea coast, a better climate, grater economic opportunities (e.g., the Gold Rush), and the absence of a border with enemies.

Several factors may account for the shrinking of the core. The most important factor seems to lie within the Israeli frontier ideology, which was so extremely antiurban that it made kibbutzim bypass urban regional entities both before (Safed, Tiberias, Afula) and after (development towns) statehood. On the other hand, it became clear very early on that anchoring an ideologically based agrarian sector in completely autonomous, autarchic regions is impossible. The solution to the dilemma, at least retrospectively, was to use the city as little as possible; thus, all the agrarian central institutions as well as rural-urban business transactions were concentrated in *one* city, Tel Aviv (with *some* business conducted through Haifa, as well). This gave Tel Aviv immense political and economic power, which eventually contributed to a peripheralization of frontier regions. At earlier stages, however, expanding the frontiers through collective and cooperative settlements also added strength to Tel Aviv, and thus aided the geographical shrinking of the core.

The continued growth of the large city has brought about the evolution of urban values, culminating in the emergence of social

Zionism among the Left and suburban residential values in urban society at large. The transition to social Zionism by the Left has dimmed the Labor movement's frontier culture, and contributed to the turning of frontiers into peripheries. The Right, which was a newcomer to territorial Zionism vis-à-vis settlements, was able to achieve some success in its frontier in the occupied territories, but only as long as the settlement activity matched new suburban residential values.

The transition of the Israeli collectivity from one frontier to another, using Elazar's (1986, 1987) interpretations (i.e., moving from rural to industrial, technological, and eventually to cybernetic frontiers), has increasingly required an urban leadership. The earlier two-way transmission of myth values between cores and frontiers has not been necessary anymore. The development of technological and cybernetic frontiers tends to be centralized and may require more international and inter-world city than domestic contacts. Thus a prospering core may be concentrated and centralized (from a national perspective, though not in terms of its internal spatial structure).

Table 2.2 presented the changing priorities in Zionist ideology alongside transitions in settlement ideals. It showed the increasing role of the territorial aspect during the two decades prior to statehood. The emphasis on territorial achievements through kibbutzim then formed the essence of the primary frontier jointly with the mountainous myth of boundary determination through settlement activity. The other two settlement ideals, development towns and the West Bank settlement project, have not served as myth creators. The idea of immigration absorption and integration was a national concept, in that these goals should have been reached by all sectors, not exclusively by development towns. This also applied to the idea of population dispersal, which again was not formulated purposefully for development towns, but was relevant for the rural sector, as well.

The settlement of the occupied territories could not create a myth, mainly because the issue has been the subject of sharp dispute in Israeli political life between two large, equally sized political sectors, one opposing and the other favoring the project. Even if political conditions were different, however, several other aspects would restrict the evolution of a myth surrounding the settlement of Judea, Samaria, and Gaza. This settlement project has used an existing myth, the mountainous one, which was originally developed in the 1920s and which concerns the use of settlements for boundary determination and territorial holding. Moreover, the Likud came into power at a time when it was already difficult to develop new pioneering myths in Israeli society. It may well be, however, that the emerging new residential values in regard to community settlements will eventually become a civic myth similar to the "American dream" relating to suburban, single-family dwellings.

Chapter 8

Society and Settlement in the Jewish Land of Israel: Past, Present, and Future

"Man is the mold of his fatherland's landscape," the Hebrew poet Shaul Tchernichovski observed. If we refer to *Man* as representing not just the individual but the nation and its social sectors, as well, then this phrase has its obverse: "the fatherland's landscape is the mold of its children." These two sides of the coin combine to reflect a process by which a collectivity constructs and develops its country according to certain value systems; simultaneously, the settlements in which members of this collectivity reside participate in the formation of those value systems.

This final chapter will attempt to summarize the several components of this argument, which constituted the heart of the analysis of modern Israeli society in this essay, by assessing the outcome of vision versus practice and outcome as this dialectic was presented in the foregoing chapters. A summary table, Table 8.1, combines Table 7.2, which summarized Parts 2 and 3, with Table 2.2, and thus attempts to display territorial and cultural developments in the cores and frontiers-peripheries of Israel together with changing priorities in Zionist objectives and transitions in the preferred settlement forms.

It was tempting to organize the whole study continuously along time. Such an approach, however, would have eliminated a focus on the interrelationships between society and settlements, which has been the raison d'être of the book. Ideological and cultural aspects of this interelationship provided one of the two central foci in every chapter. The other focus, the geographical aspect, changed from part to part. Part 1 emphasized innovative settlement forms; Part 2 dealt with conventional settlement forms and their geographical settings; Part 3 was devoted entirely to geographical settings. The temporal framework that accompanied all three discussions separately is, however, a proper one for a unifying summarizing discussion.

Four major phases or periods may be identified in the constant dialogue between society and space in modern Jewish Land of Israel. These four major phases in the emerging relationship between society and settlements in Israel may be defined as incu-

Table 8.1. Society and Settlement in the Modern Jewish Land of Israel

PHASE	PERIOD	PRIORITIES IN ZIONIST GOALS	TERRITORIAL EVOLUTION IN THE CORES	VALUE CREATION IN THE CORES	TERRITORIAL EVOLUTION IN THE FRONTIER-PERIPHERY	VALUE CREATION IN THE FRONTIER	PREFERRED SETTLEMENT FORM
1. Incubation	1880s–1920s	1. Mode of Life 2. Territory 3. Population	Spreading the settlement N.	*Rural:* Cooperation; equality; labor; pioneering; defense. *Urban:* Hebrew language; secular Hebrew culture.	Evolution of a primary frontier, notably in the North.	*The valley myth:* Occupying the unsettled; draining the swamps; agriculture and cooperativeness.	Colony (moshava); kibbutz
2. Formation	1920s–1940s	*Until the 1930s:* 1. Mode of Life 2. Territory 3. Population *As of the 1930s:* 1. Territory 2. Mode of Life 3. Population	The valleys decline as a core; Tel Aviv becomes the largest city.	Autonomy in all spheres and levels; organized Jewish labor (Haifa). The preceding continues.	Continued primary frontier: Reinforcement of the N and its joints; spreading new arms in the North and the South.	*The mountain myth:* Boundary determination through settlement.	Kibbutz; moshav
3. Maturation	1950s–1960s	*The 1950s:* 1. Population 2. Territory 3. Mode of Life	The decline in the status of Haifa.	Attempts to integrate the preceding within state frameworks.	*Until 1963:* Diversion of the effort to the Negev as a secondary frontier.	*The desert myth:* Occupying the unsettled; making the desert bloom; exploitation of	Development town; kibbutz; moshav

Table 8.1. (Continued)

PHASE	PERIOD	PRIORITIES IN ZIONIST GOALS	TERRITORIAL EVOLUTION IN THE CORES	VALUE CREATION IN THE CORES	TERRITORIAL EVOLUTION IN THE FRONTIER-PERIPHERY	VALUE CREATION IN THE FRONTIER	PREFERRED SETTLEMENT FORM
		The 1960s: 1. Territory 2. Population 3. Mode of Life			*1963–1967:* Similar attempt in the Galilee.	Negev resources.	
4. Turbulence 1970s–1980s	*Judea and Samaria*	*The 1970s:* 1. Territory 2. Mode of Life 3. Population	The rise of Jerusalem; Tel Aviv becomes a world city.	Social Zionism versus territorial Zionism. State and religious centrality in Jerusalem.	Evolution of a disputed primary frontier in Judea, Samaria, and Gaza. Additional secondary frontier in the Galilee. The North and the South turn into peripheries in the 1980s.	The mountain myth implemented in Judea, Samaria, and Gaza.	Community settlement
		The 1980s: 1. Population 2. Territory 3. Mode of Life					
		Social Zionism: 1. Mode of Life 2. Population 3. Territory					

bation (1880s–1920s), formation (1920s–1940s), maturation (1950s–1960s), and turbulence (1970s–1980s). As a general overview, Table 8.1 reveals several interesting trends. Each of the four phases was typified by a different leading Zionist objective, coupled with the introduction of a new settlement form. In the incubation phase, the emphasis was on mode of life, which was coupled with the introduction of the kibbutz. The formative phase was characterized by an accent on territory, and the emergence of the moshav. The maturation phase required major attention to population and witnessed the establishment of development towns. The fourth phase, which is still ongoing, is one of turbulence, its emphasis being once again on territory and a secondary emphasis on mode of life, which yielded the community settlement. These seemingly discrete changes were accompanied by two continuous trends: the expansion of the frontier areas and the contraction of the core areas. Each of the first three phases was characterized by new frontier myths; the fourth has not produced a myth, but has witnessed the emergence of new core values (social Zionism) for the first time since the incubation phase. These trends attest to the strong underlying territorial dimension of the Zionist enterprise, on the one hand, and to its constantly changing nature, even under the long domination of one ideology (Labor), on the other.

The four phases were accompanied by the emergence of several types of spatialities and temporalities (described in detail in Kellerman, 1989), which reflected the transition, first, from a traditional Jewish society to a pioneering-socialist society and, later, to a more capitalist-hedonist society. The three patterns of spatiality and temporality have not completely replaced each other; rather, they have left deep impressions in the evolving Israeli society. Thus, Jewish tradition conceives of time and space as sacred dimensions, with more importance attached to time than to space. Socialist-pioneering Zionism referred to these dimensions as political resources, with greater significance attributed to space. In modern Israel and its slowly evolving market economy and mass consumption, time and space are being viewed and used as economic resources, with more importance given to time, as is common in Western societies (see also Gross, 1985).

Incubation

The incubation period for the modern Jewish-Zionist settlement of Palestine did not emerge from a tabula rasa in terms of preexisting structures. Indeed, such structures though limited to the urban sector, had major impact on later patterns and processes. These preexisting structures were the cities of Jerusalem and Jaffa, which not merely existed in Palestine before the onset of the new settlement enterprise, but had already fulfilled some of their later major functions. The roots of Jerusalem as both a holy-spiritual center and a capital city go back to early history. Even in the modern era, physical modernization of the Jewish community in Jerusalem started a generation before the First Aliya, with the construction of the first quarters outside the walled city. The evolution of Jaffa into a major urban entity, and later into the largest coastal city, may have started only in the nineteenth century, but it was still earlier than the First Aliya. The seeds were planted earlier and were not unique to Jaffa alone, even if the First Aliya and the development of Jerusalem contributed much to its rapid growth.

The First Aliya presented a double original commencement in the *rural* sector: enterprising agriculture and the introduction of a new culture. In the *urban* sector, in Jaffa, however, original beginnings were of a more restricted sense. Economic growth had already been experienced there; and a productive Jewish community, into which the new, imported ideas and modes of life were blended, already existed in the town. The Second Aliya, which was the first Zionist *aliya,* did not start from zero, neither in agriculture nor in its emphasis on a new secular Hebrew culture. It introduced, however, a fresh start so far as cooperation and collectivism of the Jewish working class. This was also true for the incubation of several other values that were to become the characteristics of the Hebrew frontier settler and pioneer: self-defense, economic self-reliance, simplicity, and volunteerism. The Second Aliya took place at a time when Jaffa was already a center for many new organizations and institutions. The domestic nesting of the new ideas of the Second Aliya occurred in the colonies of the First Aliya, notably in the North, though they obviously incorporated imported ideas, particularly from Russia.

These observations have three implications. First, the initial advantage of Jaffa, along with the urban tendency of Jews and the attraction for the settlement of immigrants provided by the arrival port, turned out to be crucial for the future development of Jewish Palestine. Neither the later construction of modern international transportation facilities in Haifa nor the ancient, permanent, and growing importance of Jerusalem could cope fully with these conditions. Second, despite these conditions, Jerusalem, or the old and the mountainous, continued to offer a central focus in the spatial as well as in the cultural organization of the emerging national entity. Though the three other mountainous old urban Jewish communities either declined or were abandoned, Jerusalem continued to grow. Third, the rural collectivist project of the Second Aliya did not emerge in an urban vacuum or under circumstances of a weak urban sector.

The new, communal, and pioneering mode of life started completely from below, in contrast to both the urban and the rural modes of life in the colonies. As such, human agency contributed to effecting change in the existing social and spatial structures. The new settlement forms emerged jointly with a new core in the plains and the valleys. The development of the new core was strongly tied to Arabs' readiness to sell land, and to the penetration of Jews into Palestine from the West. The emphasis on agriculture proved itself, not only economically and socially but also spatially. It brought about large-scale land purchases and the evolution of a new N core. The myth that evolved during this period was thus a very basic one: that of the preparation of land for settlement by draining swamps.

Formation

In the formation era, the new mode of life soon predominated ideologically, politically, and spiritually. At the same time, the urban system was formed around three large cities with specific relative sizes and functions. Also, the territorial idea matured in terms of its recognition by the settlement institutions. This led to a contradiction between *urban concentration*, on the one hand, and *rural cooperative* mode of life and territorial *expansion*, on the other.

The strengthening of Labor ideas and landscapes was impressive, especially when one considers the small numbers and population share of the pioneers among all immigrants of the Second and Third Aliyas. They were able to turn the kibbutz and later the moshav into leading and eventually exclusive forms of rural settlement. Their values suffused the social, cultural, and political life of the new Jewish community. From the mid-1930s, this group also became the leading sector in Zionist elected and executive institutions. The zealous advocacy of pioneering in word and deed could be attributed at least partially to these achievements.

Despite the acceptance of the *idea* that communal, pioneering, and frontier life were superior to an urban existence, most

Labor and, obviously, non-Labor, immigrants preferred the big cities. During this period Tel Aviv became the largest city, Jerusalem turned into a capital, and Haifa became the major port. Moreover, Labor contributed to these developments, especially in Tel Aviv and to a lesser degree in Haifa as well. The basing of almost all economic, organizational, political, and cultural institutions of the Labor movement in Tel Aviv, the condemned but only fully Hebrew city, assisted in its population growth as well as in the very importance of the city. This development meant a decline in the status of the valleys as a core area. Hence, there somehow evolved a reverse duality between structures and human agency when the incubation period is compared to the formation era. In the former, the communal-rural ideal represented human agency; this turned into a structure in the latter period. Towns and colonies were the structures of the past; whereas the flow of immigrants into the cities during the formation period was accompanied by individual work, with but little Zionist institutional and direct assistance in the form of housing, industrial construction, and so forth.

The rural sector percentage of the Jewish population grew in this period, though it never reached even a third of the total population. The special social characteristics of the rural sector and the political, economic, and moral support it received from the urban sector helped the territorial concept to emerge as a leading goal. The territorial concept had its roots in early plans, notably Ruppin's, in the beginning of the twentieth century. In the mid-1930s, it became apparent that some partition solution for Palestine would be formulated. The mountainous myth of boundary determination through settlement, which had evolved since the early 1920s, now became crucial for the expansion and strengthening of the new Jewish settlement N. Though this mountainous myth was mostly applied in nonmountainous areas, it proved useful for the arms and the joints of the growing N. The socially compact, highly ideologically charged kibbutz was used as an intrusion tool. The moshav, originally created as a cooperative rather than a communal settlement form, was used to enhance settlement activity in areas already settled by kibbutzim.

A spatial event, the Tel Hai affair, turned into a social-political symbol, which contributed to the shaping of the territorial scope of the Jewish entity. As such, this incident can be interpreted as representing a structuration process between society and space. Space was a medium through which social and political values were shaped and then implemented back into space in the form of settlements. In a similar way, the kibbutz and the moshav were

rural communities with a special social character; simultaneously
they also fulfilled definite territorial objectives.

Maturation

The first two decades of statehood were associated with three
major aspects of maturation in terms of the relations between society and settlement: (1) continued growth through a restructuring of
the large cities; (2) the institutionalization of the frontier; and (3)
the construction of lower-level towns in the urban system.

For Tel Aviv and Jerusalem, statehood meant a strengthening of their status as decision-making loci. Although the formal status was granted to Jerusalem as the capital, the unique circumstances of Jerusalem's being a border city imparted to Tel Aviv
even more power. The maturation of Jerusalem as a cosmopolitan
spiritual center had to await the 1967 war and the turbulence period. Tel Aviv developed into the informal center of the new Jewish
state; central agencies and organizations, many of which had existed there before, now took on formal and informal bureaucracies.
The decline of Haifa as an international gateway when international land borders with the Arab nations were closed in 1948 also
enhanced the status of Tel Aviv as headquarters for all sectors of
the Israeli economy. The cultural life of Israel, too, centered on Tel
Aviv. The significance of these processes lay in the vast growth of
the large cities in general, and of Tel Aviv in particular; the result
was that in the 1960s metropolitan areas sprung up around Tel
Aviv and Haifa.

The decline of Haifa as a core city was related not only to its
loss of international activity; it was also the result of its restricted
ability to attract new non-high-tech industries owing to the strong
power of the Histadruth in the city. Tel Aviv, which was the center of private enterprise, flourished. The delicate balance between
the private and the public was thus preserved, despite the immense
power of government and the Histadruth.

The institutionalization of the frontier did not merely signify
the replacement of the primary frontier with secondary frontiers
following the establishment of the state. It also meant the use of
statehood to promote the rural cooperative sector and the replacement of volunteerism by institutional, mainly state, action. This
substitution was demonstrated by the extensive legislation in
regard to agriculture development and by the official status granted
to the Jewish Agency as the responsible unit for settlement con-

struction and fostering. No new rural settlement form was created, however, perhaps because the ideological tensions characterizing the prestatehood mode of life and territorial challenges were now replaced by a desire to maintain and nurture existing patterns through the use of political power in state institutions. This preservation tendency coupled with the use of state power was demonstrated in the Negev development project.

The vision of "occupying the unsettled" that prevailed in this period was not new; it was originally developed in early days of Zionist settlement. Whereas, the earlier vision had dealt with water surplus in the valleys, the new theme related to water shortages in the Negev. The second Negev myth, concerning the use of natural resources, had earlier roots, too, through the two plants for potash production that were built on the shores of the Dead Sea before the establishment of the state. The Negev project thus involved new as well as old mythological elements. Statism was reflected in the construction of an extensive infrastructure of transportation and water facilities, industrial plants, and housing. The majority of the population in the new urban and rural settlements were new immigrants, who had come to the country during its first years of statehood. Each of these three components— vision, economic resources, and human resources—had not yet been sufficiently developed and implemented when national attention was directed to the Galilee in 1963.

The way in which the new State of Israel coped with lower levels of the urban hierarchy was in the form of the establishment of development towns all over the country. These towns represented the major challenge for Israel during its years of maturation: the absorption of an extensive immigration wave. The new development towns were supposed to provide the rural sector with the missing regional urban component, but the objection of the rural sector to conventional urban-rural relationships made their growth painful; consequently, development towns were eventually smaller than planned and based on industry. Jointly with the rural sector, however, development towns constituted the spatial element of the national effort at population dispersal, or the secondary frontier.

During the first two decades of statehood, there was an inability to assess Zionist visions versus realities in at least three major areas. First, the permanency of the growth, vitality, and necessity of the large Israeli city, particularly Tel Aviv. Second, the impossibility of the attempt to develop several regions at a time, given the ideological, population, and capital constraints. Third, the limited role that statism could play as a substitute for volunteerism, ideological zeal, and pioneering. It was still believed then that the enhanced powers of government, Zionist institutions, the Histadruth, and political parties could under the conditions of Jewish sovereignty, do it all.

Turbulence

The June 1967 war marked the beginning of many transitions in Israeli society. Of interest to our discussion were the following: the alteration in the territorial scope of Israel; changes in the residential values of the urban population; the discovery of the territorial concept by the Right; the evolution of social Zionism among the Left; and the crisis in the labor economy.

The larger territory that came under Israeli control has meant, foremost, the maturing of Jerusalem as a capital city, a tourist attraction, and a spiritual center. Jerusalem also became more attractive for the religious sector, so that together with the high natural growth of the ultraorthodox population, the religious sector of Jerusalem has grown. A second territorial aspect was the introduction of various new primary consensual frontiers in the lower Jordan Valley, Gush Etzion, the Golan Heights, and Sinai. Thus, the resources that were to be diverted to the previous settlement frontiers in the Galilee and in the Negev were further restricted, in both human and economic terms. The large settlement project of Judea, Samaria, and Gaza by the Likud beginning in 1977, coupled with the waning ideological pioneering power of Labor, contributed to the transformation of the North and the South into peripheries.

A second major transition has involved the change in residential values. The metropolitan areas, especially the one around Tel Aviv, expanded into additional rings, while the population of the core city has decreased continuously since 1964 (Table 8.2). This trend has been accompanied by a tendency to buy larger housing units (Table 8.3). Thus, by 1983 the share of larger units (apartments with more than three bedrooms) accounted for over 30 percent of the Jewish housing market, compared to about 13 percent just a decade earlier. Though data are not available for the construction of mainly exurban single-family dwellings, this housing form has been sharply on the rise. There was also a rising level of car ownership, so that over half of the households in the large metropolitan areas enjoy the use of a private car. Although such trends in urban housing and transportation modes are well known

Table 8.2.   Suburban Growth in the Metropolitan Areas of Tel Aviv and Haifa, 1972–1983 (in Percents)

| AREA | POPULATION | | | CHANGE |
	1972[b]	1972[c]	1983	1972–1983
Metropolitan Tel Aviv				22.9
Core	28.5	33.3	21.1	-9.2
Inner Ring	35.0	40.8	33.8	18.8
Middle Ring	22.3	25.7	28.6	57.2
Outer Ring[a]	14.0		16.3	43.5
Metropolitan Haifa				15.1
Core	64.6	65.3	58.2	3.8
Inner Ring	31.4	31.7	37.5	37.6
Outer Ring	3.9	2.9	4.1	21.5

[a]Not included in metropolitan Tel Aviv in 1972.

[b]1972 data by the 1983 metropolitan definition.

[c]1972 data by the 1972 metropolitan definition.

Source: Central Bureau of Statistics, 1983.

Table 8.3.   Distribution of Dwelling Units in Jewish Households, by Number of Bedrooms, 1972–1983 (in Percents)

NUMBER OF BEDROOMS	1972	1983	PERCENT CHANGE
Studio apts.	6.4	2.5	-60.9
1	33.2	18.4	-44.6
2	47.0	48.4	3.0
3	10.9	24.1	121.1
4+	2.0	6.7	235.0

Sources: Central Bureau of Statistics 1979; 1984.

in the Western world, the emergence of a sizable middle class in Israel has had both territorial and cultural-ideological effects, some of which were differently divided between the Right and the Left.

The Right discovered the territorial concept regarding the use of settlements for boundary determination just when the Left seemed to have tired of it in the mid-1970s. The rise of Gush Emunim, followed by the change in administration from Left to Right, brought about a disputed primary frontier in the West Bank and Gaza. This development has turned the territorial dimension of Zionism into the central issue in Israeli politics. The extensive effort that has been invested in this settlement project has not yielded any new myth, but it did result in the establishment of a new settlement form, the community settlement. The introduction of this nonagricultural exurban community type, and the location of the West Bank within the urban fields of both Tel Aviv and Jerusalem made this area, especially during its third phase settlement, attractive for urban young and middle-aged, middle-class Israelis.

The Left discovered the big city in several ways. The increasing power of the Likud among the working class has turned the Labor party into a middle-class metropolitan party. The opening up of Israel to Western mass culture and the widening rift between Israel and the Eastern block at the time have turned Tel Aviv into a world city from a cultural perspective. Along with increasing international trade and tourism, the city became a world city from an economic perspective as well. Thus, the decline in pioneering and settlement ideology, the loss of power by the working class, the resentment of Likud settlement activity, and the increasing exposure to Western cultural-social and economic trends all led to the Left's advocacy of modern metropolitan values: civil rights, pluralism, and emancipation from religious norms. The more religious developments in Jerusalem once again raised an old conflict between Jerusalem and Tel Aviv; at the same time, the evolving specializations of the two cities, as well as the improved transportation between them, emphasized their complementarity, therefore helping to turn the North and the South into peripheries. The two cities have now become the exclusive loci for national decision making in all spheres; Tel Aviv has displayed more elements of a social Zionism, whereas Jerusalem has been characterized by a more territorial Zionism.

A fifth important transition element has emerged, particularly from the mid-1980s; this is a structural crisis in the labor economy. The economy served as the ideological, political, and economic backbone of Labor. An austerity plan, originally put into effect by both Likud and Labor following exceptionally high inflation rates in the early 1980s, meant a deep cut in government support of the agricultural sector and Histadruth industries. The effects of this major change, which may eventually end up in a structural change in the Israeli economy and society at large, are as yet difficult to assess. Some possible avenues, however, will be discussed in the next section.

What Next?

Before moving to some comments on possible future developments, several remarks have still to be made with regard both to the past and the present by assessing two questions: First, did the Zionist settlement enterprise as a whole impose a completely new spatial structure on Palestine? Second, do the trends that have emerged during the last two decades point to the opening up of a new cycle in the spatial-social organization of the Land of Israel?

During the First Temple era, as was noted in Part 2, the Israelite entity was spatially characterized by three major components: (1) the settlement of the mountainous areas; (2) a division of the country into twelve lots (for the twelve tribes); and (3) the making of Jerusalem into the religious center and capital (since the time of King David; later, as a capital only for Judea). During the Second Temple era, the division into twelve lots disappeared. In the modern era, another component disappeared, namely the almost exclusive Jewish mountainous settlement. The new Jewish core on the plains and in the valleys, the settlement *N*, is, thus, new from a Jewish historical perspective. It has also constituted a new core for Palestine in general after centuries of a heavier mountainous settlement accent.

The Jewish mountainous roots and the connection with past modes of spatial organization of the country are, however, still part of the modern Israeli experience in two ways: in making Jerusalem the capital and spiritual center and in the struggle for the settlement of the Galilee, Judea, and Samaria. The consensual Israeli connection with Jerusalem not only symbolizes past roots and cultures, it also symbolizes the existence in Israeli society of a growing religious sector with various levels of attachment to current and ancient modes of social organization. The struggle in the mountains, whether the Galilee, which is under Israeli sovereignty, or the West Bank, which is under Israeli military control, symbolizes unresolved relations with the Palestinians in particular and with the Arab world in general. The spiritual struggle being waged by several segments of Israeli society around Jerusalem, and the territorial struggle around West Bank settlements symbolize two facets of the cultural-political debate in Israel over the past heritage of the Jewish people: Which cultural-religious elements and which territorial aspects of the past should be carried into contemporary and future Israeli society?

The new Israeli settlement *N* and its additional branches

have been established, constructed, and developed under the guidance of a unique socialist Zionism. Thus, both the new social thinking and the new spatial organization of Israeli society have been symbolized by this *N*, characterized by changing relationships among its arms and eventual domination by Tel Aviv as a cultural, economic, and entrepreneurial focus.

There has been, therefore, much that is new in the spatial and social organization of modern Jewish society in Palestine-Israel, but much of the old has also remained. Earlier pioneering attempts to destroy or ignore the old Jewish as well as the old Arab failed. Lustick (1987) noted the problematic of Israel's acting as a European society in a new, supposedly empty frontier, confronted by the Arabs, who adopted Third World nationalism. It seems, then, that a major challenge for Israeli society would be to develop a true pluralism in a four-sector society, consisting of the two big sectors, the Left and the Right, and two smaller sectors, the religious and the Arab. This is a particularly demanding challenge for a society that, despite continuous, heated political debate, has been used to one leading ideology. The division into four ideological-political sectors reflects the three major ideological-political problems on the Israeli social agenda: economic organization, the Palestinian-Arab question, and the religious-cultural dilemma. These three problem areas have three different geographical loci on the map of Israel. The economic problem and its social-political ramifications for the Left center on the *N* and focus on Tel Aviv; the Palestinian problem is concentrated in the mountains and has several centers (Nazareth, Nablus, and Jerusalem); the religious problem is centered on Jerusalem.

Have the past two decades of turbulence signified the possible beginning of a new cycle of incubation-formation-maturity in the social-spatial organization of Israel? This seems to be the case, but not in a revolutionary way. In other words, as much as the first cycle was built at least to some extent on several past elements, despite its revolutionary nature, this construction would be even more true for a second possible round of Jewish social-spatial organization of Israel; the new round would nest within existing social-spatial structures.

The economic issue relating to the status and size of the public (governmental and union) economy seems to be treated more constructively than the two other issues, though even this issue is not handled in a planned, orderly way. Rather, it has responded to crises, first in the rural sector and later in the industrial sector. Kimmerling (1983a, pp. 150–151) concluded his book on Zionism and the economy by stating that Jewish settlement in the Land of Israel has probably been the most expensive and least sustained among national settlement projects in the world. The reason for this is that Jews have had to pay for land; moreover, most of the international capital-rich corporations have avoided investment in Israel, given its perception of risk. Thus, the success of the Zionist enterprise has been achieved largely because of the superiority of the ideological element over the economic. This dominance was demonstrated by the extensive use of public capital in specific ideologically determined ways.

These unique circumstances now seem to have come to an end. The ideological-pioneering spirit of the Left has been waning; the ideology of the Right has been tied mainly to urban values and modes of life. The loss of exclusive political power by the Left, along with the long-declared policy of preference for a market economy by the Right; the increasing domestic and foreign debt of the Israeli economy; and the emergence of a global economy provide additional factors in this regard. The rising middle-class urban character of Labor may assist in the gradually evolving economic change, which requires public services to function with less subsidies or none at all and requires agriculture and manufacturing to be profitable. The change in the economic structure of Israel may eventually draw both Left and Right closer to each other in this historical central issue of conflict; the difference between them may then be reduced to the nuances that are common between the two leading parties in Western societies. In Israel, however, the differences between the two major political camps may sharpen in regard to the territorial-Arab conflict or the cultural-religious argument or both.

The major geographical manifestation of the economic issue takes the form of the northern and southern frontiers turning into peripheries. The peripheries consist of four sectors: development towns, kibbutzim, moshavim and the Arab sector. The kibbutzim are generally the strongest of the four in terms of their economic power and in their potential for being enterprising. Chapter 3 briefly referred to the industrialization of the kibbutzim. This extensive process, which has brought industry into virtually every kibbutz, has caused many of the kibbutzim to depend more on industry than on agriculture for income. The kibbutzim, which constitute only approximately 3 percent of the Jewish population and about one-third of the rural sector, produce two-thirds of Israeli agricultural output plus 6 percent of its industrial output. The kibbutz has undergone many social and institutional changes since its inception, and these have received wide attention (e.g., Blasi, 1986; Rosner, 1988). Here the focus will be on several recent changes stemming from Israel's economic crisis of the late 1980s. The kibbutzim have become increasingly connected to the large city. The service economy of the kibbutzim, for one, has been directed toward the urban sector for a long time in providing motel lodging and some food services on road junctions. These services will be expanded as the kibbutz has been opening itself up in other ways, such as renting out the use of its on-site recreational, educational and catering services. The growing and sophisticated kibbutz industries have become more and more dependent on urban producer services. Many kibbutz members themselves work as professionals in the large cities and commute daily or weekly to their home villages. Throughout the last two decades, the kibbutzim have generally maintained an urban middle-class life standard.

These new trends leading to the blurring of physical and social boundaries between the kibbutz and the city—trends that have been even more profound as far as moshavim are concerned—could potentially break down the boundaries between the kibbutzim, the development towns, and the moshavim in the peripheries as well. Indeed, this dismantling has already happened to some extent with the establishment of the all-encompassing Negev Council. Cooperation among these sectors, possibly including the Arab sector, as well, could potentially renew initiative in the periphery, this time in the form of *economic*, rather than ideological, enterprise. Combining forces, especially those of kibbutz enterprise and the emerging development town political leadership may provide a new future for regions that the core is unable or unwilling to nurture anymore. The coming introduction of regional media may assist in sustaining such a trend. The kibbutzim have lost much of their *national* power; for example, fewer members of Knesset, fewer ministers, even in Labor-led governments (Rosner, 1988). *Regional* cooperation with other settlement sectors may provide kibbutzim with a different image and a new focus.

The kibbutzim have undergone numerous changes in their daily conduct of collectivism since the establishment of the first kvutza. These transitions have been debated and opposed as importing urban bourgeois elements into the kibbutz mode of life. In recent years, the very basics of the collective way of life has been challenged with debate over the possible introduction of financial rewards for work by kibbutz members. If these trends continue, they may eventually split the kibbutzim into various modes of collective settlements, as happened in several moshavim. This will

be an interesting development in terms of settlement-society relations. It would symbolize a "victory" for the much-condemned Tel
Aviv, as chaneled through the community settlement entity. The
community settlements symbolized the adoption of Leftist territorial concepts by the Right. An interesting symbiosis of once-antago-
nistic settlement means, symbols, and objectives may thus emerge
between Right and Left.

It is much more difficult to assess the geographical ramifications of the Palestinian and the religious conflicts, because they are
more complex and less mature. It seems clear that any peaceful
solution to the Palestinian problem, in the form of Palestinian
statehood, autonomy, or a federation with Jordan would bar continued Jewish settlement on the West Bank. This situation could
create many pressures on land, especially on the central coastal
plain, given the current aspirations for low-density housing and the
renewed mass immigration from the Soviet Union. The long-stand-
ing policy of preference for agricultural land uses would then have
to be reassessed, as would the establishment of a new hilly and
mountainous urban corridor connecting Jerusalem and Tel Aviv.
On the other hand, continued Jewish settlement on the West Bank
might result in one of the two scenarios presented at the conclusion
of Chapter 3; namely, that the West Bank could become increasingly attractive for most Israeli political groups, or that geographical sectors may be created around the major cities, each sector settled by a different political group.

The religious conflict seems to be the most serious of the
three major struggles, because it relates to the very identity of Jew-
ishness in a modern era and under the conditions of Jewish sovereignty. The growth in the size and political power of ultraorthodox
groups has already led to increased spatial segregation and further
pressure by both secular and religious groups for social and legal
changes. The emergence of social Zionism is related, in part, to
desires to reformulate the Zionist-Israeli social arena along Western civic values and less, or even not at all, along elements reflecting the Jewish tradition. The Zionist religious party that used to
serve as a bridge between several camps has been weakened in
these circumstances. The desire to reformulate Zionism along
Western values amounts to a return to Herzl's original ideas on the
nature of the Jewish state. Ironically this has occurred at a time
when the Israeli Right has abandoned Herzl's political approach,
according to which an international charter is needed to attain
Jewish sovereignty in the Land of Israel.

Two additional factors for a reshaping of relationships

between society and space have emerged when the writing of this book came into conclusion: the water problem and massive immigration from the Soviet Union. Following several years of drought it became apparent that water usage in Israel, especially for irrigation, will have to be reviewed. It seems that drastic cuts in the water supply for agriculture may enhance current trends for a heavier accent on manufacturing, tourism, and services in the rural sector at large, as well as tendencies toward more flexible forms of social and economic organization of the rural sector.

It is as yet difficult to assess the sociospatial impact of the huge immigration wave from the Soviet Union that started in 1990. The new absorption policy permitting immigrants to choose their place of residence and the shortage in housing in the early 1990s caused many Soviet immigrants to live in temporary residences. This immigration wave may potentially change the demographic balance between Jews and Arabs in the mountainous Galilee. It is questionable, however, whether the status of the southern and northern peripheries will change if most immigrants settle in the veteran urban areas. The hundreds of thousands of immigrants may in the end supply their own inputs to a new cycle of incubation and formation in society and settlement in Israel.

References

Aaronson, R. (1989). "Jerusalem in the Eyes of Second Aliya People." In H. Lavsky (ed.), *Jerusalem in Zionist Conception and Work* [Hebrew], pp. 47–66. Jerusalem: The Zalman Shazar Center and the Hebrew University.

Ackerman, A. (1982). *Zionism in Struggle* [Hebrew]. Jerusalem: Good Times.

Agnon, S. Y. (1971). *Shira* [Hebrew]. Tel Aviv: Schocken.

Aharonowitz, Y. (1941). *The Writings of Yoseph Aharonowitz* [Hebrew]. Tel Aviv: Am-Oved.

Akzin, B., and Dror, Y. (1966). *Israel: High Pressure Planning.* New York: Syracuse University Press.

Alkalai, Y. (1876). *Hahavatzelet* [Hebrew] no. 6, 43 (Elul 19, 5636; September).

Althusser, L., and Balibar, E. (1970). *Reading "Capital."* London: New Left Books.

Altman, E. A., and Rosenbaum, B. R. (1973). "Principles of Planning and Zionist Ideology: The Israeli Development Towns." *Journal of A.I.P.* 39: 316–325.

Amiran, D., and Shachar, A. (1959). "The Large Cities of Israel: A Geographical Comparison" [Hebrew]. *Studies* 1: 134–156.

———. (1969). *Development Towns in Israel.* Jerusalem: The Hebrew University.

Anderson, J. (1973. "Ideology in Geography." *Antipode* 5: 1–6.

Applebaum, L., and Margolis, H. (1983). *The Non-Agricultural Village in Israel as a Development Tool—Background, Problems, Chances* [Hebrew]. Working paper 8, Rehovot: The Settlement Research Center.

Aronoff, M. J. (1973). "Development Towns in Israel." In M. Curtis and M. S. Chertoff (eds.), *Israel: Social Structure and Change*, pp. 27–45. New Brunswick, N.J.: Transaction Books.

Aronson, G. (1990). *Israel, Palestinians and the Intifada: Creating Facts on the West Bank.* London: Kegan Paul International.

Avidar, Y. (1980). "The 1929 Riots: Political and Security Implications" [Hebrew]. *Ma'arachot* 272: 42–47.

Avigur, S. (1978). *With the Defense Generation* [Hebrew], vol. 2. Tel Aviv: Ma'arachot.

Avneri, A. L. (1980). *The Jewish Land Settlement and the Arab Claim of Dispossession (1878–1948)* [Hebrew]. Tel Aviv: Hakibbutz Hameuchad.

Bagelman, S., ed. (1984–1987). *Statistical Yearbook for Jerusalem 1982–1985* [Hebrew]. Jerusalem: The Municipality of Jerusalem and the Jerusalem Institute for the Study of Israel.

Bar-Gal, Y. (1982). "Ruralization Rate and Migration Balance under Core/Periphery Conditions—The Israel Case." *GeoJournal* 6: 165–171.

———, and Shamai, S. (1983). "The Jezreel Valley Swamps—Legend and Reality" [Hebrew]. *Cathedra* 27: 163–174.

Bein, A. (1953) *The History of the Zionist Settlement in the Land of Israel* [Hebrew]. Jerusalem: Massada.

Bell, G. (1962). "Changes in City Size Distribution in Israel." *Ekistics* 13.

Ben-Arieh, Y. (1977). *A City in the Reflection of an Era: Jerusalem in the Nineteenth Century—The Old City* [Hebrew]. Jerusalem: Yad Yitzhak Ben-Zvi.

———. (1979). *A City in the Reflection of an Era: New Jerusalem in Its Beginning* [Hebrew]. Jerusalem: Yad Yitzhak Ben-Zvi.

———. (1981). "The Twelve Largest Settlements in Palestine in the Nineteenth Century" [Hebrew]. *Cathedra* 19: 83–144.

———. (1982). "Historical Geography in Israel: Retrospect and Prospect." In A. R. H. Baker and M. Billinger (eds.), *Period and Place: Research Methods in Historical Geography*, pp. 3–9. Cambridge: Cambridge University Press.

———. (1987). "The Population of Palestine and Its Settlement at the Eve of the Zionist Settlement Project." In Y. Ben-Arieh, Y. Ben-Artzi, and H. Goren (eds.), *Studies in the Historical-Settlement Geography of the Land of Israel* [Hebrew], pp. 1–24. Jerusalem: Yad Yitzhak Ben-Zvi.

Ben-Artzi, Y. (1989). "The Uniqueness of Haifa and Its Development During the Mandate Period." In M. Naor and Y. Ben-Artzi (eds.), *Haifa in Its Development 1918–1948* [Hebrew], pp. 27–37. Jerusalem: Yad Yitzhak Ben-Zvi.

Ben-Azar, E. (1989). "I Have Something Against Jerusalem." In H. Lavsky (ed.), *Jerusalem in Zionist Conception and Work*

[Hebrew], pp. 456–462. Jerusalem: The Zalman Shazar Center and the Hebrew University.

Ben-Gurion, D. (1951). *In the Battle* [Hebrew], vol. 5. Tel Aviv: Mapai.

———. (1955). *In the Battle* [Hebrew], vol. 2. Tel Aviv: Ayanot.

———. (1969). *The Renewed State of Israel* [Hebrew], vol. 1. Tel Aviv: Am-Oved.

———. (1971). *Memoires* [Hebrew], vol. 1. Tel Aviv: Am-Oved.

———. (1979). "To the South." In Y. Gradus and A. Shmueli (eds.), *The Land of the Negev: Man and Desert* [Hebrew], vol. 1, pp. xi–xvi. Tel Aviv: Misrad Habitahon.

———. (1982). *Memoires* [Hebrew], vol. 5. Tel Aviv: Am-Oved.

"The Ben-Gurion Plan for Security and Fortification in the Year 1929" [Hebrew]. (1963). *Molad* 21: 276–279.

Ben-Horin, Z. (1983). *Kibbutzim and Development Towns (from Paternalism to Partnership)* [Hebrew]. Haifa: The University of Haifa and the University Kibbutz Center 57.

Ben-Shalush, M. H. (1956). "The History of Jerusalem During the First Temple Era." In M. Avi-Yonah (ed.), *The Jerusalem Book* [Hebrew], vol. 1. *The Natural Conditions and the History of the City Since Its Beginning Until the Destruction of the Second Temple*, pp. 111–135. Jerusalem and Tel Aviv: Bialik Institute.

Benvenisti, M. (1981). *Jerusalem: A City and a Wall in Its Center* [Hebrew]. Tel Aviv: Hakibbutz Hameuhad.

———. (1984). *The West Bank Data Project.* Washington, D.C.: American Enterprise Institute for Public Policy Research.

Bezek (Israel Telecommunications Co.) (1986a). *Bezek Yearbook 1985–86* [Hebrew]. Jerusalem: Author.

———. (1986b). *The Telex and Fax Directory 1986–87* [Hebrew]. Tel Aviv: Dapei Zahav.

Bialer, A. (1985). "A Road to the Capital—Turning Jerusalem into the Formal Seat of the Government of Israel in the Year 1949" [Hebrew]. *Cathedra* 35: 163–193.

Bigger, G. (1976). "The Contribution of the British Ruling to the Development of Jerusalem in the Beginning of Its Governing in the Country (1918–1925)" [Hebrew]. *Studies* 9: 175–200.

———. (1983). *A Crown Colony or a National Homeland: The Impact of the*

> *British Ruling over Palestine 1917–1930: A Geographical-Histori-*
> *cal Examination*[Hebrew]. Jerusalem: Yad Yitzhak Ben-Zvi.

———. (1986). "The Urban Hierarchy in Palestine During the Mandate"
[Hebrew]. *Studies* 12: 87–98.

———. (1989). "The Strategic Conception of Haifa by the British Admin-
istration." In M. Naor and Y. Ben-Artzi (eds.), *Haifa in Its
Development 1918–1948* [Hebrew], pp. 59–67. Jerusalem: Yad
Yitzhak Ben-Zvi.

Blasi, J. (1986). *The Communal Experience of the Kibbutz.* New Brunswick,
N.J.: Transaction Books.

Borukhov, E., and Werczberger, E. (1980). *Factors Affecting the Development of New Towns in Israel.* Tel Aviv University: Pinhas Sapir
Center for Development.

Bretzki, N. (1988). "When I'll Be Grown Up I Want to Be Young." *Maariv*
[Hebrew] (September 23).

Brutzkus, E. (1970). *Regional Policy in Israel.*Jerusalem: Ministry of Interi-
or, Town and Planning Department.

Burghardt, A. (1969). "The Core Concept in Political Geography: A Definition of Terms." *Canadian Geographer* 13: 349–353.

Carmel, A. (1969). *The History of Haifa During the Turkish Period*
[Hebrew]. Haifa: The University Institute of Haifa.

Central Bureau of Statistics. *List of Settlements in Israel,* published annually
or biannually. Jerusalem: Author.

———. (1959–1987). *Tourism in Israel 1958–1987.* Special Publication Series,
published annually. Jerusalem: Author.

———. (1965–1988). *Statistical Yearbook for Israel.* Jerusalem: Author (an
annual publication).

———. (1979). *Population and Housing Census 1972.* Housing Conditions,
Publication B. Jerusalem: Author.

———. (1983). *Population and Housing Census 1983.* Population and Households, Temporary Results, Publication 1, Jerusalem: Author.

———. (1985). *Industry and Manufacturing Survey 1982,* Part A. Special
Publications Series 768, Jerusalem: Author.

———. (1987). *Industry and Manufacturing Survey 1983,* Part A. Special
Publications Series 796, Jerusalem: Author.

Christaller, W. (1935). *Die Zentralen Orte in Sueddeutschland.* Jena: Fischer.

Cohen, E. (1969). "Dispersing and Integrating Exiles as Contradictory Tasks." In *Integration of Exiles, Study Days at the Hebrew University in Jerusalem,* pp. 143–157 [Hebrew]. Jerusalem: Y. L. Magnes, The Hebrew University.

––––––. (1970a). *The City in Zionist Ideology.* Jerusalem Urban Studies 1, Jerusalem: Institute of Urban and Regional Studies, The Hebrew University.

––––––. (1970b). "Development Towns—The Social Dynamics of 'Planted' Urban Communities in Israel." In E. Eisenstadt, R. Bar-Yosef, and C. Adler (eds.), *Integration and Development in Israel,* pp. 587–617. Jerusalem: Israel University Press.

––––––, Peres, Y., and Heller, A. n.d. *The Absorption Capacity of Development Towns* [Hebrew]. Tel Aviv: Yissum Mehkarim and the Ministry for Aliya Absorption.

Cohen, G. (1988). "Tourists and Pilgrims." In Y. Praver and O. Ahimeir (eds.), *Twenty Years in Jerusalem 1967–1987* [Hebrew], pp. 162–167. Tel Aviv: Misrad Habitahon and the Jerusalem Institute for the Study of Israel.

Cohen, H. (1988). "The Status of Jerusalem in the Law of the State of Israel." In Y. Praver and O. Ahimeir (eds.), *Twenty Years in Jerusalem 1967–1987* [Hebrew], pp. 246–267. Tel Aviv: Misrad Habitahon and the Jerusalem Institute for the Study of Israel.

Cohen R. B. (1981). "The New International Division of Labor, Multinational Corporations and Urban Hierarchy." In M. Dear and A. J. Scott (eds.), *Urbanization and Urban Planning in Capitalist Society,* pp. 287–315. New York: Methuen.

Cohen S. B. (1977). *Jerusalem: Bridging the Four Walls.* New York: Herzl Press.

––––––, and Kliot, N. (1981). "Israel's Place-Names as Reflection of Continuity and Change in Nation-Building." *Names* 29: 227–248.

Cohen, Y. (1967). *Commercial Influence Spheres of the Urban Settlements in the Southern Coastal Plain of Israel* [Hebrew]. Publications in Problems of Regional Development 4, Rehovot: The Settlement Study Center.

The Community Settlement—An Organizational Structure [Hebrew]. (1978).Tel Aviv: The Jewish Agency and the World Zionist Organization.

Daniels, P. W. (1982). *Service Industries: Growth and Location.* Cambridge: Cambridge University Press.

de Blij, H. J. (1973). *Systematic Political Geography,* 2d ed. New York: John Wiley.

de Fries, D. (1989). "The Roots of 'Red Haifa'." In M. Naor and Y. Ben-Artzi (eds.), *Haifa in Its Development 1918–1948* [Hebrew], pp. 79–94. Jerusalem: Yad Yitzhak Ben-Zvi.

Dickinson, R. E. (1964). *City and Region.* London: Routledge and Kegan Paul.

Dodgshon, R. A. (1987). *The European Past: Social Evolution and Spatial Order.* London: Macmillan.

Efrat, E. (1981). "Patterns of Marginal Settlements in Israel" [Hebrew]. *Studies* 11: 87–99.

Eisenstadt, S. N. (1967a). "Israeli Identity: Problems in the Development of the Collective Identity of an Ideological Society." *Annals of the American Academy of Political and Social Science* 370: 116–123.

———. (1967b). *Israeli Society.* London: Weidenfeld and Nicholson.

Elazar, D. J. (1970a). *Israel: From Ideological to Territorial Democracy.* New York: General Learning Press.

———. (1970b). *Cities of the Prairie: The Metropolitan Frontier and American Politics.* New York: Basic Books.

———. (1986). *Israel: Building a New Society.* Bloomington: Indiana University Press.

———. (1987). *Building Cities in America: Urbanization and Suburbanization in a Frontier Society.* Lanham, Md.: Hamilton Press.

Elon, A. (1971). *The Israelis: Founders and Sons.* New York: Holt, Reinhart and Winston.

———. (1990). *Jerusalem: City of Mirrors.* London: Weidenfeld and Nicolson.

Felsenstein, D. (1986). *The Spatial Organization of High Technology Industries in Israel.* Jerusalem: The Hebrew University, Department of Geography and Institute of Urban and Regional Studies.

———. (1988). *Issues in the Development of High-Tech Industry in Jerusalem* [Hebrew]. Jerusalem: The Jerusalem Institute for the Study of Israel.

Fifer, J. V. (1976). "Unity by Inclusion: Core Area and Federal State at American Independence." *The Geographical Journal* 142: 462–470.

————. (1981). "Washington, D.C.: The Political Geography of a Federal Capital." *Journal of American Studies* 15: 5–26.

Figures (and Facts of the Community and Economy in Palestine). Vols. 8–9. (1947).

Fischer, Y. (1988). "Cultural and Spiritual Life." In Y. Praver and O. Ahimeir (eds.), *Twenty Years in Jerusalem 1967–1987*[Hebrew], pp. 193–245. Tel Aviv: Misrad Habitahon and the Jerusalem Institute for the Study of Israel.

Friedman, M. (1988). "The Yeshivot World." In Y. Praver and O. Ahimeir (eds.), *Twenty Years in Jerusalem 1967–1987* [Hebrew], pp. 174–178. Tel Aviv: Misrad Habitahon and the Jerusalem Institute for the Study of Israel.

Gelber, Y. (1989). "Immigrants from Germany in Haifa in the 1930s and 1940s." In M. Naor and Y. Ben-Artzi (eds.), *Haifa in Its Development 1918–1948* [Hebrew], pp. 95–110. Jerusalem: Yad Yitzhak Ben-Zvi.

Giddens, A. (1979). *Central Problems in Social Thoery.* London: Macmillan.

————. (1981). *A contemporary Critique of Historical Materialism.* Berkeley: University of California Press.

————. (1984). *The Constitution of Society: Outline of the Theory of Structuration.* Berkeley: University of California Press.

————. (1985). *The Nation-State and Violence.* Cambridge: Polity Press.

Giladi, D. (1973). *The Yishuv During the Fourth Aliya (1924–1929)* [Hebrew]. Tel Aviv: Am-Oved.

————. (1985). "Economy and Society During the Second Aliya." In M. Naor (ed.), *The Second Aliya 1903–1914* [Hebrew], pp. 4–25. Edan Series. Jerusalem: Yad Yitzhak Ben-Zvi.

Glasmeier, A. K., Hall, P., and Markusen, A. R. (1983). *Recent Evidence on High-Technology Industries' Spatial Tendencies: A Preliminary Investigation.* Working Paper 417, Berkeley: University of California, Institute of Urban and Regional Development.

Glassner, M.I., and de Blij, H. J. (1980). *Systematic Political Geography,* 3d ed. New York: John Wiley.

Goldberg, G., and Ben-Zadok, E. (1983). "Regionalism and a Territorial Rift in the making: The Jewish Settlement in the Administered Territories" [Hebrew]. *State, Government and International Relations* 21: 69–94.

Gottmann, J. (1952). "The Political Partitioning of Our World: An Attempt at Analysis." *World Politics* 4: 512–519.

————. (1973). *The significance of Territory*. Charlottesville: University Press of Virginia.

Government of Palestine. (1938). *Statistical Abstract of Palestine 1937–38*. Jerusalem: Government Printing Press.

Government Yearbook (1950–1984). [Hebrew]. Jerusalem: Governmental Printer, annual publication.

Gradus, Y. (1983). "The Role of Politics in Regional Inequality: The Israeli Case." *Annals of the Association of American Geographers* 73: 388–403.

————, and Einy, Y. (1980). "The Industrial Gap Between Center and Periphery in Israel" [Hebrew]. *Economics Quarterly* 106: 262–275.

————, and Krakover, S. (1976). "The Level of Industrialization and Its Characteristics in the Central and Development Regions" [Hebrew]. *Economics Quarlerly* 88–89: 66–78.

Gregory, D. (1978). *Ideology, Science and Human Geography*. London: Hutchinson.

Greiczer, I. (1982). "The Workers Neighborhood: Experiments in the Formation of Urban Landscape by Social Ideology in British Mandate Palestine" [Hebrew]. Ph.D. dissertation, Jerusalem, The Hebrew University.

Gross, D. (1985). "Temporality and the Modern State." *Theory and Society* 14: 53–82.

Grossman, D. (1977). "The Geographical Significance of the Settlement Process—The Case of Israel." In R. C. Eidt et al. (eds.), *Man, Culture and Settlement*, pp. 316–321. New Delhi: Kalyani.

Guelke, L. (1974). "An Idealist Alternative in Human Geography." *Annals of the Association of American Geographers* 64: 193–202.

Gur, O. (1967). *The Service Industries in a Delveloping Economy: Israel as a Case Study*. New York: Praeger Books.

Guri, H. (1989). "Between Tel Aviv and Jerusalem." In H. Lavsky (ed.), *Jerusalem in Zionist Conception and Work* [Hebrew], pp. 451–455. Jerusalem: The Zalman Shazar Center and the Hebrew University.

Guvrin, N. (1989). "Jerusalem and Tel Aviv as Metaphors in the Hebrew Literature: The Development of an Image." In H. Lavsky (ed.), *Jerusalem in Zionist Conception and Work* [Hebrew], pp. 434–450. Jerusalem: The Zalman Shazar Center and the Hebrew University.

Gvatti, H. (1981). *One Hundred Years of Settlement* [Hebrew]. Tel Aviv: Hakibbutz Hameuhad.

Hagerstrand, T. (1970)."What About People in Regional Science?" *Papers and Proceedings of the Regional Science Association* 24: 7–21.

Harel, H. (1989). "Herzl's Attitude to Jerusalem." In H. Lavsky (ed.), *Jerusalem in Zionist Conception and Work* [Hebrew], pp. 75–90. Jerusalem: The Zalman Shazar Center and the Hebrew University.

Harel, M. (1969). *This Is Jerusalem* [Hebrew]. Tel Aviv: Am-Oved.

———. (1987). "On the Love Between a Nation and Its Fatherland." In *Between a Nation and Its Fatherland* [Hebrew], pp. 24–34. Jerusalem: World Zionist Organization.

Harper, R. E. (1987). Personal communication.

Harris, W. W. (1980).*Taking Root: Israeli Settlement in the West Bank, the Golan and Gaza-Sinai, 1967–1980.* New York: Research Studies Press (John Wiley).

Harvey, D. (1969). *Explanation in Geography.* New York: St. Martin's Press.

———. (1973). *Social Justice and the City.* London: Arnold.

Hasson, S. (1981). "Social and Spatial Conflicts: The Settlement Process in Israel During the 1950s and the 1960s." *L'Espace Geographique* 3: 169–179.

———. (1987). "Tel Aviv—The Holy City" [Hebrew]. *Politics* 18: 48–51.

———, and Gosenfeld, N. (1980). "Israeli Frontier Settlements: A Cross-Temporal Analysis." *Geoforum* 11: 315–334.

Hayuth, Y. (1974). "Settlement Development in the Qrayot Area of Metropolitan Haifa" [Hebrew]. M.A. thesis, Jerusalem, The Hebrew University.

Henrikson, A. K. (1983). "A Small, Cozy Town, Global in Scope." *Ekistics* 299: 123–145.

Hepworth, M. E., Green, A. E., and Gillespie, A. E. (1987). "The Spatial Division of Information Labor in Great Britain." *Environment and Planning A* 19: 793–806.

Horowitz, D., and Lissak, M. (1978). *Origins of the Israeli Polity: Palestine under the Mandate.* Chicago: University of Chicago Press.

Illeris, S. (1987). "The Role of Big City Regions in Western Europe." Paper presented at the European Science Foundation Workshop, Jerusalem.

The Interim Government, *Declaration on the Establishment of the State of Israel*, 1948 [Hebrew].

The Interministerial Committee for the Study of the Condition of Transitory Camps. (1954). *Report* [Hebrew]. Jerusalem: Author.

Isranet. (1986). Subscribers List [Hebrew].

Jabotinski, Z. (1937). *A Stenographic Report of the Witness Before the Royal Committee (London, February 11, 1937)* [Hebrew]. Tel Aviv: Board of the New Zionist Organization in the Land of Israel.

———. (1981). *Guiding Principles to Current Problems* [Hebrew]. Tel Aviv: Jabotinski Institute.

Jefferson, M. (1939). "The Law of the Primate City." *The Geographical Review* 29: 226–232.

Kaniel, Y. (1981). "The Struggle Between Jerusalem and Jaffa over the Hegemony in the Jewish Community During the Period of the First and Second Aliya (1882–1914)." In Y. Hacker (ed.), *Shalem* 3 [Hebrew], pp. 185–212. Jerusalem: Yad Yitzhak Ben-Zvi.

Kark, R. (1974). *The History of Settlement in the Negev Until 1948* [Hebrew]. Tel Aviv: Hakibbutz Hameuhad.

———. (1976). "The Development of the Towns Jerusalem and Jaffa During the Years 1840 until World War I (a Study in Historical Geography)" Ph.D. dissertation, Jerusalem, The Hebrew University.

———. (1977). "The Development of Jerusalem and Jaffa at the End of the Ottoman Period" [Hebrew]. *Landscape* 9–10: 106–114.

———. (1984). *Jaffa: The Growth of a City 1799–1917* [Hebrew]. Jerusalem: Yad Yitzhak Ben-Zvi.

———. (1990). "The Changing Status of the Coastal Cities During the Nineteenth Century." In B. Z. Kedar, T. dotan, and S. Safrai (eds.), *Chapters in the History of Commerce in the Land of Israel* [Hebrew], pp. 324–337. Jerusalem: Yad Yitzhak Ben-Zvi.

Karmon, Y. (1971). *Israel: A Regional Geography*. New York: John Wiley.

Karton-Bloom, R. (1989). "The Giant Past Is Reflected in Distortion." In H. Lavsky (ed.), *Jerusalem in Zionist Conception and Work* [Hebrew], pp. 431–433. Jerusalem: The Zalman Shazar Center and the Hebrew University.

Katz, Y. (1986). "Ideology and Urban Development: Zionism and the Origins of Tel Aviv, 1906–1914." *Journal of Historical Geography* 12: 402–424.

———. (1989). "The Turn in the Attitude of Usishkin and Hov'vei Zion Toward the Development of Jerusalem and to the Establishment of the Hebrew University Before World War I." In H. Lavsky (ed.), *Jerusalem in Zionist Conception and Work* [Hebrew], pp. 107–136. Jerusalem: The Zalman Shazar Center and the Hebrew University.

Katzenelson, B. (1969). "Chapters in the History of the Workers Movement." In S. N. Eisenstadt, H. Adler, R. Bar-Yoseph, and R. Kahana (eds.), *The Social Structure of Israel* pp. 3–13 [Hebrew]. Jerusalem: Academon.

Kellerman, A. (1972). "The Spatial Characteristics of the Inter-Village Centers in Israel" [Hebrew]. M.A. thesis, Jerusalem, The Hebrew University.

———. (1981). "Retail Ribbon Development in the Industrial Area of Haifa, Israel." *Geoforum* 12: 371–375.

———. (1983). "The Suburbanization of Retail Trade: The Israeli Case." *Area* 15: 219–222.

———. (1984a). "Telecommunications and the Geography of Metropolitan Areas." *Progress in Human Geography* 8: 222–246.

———. (1984b). "Transitions in the Interrelationships Between Space and Society: A Terminological Structurationist Framework" [Hebrew]. *Horizons* 9–10: 81–92.

———. (1985a). "Population Dispersal: Forecasting and Reality in the Four Million Population Plan for Israel." *Geography Research Forum* 8: 53–72.

———. (1985b). "The Evolution of Service Economies: A Geographical Perspective." *The Professional Geographer* 36: 133–143.

———. (1985c). "City Profile: Tel Aviv." *Cities* 2: 98–105.

———. (1986a). "Characteristics and Trends in the Israeli Service Economy." *The Service Industries Journal* 6: 205–226.

———. (1986b). "Telecommunications as a Tool for Closing Center-Periphery Gaps" [Hebrew]. *Economics Quarterly* 128: 547–554.

———. (1987). "Retail Supply and Demand in a System Under Transition: The Case of Israel." *GeoJournal* 15: 31–38.

———. (1989). *Time, Space and Society: Geographical Societal Perspectives.* Dordrecht: Kluwer (D. Reidel).

Kimhi, Y. (1988). "Demographic, Economic and Metropolitan Development." In Y. Praver and O. Ahimeir (eds.), *Twenty Years in Jerusalem 1967–1987* [Hebrew], pp. 68–81. Tel Aviv: Misrad Habitahon and the Jerusalem Institute for the Study of Israel.

Kimmerling, B. (1974). "The Influence of Land and Territorial Factors in the Jewish-Arab Conflict over the Structuring of the Jewish Society in the Land of Israel (Since the Beginning of Settlement Until 1955)" [Hebrew]. Ph.D. dissertation, Jerusalem, The Hebrew University.

———. (1982). "Change and Continuity in Zionist Territorial Orientations and Politics." *Comparative Politics* 14: 191–210.

———. (1983a). *Zionism and Economy.* Cambridge, Mass.: Schenkman.

———. (1983b). *Zionism and Territory.* Berkeley: University of California, Institute of International Studies, Research Series No. 51.

———. (1985). "Between the Primordial and the Civil Definitions of the Collective Identity: Eretz Israel or the State of Israel?" In E. Cohen, M. Lissak, and U. Almagor (eds.), *Comparative Social Dynamics,* pp. 262–283. Boulder, Colo.: Westview Press.

———. (1989). "Boundaries and Frontiers of the Israeli Control System: Analytical Conclusions." In B. Kimmerling (ed.), *The Israeli Society: Boundaries and Frontiers,* pp. 265–284. Albany: State University of New York Press.

Kipnis, B. (1983). "The Development of the Jewish Urban Settlement in the Galilee During the Years 1948–1980." In A. Shmueli, A. Sofer, and N. Kliot (eds.), *The Lands of Galilee* [Hebrew], pp. 723–744. Haifa: Hevra Lemehkar Madai Shimushi.

Kiryati, Y. (1986). "Tokyo, Jerusalem...and Tel Aviv" [Hebrew]. *Muzot* 4: 58–59.

Kliot, N. (1978). "The Political Landscape: A Geographical Analysis of the Impact of Ideology on the Landscape." Ph.D. dissertation, Worcester, Mass., Clark University.

Knight, D. B. (1977). *A Capital for Canada.* Chicago: University of Chicago, Department of Geography, Research Paper 182.

Knight, R. V., and Gappert, G. (1984). "Cities and the Challenge of the Global Economy." In R. D. Bingham and J. P. Blair (eds.), *Urban Economic Development,* pp. 63–78. Urban Affairs Annual Reviews 27, Beverly Hills, Calif.: Sage.

Kohavi, M. (1984). "The Settling Period." In *The History of the Land of Israel* [Hebrew], vol. 2. *Israel and Judea During the Biblical Period,* pp. 21–84. Jerusalem: Keter and Yad Yitzhak Ben-Zvi.

Kook, A. Y. H. (1937). *I'll Remember* [Hebrew], vol. 1, Sabbath and Holiday Series, ed. Y. L. H. Fischman. Jerusalem: Rabbi Kook Institute.

Krakover, S. (1985). "Spatio-Temporal Structure of Population Growth in Urban Regions: The Case of Tel Aviv and Haifa, Israel." *Urban Studies* 22: 317–328.

———, and Dover, S. (1987). "Regional Growth Nuclei." *Geoforum* 18: 89–101.

Kruyanker, D. (1988). "The City's Lookings." In Y. Praver and O. Ahimeir (eds.), *Twenty Years in Jerusalem 1967–1987* [Hebrew], pp. 11–67. Tel Aviv: Misrad Habitahon and the Jerusalem Institute for the Study of Israel.

Kulat, Y. (1964). "Ideology and Reality in the Labor Movement in Palestine 1905–1919" [Hebrew]. Ph.D. dissertation, Jerusalem, The Hebrew University.

Lanir, Y. (1979). "Behavioral Aspects in the Historical Development of the Kibbutz" [Hebrew]. *The Kibbutz* 6–7: 92.

Lavsky, H., ed. (1989). *Jerusalem in Zionist Conception and Work* [Hebrew]. Jerusalem: The Zalman Shazar Center and the Hebrew University.

Lefebvre, H. (1976). "Reflections on the Politics of Space," trans. M. Enders. *Antipode* 8: 30–37.

Livne, E. (1969). *Aharon Aharonson—The Man and His Time* [Hebrew]. Jerusalem: Bialik Institute.

———. (1972). *Israel and the Western Civilization Crisis* [Hebrew]. Tel Aviv: Schocken.

Lorch, N. (1989). "Ben-Gurion and the Making of Jerusalem into Israel's Capital." In H. Lavsky (ed.), *Jerusalem in Zionist Conception and Work* [Hebrew], pp. 377–403. Jerusalem: The Zalman Shazar Center and the Hebrew University.

Luft, Z. (1923). "Field Neighborhoods" [Hebrew]. *The Young Laborer* 10, nos. 17–18: 7–9.

Lustick, I. (1987). "Israeli State-Building in the West Bank and the Gaza Strip: Theory and Practice." *International Organization* 41: 151–171.

———. (1988). *For the Land and the Lord: Jewish Fundamentalism in Israel* New York: Council on Foreign Relations.

Maimonides (Moses Ben Maimon). (1955). *The Code of Maimomides.* New Haven, Conn.: Yale University Press.

Margalit, A. (1980). "The Socialist-Zionist Labor Movement in Palestine in the 1920s: An Attempt for Synthesis" [Hebrew]. *Cathedra* 16: 79–92.

Matras, J. (1973). "Israel's New Frontier: The Urban Periphery." In M. Curtis and M. S. Chertoff (eds.), *Israel: Social Structure and Change,* pp. 3–14. New Brunswick, N.J.: Transaction Books.

Meinig, D. W. (1978). "The Continuous Shaping of America: A Prospectus for Geographers and Historians." *American Historical Review* 83: 1186–1217.

Meir A., (1980). "The Diffusion of Industy Adoption by *Kibbutz* Rural Settlements in Israel." *The Journal of Developing Areas* 14: 539–552.

Meiron, d. (1985). "If There Will Not Be Jerusalem" [Hebrew]. *Politics* 2: 10–12.

Mikesell, M. W. (1960). "Comparative Studies in Frontier History." *Annals of the Association of American Geographers* 50: 62–74.

Moyal, A. (1979). "Vision and Reality in the Negev Development." In A. Shmueli and Y. Gradus (eds.), *The Land of the Negev* [Hebrew], vol. 2, pp. 718–724. Tel Aviv: Misrad Habitahon.

Muvhar, A. (1983). "The Rural Settlement in the Mountainous Galilee During the Years 1967–1977." In A. Shmueli, A. Sofer, and N. Kliot (eds.), *The Lands of the Galilee* [Hebrew], pp. 705–716. Haifa: Hevra Lemehkar Madai-Shimushi.

Naor, M. (1983). "Pinhas Sapir (During the Years 1930–1949)" [Hebrew]. Ph.D. dissertation, Tel Aviv, Tel Aviv University.

———. (1989). "Haifa and the Struggle." In M. Naor and Y. Ben-Artzi (eds.), *Haifa in Its Development 1918–1948* [Hebrew], pp. 184–194. Jerusalem: Yad Yitzhak Ben-Zvi.

The National Committee. (1947). *The Community Economy Book for the Year 1947* [Hebrew]. Tel Aviv: Defus Sefer.

Near, H. (1979). "Ein Harod—Hakibbutz Hameuhad—Continuation and Change" [Hebrew]. *The Kibbutz* 6–7: 55.

———. (1987). *Frontiersmen and Halutzim: The Image of Pioneer in North America and Pre-State Jewish Palestine.* Discussion Paper 69, Haifa: University of Haifa, The Kibbutz University Center.

Nedava, Y., ed. (1982). *Jabotinski in Reflection over Generations* [Hebrew]. Tel Aviv: The Beitar Alumni Association.

Newman, D. (1984a). "Ideological and Political Influences on Israeli Urban Colonization: The West Bank and Galilee Mountains." *Canadian Geographer* 28: 142–155.

———. (1984b). "The Development of the Yishuv Kehillati in Judea and Samaria: Political Process and Settlement Form." *Tijdschrift voor Economische en Sociale Geografie* 75: 140–150.

———. (1989). "Frontier Settlement in the 1980s: A Cross Regional Comparison" [Hebrew]. *Merhavim (Spaces)* 3: 63–80.

Noyelle, T. J., and Stanback, T. M., Jr. (1984). *The Economic Transformation of American Cities.* Totowa, N.J.: Rowman and Allenheld.

Olizur, A. (1939). *The National Capital and the Construction of the Country* [Hebrew]. Jerusalem: Keren Hayessod.

Ophir, A (1985). "And There Is Still Jerusalem" [Hebrew]. *Politics* 3: 45–46.

Oren, E. (1978). *Settlement During Years of Struggle* [Hebrew]. Jerusalem: Yad Yitzhak Ben-Zvi.

———. (1979a). "The Tel-Hai Heritage in the Test of Practice" [Hebrew]. *Roots* 1: 172–207.

———. (1979b). "The Negev in the Revolt, the Struggle and the Independence War, Since the Year 1938 Until the Year 1949." In Y. Gradus and A. Shmueli (eds.), *The Land of the Negev: Man and Desert* [Hebrew], vol. 1, pp. 380–413. Tel Aviv: Misrad Habitahon.

———. (1980). "The Tel Hai Heritage in the Test of the Settlement Practice" [Hebrew]. *Landscapes* 15: 21–29.

———. (1983). "Settlement Policy in the Galilee in Pre-Statehood." In A. Shmueli, A. Sofer, and N. Kliot (eds.), *The Lands of Galilee* [Hebrew], pp. 787–818. Haifa: Hevra Lemehkar Madai-Shimushi.

Orni, E. (1979). "Land Purchase in the Negev and Development Projects of the Jewish National Fund." In Y. Gradus and A. Shmueli (eds.), *The Land of the Negev: Man and Desert* [Hebrew], vol. 2, pp. 417–439. Tel Aviv: Misrad Habitahon.

Paran, U. (1970). "Kibbutzim in Israel: Their Development and Distribution." *Jerusalem Studies in Geography* [Hebrew]: 1–36.

Paz, Y. (1989). "The Attempts to Create a Jewish Land Continuum Between Tel Aviv and Jerusalem in the Mandate Era." In H. Lavsky (ed.), *Jerusalem in Zionist Conception and Work* [Hebrew], pp. 279–302. Jerusalem: The Zalman Shazar Center and the Hebrew University.

Peldi, U. (1972). *"Regional Urban Systems" as a Factor in Population Dispersal in Israel* [Hebrew]. Tel Aviv: Housing Ministry.

Perlmutter, H. (1979). "Philadelphia: The Emerging International City." Philadelphia: La Salle College.

Phillips, R. S., and Vidal, A. C. (1983). "The Growth and Restructuring of Metropolitan Economies." *Journal of the American Planning Association* 49: 291–306.

A Plan for the Geographical Distribution of Population in a Five Million Israel [Hebrew]. (1972). Jerusalem: Interior Ministry and Finance Ministry.

Portugali, J. (1976). "The Effect of Nationalism on the Settlement Pattern of Israel." Ph.D. dissertation, London, London School of Economics.

Pounds, N. J. G. (1972). *Political Geography,* 2d ed. New York: McGraw-Hill.

Premus, R. (1984). "Urban Growth and Technological Innovation." In R. D. Bingham and J. P. Blair (eds.), *Urban Economic Development,* Urban Affairs Annual Reviews 27, pp. 47–61. Beverly Hills, Calif.: Sage.

Prescott, J. R. V. (1978). *Boundaries and Frontiers.* London: Croom-Helm.

Raanan, Z. (1980). *Gush Emunim* [Hebrew]. Tel Aviv: Sifriyat Poalim.

Rabinowitz, Y. (1976). "The Settlement Term in the Works of Yitzhak Tabenkin" [Hebrew]. *From the Inside* 38: 233–246.

Ram, H. (1982). "The Jewish Community in Jaffa Since the Second Half of the Eighteenth Century Until the First Years of the British Mandate Government" [Hebrew]. Ph.D. dissertation, Ramat Gan, Bar-Ilan University.

Razin, E. (1984). *The Location of Industrial Companies in Israel* [Hebrew]. Jerusalem: The Jerusalem Institute for the Study of Israel.

Redfield, R., and Singer, M. (1954). "The Cultural Role of Cities." *Economic Development and Cultural Change* 3: 53–73.

Reichman, S. (1975). "Three Dilemmas in the Development of the Jewish Community in the Land of Israel: Settlement, Population and Reconstruction" [Hebrew]. *City and Region* 2: 47–56.

———. (1977). "New Urban Settlement Forms in Israel" [Hebrew]. *City and Region* 3: 3–19.

———. (1979). *From a Holding Post to a Settled Land: The Creation of the Jewish Settlement Map in the Land of Israel 1918–1948* [Hebrew]. Jerusalem: Yad Yitzhak Ben-Zvi.

————. (1984). "Geographical Elements in the Crystallization of the Zionist Settlement Method at the End of the Ottoman Period" [Hebrew]. *The land of Israel* 17: 117–127.

————, and Hasson, S. (1984). "A Cross-Cultural Diffusion of Colonization: From Posen to Palestine." *Annals of the Association of American Geographers* 74: 57–70.

————, and Yehudai, M. (1984). *Chapters in the History of Physical Planning in Israel: A Survey of Initiating Physical Planning 1948–1965* [Hebrew], vol. 1. Jerusalem: Interior Ministry and The Hebrew University.

Rilke, R. M. (1955). "Duineser Elegien: Siebente Elegie." *Saemtliche Werke*, vol. 1, p. 711. Wiesbaden: Insel Verlag.

Rosen, M. (1984). *The Jewish community in Jerusalem in the Seventeenth Century* [Hebrew]. Tel Aviv: Tel Aviv University and Misrad Habitahon.

Rosenman, A. (1983). "Problems in Jewish Rural Mountainous Settlement in the Galilee During the Last Thirty Years." In A. Shmueli, A. Sofer, and N. Kliot (eds.), *The Lands of the Galilee* [Hebrew], pp. 683–704. Haifa: Hevra Lemehkar Madai-Shimushi.

Rosner, M. (1988). *The Kibbutz Movement in the Eighties.* Publication 73, Haifa: The Kibbutz University Center, University of Haifa.

Rubinstein, A. (1980). *From Herzl to Gush Emunim and Back* [Hebrew]. Tel Aviv: Schocken.

Rubinstein, D. (1982). *Those for God Come to Me: Gush Emunim* [Hebrew]. Tel Aviv: Hakibutz Hameuhad.

Ruppin, A. (1968). *The Chapters of My Life: The Beginning of My Work in the Country 1907–1920* [Hebrew]. Tel Aviv: Am-Oved.

Sack, R. D. (1981). "Territorial Bases of Power." In A. D. Burnett and P. J. Taylor (eds.), *Political Studies from Spatial Perspectives*, pp. 53–71. New York: John Wiley.

Salomon, I., and Razin, E. (1985). "Potential Impact of Telecommunications on the Economic Activities in Sparsely Populated Regions." In Y. Gradus (ed.), *Desert Development: Man and Technology in Sparselands*, pp. 218–232. Dordrecht: Reidel.

Sassen-Koob, S. (1985). "Capital Mobility and Labor Migration: Their Expression in Core Cities." In M. Timberlake (ed.), *Urbanization in the World System*, pp. 231–265. New York: Academic Press.

Schmaltz, A. (1979). "The Population of the Negev." In A. Shmueli and Y. Gradus (eds.), *The Land of the Negev* [Hebrew], vol. 2, pp. 440–479. Tel Aviv: Misrad Habitahon.

Schweid, E. (1987). "Between a Nation and Its Fatherland." In *Between a Nation and Its Fatherland* [Hebrew], pp. 15–23. Jerusalem: World Zionist Organization.

Schweitzer, A. (1984). *Turnarounds* [Hebrew]. Tel Aviv: Zemora-Bitan.

Segev, T. (1984). *1949: The First Israelis* [Hebrew]. Jerusalem: Domino.

Segre, D. (1985). *Israel: A Society in Transition.* Oxford: Oxford University Press.

Sela, A. (1989). "The Western Wall Riots (1929)—A Turning Point Between Jews and Arabs?" [Hebrew], pp. 261–278. In H. Lavsky (ed.), *Jerusalem in Zionist Conception and Work.* Jerusalem: The Zalman Shazar Center and the Hebrew University.

Seliger, M. (1976). *Ideology and Politics.* New York: The Free Press.

Shachar, A. (1971). "Israel's Development Towns, Evaluation of National Urbanization Policy." *Journal of A.I.P.* 37: 362–372.

———. (1987). "The Global Economy and World Cities." Paper presented at the European Science Foundation Workshop, Jerusalem.

———, and Lifshitz, G. (1980). "The Spatial Pattern of Interregional Migration in Israel" [Hebrew]. *Studies* 11: 153–177.

Sharon, A. (1951). *Physical Planning in Israel* [Hebrew]. Jerusalem: The Governmental Printer.

Shilhav, Y. (1986). "'The Sacredness of the Country' as a Process of Territorial Indoctrination" [Hebrew]. *Studies* 12: 142–150.

Shilo, M. (1989). "From Jaffa to Jerusalem: The Attitude of the Zionist Organization Toward Jerusalem During the Second Aliya Period." In H. Lavsky (ed.), *Jerusalem in Zionist Conception and Work* [Hebrew], pp. 91–106. Jerusalem: The Zalman Shazar Center and the Hebrew University.

Silberberg, R. (1973). *The Population Distribution in Israel, 1948–1972* [Hebrew]. Jerusalem: The Finance Ministry.

Singlemann, J. (1978). *From Agriculture to Services: The Transformation of Industrial Employment.* Beverly Hills, Calif.: Sage.

Sofer, A. (1971). "The Location of Industries in the Haifa Bay (from a Geographical Perspective)" [Hebrew]. Ph.D. dissertation, Jerusalem, The Hebrew University.

———. (1977). "The 'Double Backbone' Plan—A Human Geographical Perspective" [Hebrew]. *Horizons* 3: 57–68.

———. (1980). "The Large Cities in Israel." In A. Sofer and B. Kipnis (eds.), *Atlas of Haifa and the Carmel,* pp. 66–67. Haifa: Hevra Lemehkar Madai Shimushi.

———. (1982). "New Solutions for the Settlement of the Mountainous Galilee" [Hebrew]. *Horizons* 5: 49–54.

———. (1986). "The Territorial Struggle Between Jews and Arabs in the Land of Israel" [Hebrew]. *Horizons* 17–18: 7–23.

———. (1988). "Attitude Contacts Between the Port and the Industry in the Haifa Area." In *Symposium Minutes: The Port, Shipping and the City of Haifa: Interrelationships* [Hebrew], pp. 91–105. Haifa: The University of Haifa.

———, and Finkel, R. (1988). *The Observation Outposts in the Galilee: Goals, Achievements, Conclusions* [Hebrew]. Publications in Problems of Regional Development 43, Rehovot: The Center for the Study of Rural and Urban Settlement.

Soja, E. W. (1980). "The Socio-Spatial Dialectic." *Annals of the Association of American Geographers* 70: 207–225.

———. (1985). "The Spatiality of Social Life." In D. Gregory and J. Urry (eds.), *Social Relations and Spatial Structures,* pp. 90–127. London: Macmillan.

———. (1989). *Postmodern Geographies: The Reassertion of Space in Critical Social Theory.* London: Verso.

Sprinzak, E. (1981). "'Gush Emunim' the 'Iceberg Model' of the Political Extremism" [Hebrew]. *State, Government and International Relations* 17: 22–49.

Stein, M. (1970). *Between the Culture of Israel and the Culture of Greece and Rome* [Hebrew]. Tel Aviv: The Writers Association in Israel.

Stern, E. Gradus, Y., Meir, A., Krakover, S., and Tsoar, H. (eds.). (1986). *Atlas of the Negev.* Beersheba: Department of Geography, Ben-Gurion University.

Stern, S. (1974). "The Development of the Urban Structure of Haifa During the Years 1918–1947" [Hebrew]. Ph.D. dissertation, Jerusalem, The Hebrew University.

———. (1989). "The Port in Haifa." In M. Naor and Y. Ben-Artzi (eds.), *Haifa in Its Development 1918–1948* [Hebrew], pp. 68–78. Jerusalem: Yad Yitzhak Ben-Zvi.

Tabenkin, Y. (1983). *The Settlements—Concept and Way* [Hebrew]. Tabenkin Works Series 1, Tel Aviv: Hakibbutz Hameuhad.

Tadmor, H. (1969). "The First Temple and the Return to Zion Periods." In H. H. Ben-Sasson (ed.), *The History of the Jewish People* [Hebrew], vol. 1, pp. 91–173. Tel Aviv: Dvir.

Telephone Directory—Jerusalem 1986–87 [Hebrew]. Tel Aviv: Dapei-Zahav.

Telephone Directory—Tel Aviv and Its Environs 1987 [Hebrew]. Tel Aviv: Dapei-Zahav.

Taylor, P. (1985). *Political Geography*. London: Longman.

Therborn, G. (1980). *The Ideology of Power and the Power of Ideology*. London: Verso.

Tischler, Y. (1947). *The Settlement of the Land of Israel: A Plan for the Construction of the Country and the Absorption of the Sons—The Builders*. Tel Aviv: Binyan Haaretz.

Tuan, Y. F. (1974). *Topophilia*. Englewood Cliffs, N.J.: Prentice-Hall.

Turner, F. J. (1928). *The Frontier in American History*. New York: Holt.

Vitkin, Y. (1961). *The Writings of Yoseph Vitkin,* ed. A. Shochat. Tel Aviv: Am-Oved.

Wachman, A. (1977). "The 'Double Backbone' Plan" [Hebrew]. *Horizons* 3: 43–56.

Waterman, S. (1979). "Ideology and Events in Israeli Human Landscapes." *Geography* 64: 171–181.

Weber, A. F. (1899). *The Growth of Cities in the Nineteenth Century: A Study in Statistics*. New York: Macmillan.

Weintraub, D., Lissak, M., and Azmon, Y. (1969). *Moshava, Kibbutz, and Moshav: Patterns of Jewish Rural Settlement and Development in Palestine*. Ithaca, N.Y.: Cornell University Press.

Weiss, A. A. (1957). *The Beginning of Tel Aviv* [Hebrew]. Tel Aviv: Ayanot.

Whittlesey, D. (1939). *The Earth and the State*. New York: H. Holt.

Williams, C., and Smith, A. D. (1983). "The National Construction of Social Space." *Progress in Human Geography* 7: 502–518.

Wolch, J., and Dear, M., eds.(1989). *The Power of Geography: How Territory Shapes Social Life*. London: Unwin Hyman.

Yaari, A. (1947). *Land of Israel Memoires* [Hebrew], vol. 1. Jerusalem: World Zionist Organization.

Yeshivot Committee in the Land of Israel. (1987). *The 5748, 1987–88 Calendar* [Hebrew]. Jerusalem: Author.

Zameret, Z. (1985). "Gordon and Brenner." In M. Naor (ed.), *The Second Aliya 1903–1914* [Hebrew], pp. 84–100. The Edan Series, Jerusalem: Yad Yitzhak Ben-Zvi.

Zohar, E. (1974). *In the Tweezers of the Government: Why Nobody Rises* [Hebrew]. Jerusalem: Shikmona.

Zur, Z. (1980). *The Settlement and the State Boundaries* [Hebrew]. Tel Aviv: Hakibbutz Hameuhad.

———. (1982). *From the partition Debate Until the Alon Plan* [Hebrew]. Research Publications 7, Ramat-Efal: Yad Tabenkin.

Index

Aaronson, R., 187
Ackerman, A., 58
Acre, 125–27, 165, 202, 205,
    223–26, 235
Activism, 22
Agnon, S. Y., 51
Agrarian, 63; ritual, 59; policy, 70;
    rural organizations, 70; sector,
    207, 260; central institutions,
    260. *See also* settlements; fron-
    tier; mode of life
Agrarianism, 187, 256, 259
Agricultural, 96, 195, 200; world,
    10, 12, 28, 49, 54, 56, 97, 229;
    activity, 16, 38, 50–51, 66–67,
    79–80, 107, 128, 131, 140, 183,
    195, 211, 218, 248, 252, 274, 277;
    sector, 207, 212, 274. *See also*
    mode of life; rural; land; settle-
    ments; region; value; village
Agriculture, 20–21, 23, 44, 51, 55,
    59, 66–67, 69, 70, 73, 79, 84–85,
    92, 96, 98, 102, 109, 130, 139,
    197, 201, 210, 220, 252, 259,
    267–68, 277, 280; cooperative,
    19; Ministry of, 67; development,
    270. *See also* Jewish
Aharonowitz, Y., 50
Airport, 224, 226, 234, 241
Akzin, B., 22
Aliya, 42, 140, 267; First, 48, 49,
    51, 107, 119, 120, 127, 129, 139,
    153, 154, 183, 187, 197, 204, 244,
    253, 267; Second, 44, 48, 49, 51,
    53, 54, 55, 58, 120, 129, 130, 153,
    187–88, 196, 199, 202, 204–5,
    207–8, 253, 267–68; Third, 48,
    52, 55, 58, 187, 202, 207–8, 268;
    Fourth, 55, 131; Fifth, 55, 229
Alkalai, Y., 152
Alon Plan, 86–91, 92
Althusser, L., 3

Altman, E. A., 76, 79, 81
Amiran, D., 75, 82, 105, 120, 126,
    132, 158, 234
Applebaum, L., 98
Arab, 12, 25, 27, 28, 35, 40, 53, 64,
    70, 74, 86, 92, 111, 121, 124, 145,
    156, 160, 185, 188, 197–99, 216,
    228, 245, 268, 275, 276–77, 280;
    settlements and regions, xiv, 15,
    27, 70, 152, 199, 212, 216,
    220–21, 228; impacts, 1, 9,
    24–28, 119; countries, 11, 27, 63,
    65, 149, 225, 230, 239, 270; riots
    and uprising, 14, 27, 55–56, 86,
    89, 131, 137, 204, 221, 256; sec-
    tor and society, 24, 26–28, 58,
    113, 124, 148, 196, 198, 205, 219,
    221, 277–78; population, 87, 89,
    94, 100, 101, 111, 120, 121, 197,
    200, 214, 217–18, 223, 244. *See
    also* Palestinian; town; Jewish;
    city; territorial
Army, 66. *See also* military
Aronoff, M. J., 74
Aronson, G., 93
Ashdod, 80, 223, 230, 236, 239, 253
Ashkenazic, 159. *See also* Jew
Autarchy, 9, 12
Avidar, Y., 25, 26
Avigur, S., 215
Avneri, A. L., 25–27
Azmon, Y., 22

Bagelman, S., 178
Balibar, E., 3
Bar-Gal, Y., 2, 210
Beersheba, 78, 80, 165, 202, 212,
    221, 223, 237, 244–45, 250–51
Bein, A., 54, 59
Bell, G., 2
Ben-Arieh, Y., 2, 5, 124, 125, 126,
    130, 151, 153, 156, 157